In the early nineteenth century, the publishing house of Taylor & Hessey brought out the work of Keats, Clare, Hazlitt, De Quincey Carlyle, Lamb, Coleridge and many more of the most important literary figures of the time, as well as the great literary journal of the period, *The London Magazine*. Tim Chilcott here examines the life and work of John Taylor, the firm's founder.

The account, which incorporates a large amount of hitherto unpublished material, is a fascinating piece of literary, social and publishing history, showing clearly the relationship between the author and his publisher, and in turn between the publisher and the reading public. Mr Chilcott also explores the ways in which Taylor and Hessey, as publishers of new literature, dealt with the pressures created by these relationships during the central period 1816 to 1826.

THE AUTHOR

Tim Chilcott was educated at Cowbridge Grammar School, Glamorgan, and then at St John's College, Cambridge, as an undergraduate and post-graduate student. He spent a year teaching in the U.S.A., and is now Lecturer in English at the United States International University in England.

A PUBLISHER AND HIS CIRCLE

A PUBLISHER AND HIS CIRCLE

*the life and work of
John Taylor,
Keats's publisher*

Tim Chilcott

*Department of English
United States International University
Ashdown Park, Sussex*

Routledge & Kegan Paul   London and Boston

First published 1972
by Routledge & Kegan Paul Ltd
Broadway House, 68–74 Carter Lane,
London EC4V 5EL and
9 Park Street,
Boston, Mass. 02108, U.S.A.
Printed in Great Britain by
The Camelot Press Ltd, London and Southampton
© Tim Chilcott 1972
ISBN 0 7100 7198 1

Contents

Preface and acknowledgments

This is a book about publishing; and more especially, about the career of one man, John Taylor, who has some claim to be considered one of the great publishers in English literary history. Yet there can be no doubt that, save in a few circles, neither his name nor his achievement are well known, and some of the reasons for this relative neglect are understandable. In terms of size and organisation, the firm which he built in London during the early 1800s with his partner James Hessey was not large. It was never able during any period of its existence to compete with the success of more renowned houses such as Murray's or Constable's, or, in terms of sales and public recognition, with the greater glories of Scott and Byron. Nor, indeed, did the two men create a tradition of publishing by establishing a firm to survive into our century, for their partnership lasted only twenty years, and the best of its work was achieved in a mere ten of these, between 1816 and 1826. Throughout their career, too, they faced a combination of financial difficulties and critical attack which was damaging enough to weaken any profound impact, in terms of sales, upon the imagination of Regency society. Yet despite these problems, there can be no doubt that they gathered about themselves during these years a circle of the highest quality; for within this brief period, they encouraged and published the work of Keats, Lamb and Hazlitt, Clare, De Quincey, Hood and Coleridge, Reynolds, Landor and Carlyle, George Borrow and Henry Cary. Few publishers before or since, indeed, can have created a list as full of imaginative literature that was destined to survive its own age. And, in its widest terms of reference, this study of Taylor's career is an attempt to assess the importance of his house to the literature which has now become a part of our common heritage.

Faced with such a wealth of personality and event, I decided early in the writing of this book to impose no set pattern upon my approach to each author of the house. Indeed, the kind of information and material available has naturally suggested different emphases, different avenues of interpretation. With Clare, to take one example, I have tried to explore in depth the literary relationship which was created between Taylor and him, whereas with Hazlitt, with whom this kind of association was clearly less important, the emphasis changes to an examination of the social and moral power exercised by the great Reviews. Similarly, certain aspects of Keats's relationship with the firm have led to an analysis of his attacks against the reading public, whereas in the case of Landor, who regarded such readers as less of an enemy, the emphasis shifts to a study of the justice and efficacy of censorship on moral and political grounds. Such changes in focus will not, I hope, prove disconcerting, for the purpose behind them is to demonstrate the many influences which Taylor, in common with every publisher, was forced to recognise in order to survive. And they will all, I trust, be seen as bound together by a common theme – the desire to illustrate the ways in which Taylor himself, on both a personal and intellectual level, helped to shape the literature of his generation.

This has proved a rich and extensive field, and inevitably in a book of this kind, some of the more intricate details of Taylor's career have had to be compressed or omitted in favour of presenting a more general picture. Yet, even with the large use I have made of previously unpublished papers, a very considerable body of unpublished material remains, revealing much about the nature of nineteenth-century publishing as well as the firm's associations with Keats and Clare, Lamb, De Quincey, and Landor. A good deal of this material I hope to present soon in a collection of letters and papers concerning Taylor and his circle.

The final belief which has guided my approach throughout this book has been, perhaps, more a question of conviction than of argument. In its simplest terms, the conviction has been that the publishing house has too often been consigned to a role of minor importance in many studies of our literature. Myth has reduced the publisher either to a shadowy figure of little significance or to an intelligent parasite who perniciously lives off his authors. Only rarely is either myth based on fact. Indeed, as I have tried to show, to examine the problems, disappointments, and applause which the publisher receives is, in a very real sense, to examine the ways in which our own literacy is fostered. The publishing house identifies and adjudicates between the interests of many parties. It must look for its survival, in Samuel Butler's phrase, both to the 'sayer' of literature and to the 'sayee'. In just this way, the house of

Taylor & Hessey was Janus-faced, looking towards Keats and Clare, Lamb and Hazlitt, for the creation of new literature; but looking also, and often with greater anxiety, towards the mass reading public to acclaim the importance of those writers, and thereby cultivate a tradition of literary excellence. Perhaps in this wider context, which includes the recognition of literature by society as well as the creation of it by the individual artist, rests indeed the firm's chief claim to attention. Taylor and Hessey are important, not simply because they so fully recognised and encouraged the writers of their house, but also because, in so doing, they showed how in a particular time the cause of literature and a literate society might be fostered and sustained.

Throughout the research for this book, I have been shown many kindnesses, and I should like here briefly to record my thanks. In England, many librarians have given their help in answer to my requests for books, manuscripts, and information; and I would like to thank the librarian and staff of the British Museum, the National Library of Scotland, the Bodleian Library, University College Library, London, and in particular, the University Library, Cambridge, for all their assistance. I owe a particular debt of gratitude to the Trustees of the British Museum and the National Library of Scotland also for their permission to quote from unpublished manuscripts in their charge. Many smaller libraries in this country have also given me invaluable help. To the late Dr Alexander Bell of Peterborough Museum, to Miss B. M. Attenborough of the Denman Library, Retford, Mr D. H. Halliday and Mr David Powell of the Northampton Public Library, Mr Barry Hall of Peterborough Public Library, Mr L. Tebbutt of Stamford Public Library, and to Mr W. R. Maidment and the staff of Keats House, Hampstead, I am much indebted for all their assistance. Again, in connection with the material I have studied in the libraries mentioned above, I must thank the Trustees of both the Peterborough City Museum and Northampton Public Library, and also the London Borough of Camden at Keats House, for permission to quote from manuscripts in their collections. In the United States, four libraries answered my requests for photostats, or allowed me to study original manuscripts when I visited them, and I should like to thank Mrs June Moll of the Miriam Lutcher Stark Library, University of Texas, Dr W. H. Bond of the Houghton Library, Harvard, the late Mr John D. Gordan, former Curator of the Berg Collection in the New York Public Library, and Mr Frederick B. Adams, now Director Emeritus of the Pierpont Morgan Library, New York, for their invaluable assistance. I must thank too the Trustees and governing bodies of the four libraries mentioned above for permission to quote from unpublished manuscripts in their charge.

Many descendants of John Taylor and James Hessey have willingly allowed themselves to be badgered for family recollections, letters, and other material. Miss Violet Wilkinson and Mrs M. P. Flecker showed me several books and manuscripts relating to the firm, and Mr Michael Brooke-Taylor of Bakewell kindly allowed me to quote letters from Hessey to Taylor in his possession. Mr Douglas Grounds, Senior History Master at Retford Grammar School, gave me much valuable information about the kind of life Taylor would have led in Retford in the 1790s, and Mr R. W. King generously sent me his notes on the relationship between Cary and Taylor & Hessey. To Mr Eric Robinson, I am indebted for an offprint of the article by him and Mr Geoffrey Summerfield which he kindly sent me in the early stages of my research. My disagreements with them over their interpretation of Taylor's relationship with Clare will not, I hope, in any way appear to lessen my obligation to them both for that most salutary of critical exercises, presenting the other point of view. I should like to thank also Miss Joyce Weston, Mrs Margaret Badham, Mrs Cecily Hessey-White of Montreal, Mr Robert D. Hessey of Council Bluffs, Iowa, Mr John C. Brooke-Taylor of Northampton, Dr A. N. L. Munby, and most especially, two former teachers, Mr Hugh Sykes Davies and Mr George Watson of St John's College, Cambridge.

In a study of this kind, covering as it does so many writers of talent and genius, it would be impossible to deny a deep indebtedness to those previous biographers, editors, and critics of the firm's authors, who have done so much to create just perspectives and sympathetic judgments. But for them, indeed, this book would scarcely have been possible, and my general indebtedness to them will, I hope, be apparent both in specific references and in general argument. There remain three men, however, to whom I owe especial thanks for their assistance. Dr Ian Jack, my former supervisor during the years of research which have led to this book, gave me much advice and sympathetic encouragement for which I am very grateful indeed. Professor Edmund Blunden, whose memoir of John Taylor has proved an invaluable guide, talked to me on several occasions about the firm, and for his suggestions and hospitality I would like here to record my sincere thanks. Mr R. W. P. Cockerton of Bakewell, a descendant of Taylor's brother James, has from the very beginning of this research shown a great interest in its progress, and for his many kindly letters of advice and encouragement, as well as for much generous hospitality, I am very grateful indeed. The frequency with which I have quoted from the hundreds of unpublished Taylor letters in his possession is, indeed, only a small indication of my great indebtedness to him.

If there should be a dedication to this book, it should go to that group of people who gave hope when the going was most difficult. Some have already been mentioned, but to them I would like to add the names of my parents, and of Mr John Crook and Mr Gaylord Meech. To them especially, and to all those other friends in Cambridge, Bakewell, and elsewhere who pushed hardest, this book is affectionately dedicated.

T. J. CHILCOTT

Ashdown Park, Sussex

Apprenticeship: 1781-1816

One story which John Taylor always delighted in relating was the tale of his grandfather's engagement. Sometime during the 1730s, a certain Miss Elizabeth Wilson, the daughter of a wealthy linen merchant of Leeds, begged a fortune teller to reveal how she should meet her future husband. The woman answered in unusually explicit detail. She would marry the man from whom she first accepted a silver snuff box. The following day, William Taylor, John's grandfather, offered Elizabeth a pinch of snuff from a silver box:[1]

> She looked earnestly at the box and he begged her acceptance of it. This however she was resolved not to do lest she should seem to rely too much on the story of the old witch whose Predictions she was resolved to disappoint. She thought she had given it back again but they sat sometime in conversation and when he was gone, to her great surprise she found the box still in her lap.

However apocryphal the story, the witch's prediction was accurate enough, for by 1745, William and Elizabeth were married and established in a prosperous drapery business in York. William himself was descended from a family of Scottish aristocrats, the Tailyours of Tailyourtoun near Montrose; and politically at least, his marriage to Elizabeth made for a dangerous partnership. Elizabeth, in the tradition of her family, was a staunch Jacobite; and William, although he refused to swerve from a nominal loyalty to George I, was sympathetic enough to the Jacobite cause to gain the confidence of the leaders of the rebellion, who dined with him several times during the turmoil of 1745–6. On at least one occasion, the Young Pretender himself was hidden in William's house and enjoyed an evening at the theatre with him, heavily disguised. But even though William refused to actively support the Jacobite cause, his sympathy for the many rebels who were his personal friends eventually cost him his life. In 1757, whilst helping the last survivors of the Pretender's army to escape by boat off the Yorkshire coast, he caught a fever and died at the age of fifty-two.

William's youngest son, James, had been born five years previously, in September 1752. Of his boyhood no details now survive; but the failure of the rebellion must have clouded the fortunes of a family with acknowledged Jacobite sympathies, and his mother, who survived until 1796, certainly faced great difficulties in providing for her children after William's death. Sometime during his early twenties, though, James met and fell in love with a girl from Newark, Sarah Drury, and on 27 September 1778 they were married in Newark church. Shortly afterwards, they moved a few miles north to Retford, a rapidly expanding commercial centre of some two thousand inhabitants. James immediately took advantage of the business opportunities that the town offered. Soon after his arrival with Sarah, he bought a house in the centre of town, in the Market Square, and there began to build up a prosperous trade as the bookseller, printer, and auctioneer for the district. In this house, on 31 July 1781, their third child John was born.

Only the barest facts now survive of Taylor's boyhood and the kind of life he led at Retford. At the age of twelve, he was attending the Grammar School at Lincoln, where he first met the young William Hilton and Peter de Wint, the artists with whom he enjoyed a close friendship for many years after their schooldays. A single but revealing glimpse of his life at this time remains. 'One of my own Characteristics as a little Boy', he later recalled, 'was that of Friendship for others older than myself':[2]

> Ned Haines, the son of a Sheriff's Officer, gave me on this account the nickname of 'Old Associate' – It was much developed when I came to London – but at Lincoln Grammar School, where I went when I was 12 years old, it was a peculiar trait with me.

This glimpse of Taylor's personality as a boy is tantalisingly brief, but it illustrates that even at this age, he possessed something of that capacity, so fully realised in his later years, for developing friendships with those who were different from him in maturity and beliefs. How long he remained a pupil at Lincoln is unknown, but it cannot have been longer than two years at most, for it is almost certain that he attended the Grammar School at Retford before he was fifteen. The school was adjacent to the parish church in Chapelgate, only two minutes' walk from his father's house in the Market Square. It taught between thirty and forty boys, mostly the sons of the better-off tradesmen, wealthy local farmers, and professional men. By the original statutes of 1552, which were still in force in the 1790s, the only subjects stipulated for instruction were Greek, Latin, and religious knowledge. But like many schools of the late eighteenth century, Retford had been forced by popular demand to widen the scope of its curriculum, and it is likely that Taylor was instructed in English and mathematics, and perhaps history and geography, as well as the traditional disciplines. His head-masters, the Rev. Ellis Stevenson and the Rev. William Trye, seem both to have been enlightened teachers. Indeed, Trye, who had not long come down from Pembroke College, Oxford, clearly regarded him as one of his best pupils, for in 1795 or 1796, there were proposals that he should continue his studies at university. Trye sounded out the opinions of his friends, and particularly asked the advice of the rector of Babworth, a village two miles from Retford where he held a curacy. But the suggestion fell on stony ground. The rector was convinced that a young man going to university without any fortune whatsoever was sure to get on badly; and it was clear that James Taylor, building up his business as well as providing for an increasingly large family, could not afford the expense of further education for his son. When John finally left school, he joined his father's shop and there began his apprenticeship in the trade of printing and bookselling.

To catch at the threads of Taylor's early life, to define those aspects of environment or education which may have moulded his future character, is difficult. Until 1802, when he was twenty-one, neither he nor his younger brother James had begun to write to each other the many letters which so fully illuminate the ideas and activities of his later life. But if many of the details are now lacking, his early education clearly instilled in him one quality at least, which was of the greatest value to him throughout his life. There is little doubt that, during his schooldays, neither Stevenson nor Trye restricted his natural curiosity by compelling him to follow a set syllabus of learning. On the con-trary, in the range of their curriculum, they may well have played a major part in fostering the breadth of outlook, the capacity to appreci-ate the disciplines of many different subjects, which he continually built upon and deepened in later years. Throughout his life, Taylor rarely attempted to compartmentalise knowledge. Connections could be made, parallels drawn, correspondences noted in subjects as diverse as Christianity and phrenology, linguistics and economic theory, literature and the Great Pyramid of Egypt – all of which were to fascinate him at various periods in his life. During his youth at Retford, and even during his early years in London, this range of interest was inevitably unrefined. The detailed knowledge and understanding of political economy or linguistic theory was to be gained only slowly, after years of painstaking study. But the impulse for this breadth of outlook had been planted. What was developing during these years, however crudely, was a largeness of mind which was later to move with remarkable fluency over many areas of experience.

In this development, books were a paramount influence. Not only in school but at home also, the printed word was a part of his everyday life. His sisters Ann and Nancy wrote youthful verses and he himself composed poetry and read extensively. When he left school, he steeped himself still more in books, in the intricacies of setting up type in his father's business, in the trade of buying and selling, estimating prices, drawing up catalogues, and engraving plates. Again, only a single trace of his way of life at this time now survives. When he was twenty, he wrote one of his first letters to his brother James and painted a brief self-portrait:[3]

> We still go on with a high hand among the Freemen –
> Drumming, Fifing, Swearing, Shouting, Drinking, Eating,
> keeping it up all Night long, nay for Weeks without ever being
> in bed. . . .

> . . . I scribble a few Verses now & then but they would not be
> worth your Singing, even if I had good Tunes. . . . Your brother
> is still the Being he always was. – Stupid, duke mad, queer,
> bookish, modest, imprudent. – Rhyming, Writing, Reading,
> Fluting, Drawing, 'Graving.

It was the time of the dilettante artist and the mild anarchist. Dabbling in poetry, music, and engraving, his career not yet decided, he lived freely, finding both in poetry and in the mug of ale equal inspiration. Yet one final impression of his youth in Retford reveals a very different side of him. Out of his many friends and relations, he chose as his particular companion his brother James, who was seven years his junior; and during these early years a friendship began which was to last for over sixty years. As this study will often show, the importance of this relationship can scarcely be over-estimated – not only because the pattern of James's life is so often woven into Taylor's own history, illuminating his ideas, but also because on several occasions, when the fortunes of the firm of Taylor & Hessey were at their lowest, the house would not have survived but for James's generosity.

In 1802, when he was only fourteen, James left home to join his elder sister Ann and her husband in their linen-drapery business in Bakewell. Taylor too began to feel confined by the provincial atmosphere of Retford, and with James gone, he had already set his sights on London. It was an understandably sincere desire to broaden his experience, but his mother, whilst accepting his arguments for leaving home, saw his desire as the mark of an ambitious man. In a letter to James, she expressed her fears:[4]

> – with tears I write it God grant I may be deceived can I doubt that all mankind deceive themselves – – – when I see my own son point out the only Error in poor Elvidge – and yet cannot see it in himself – Ambition he said was his only fault – – to be thought Great – – what he used to dispise in another. . . . our fears increce when we see pleasure and a wish to appear great, of so much consequence.

Certainly, Sarah's charge was dramatised and even exaggerated; and much of her criticism may have arisen from a maternal desire to keep John at home, which he would not accept. But as certainly, she spoke some truth when she called him ambitious. He himself indeed recognised this quality in his character:[5]

> Every day leaves me . . . without Care in the World, unless on the Score of Ambition; for I feel rather earnest to cut my figure in the World as well as others, & no Opportunity is suffered to pass away without an eye to Futurity. . . . I am always on the alert for seizing any favourable proposition that may be made to me.

That Taylor was anxious as a young man to make a mark in the world, concerned to capture and deserve the esteem of his contemporaries, is clear; and a desire which would perhaps have been forgiven in the Benjamin of the family was not altogether forgiven in him. But whatever tension his ambitions created at home during the summer of 1803, the dissension was short-lived, for, in the autumn of that year, his wish to leave Retford was realised. Determined as he was to continue in the trade of printing and bookselling, London was the only possible destination for him. It was the centre of the book trade in England and dominated the readership of even the largest provincial towns. The greater proportion of the reading public in the whole country was estimated to live in the city.[6] It housed well over two-thirds of the master printers in the kingdom, and the great nucleus of publishing houses which sent books to the provinces directed practically all their business from Fleet Street and Paternoster Row. For Taylor, the trade of a country bookseller had now become too restricted to satisfy his mind, and although in his first years away from Retford, he was often to write home bitterly despondent at the fever and loneliness of the city, London was always to be the inevitable testing-ground for his ambitions. His apprenticeship as a city bookseller and publisher was far longer and more arduous than a similar apprenticeship in Retford. But by the same token, the rewards the city gave in terms of opportunity and recognition were far greater than could ever have been gained in a small provincial town.

By the beginning of December 1803, Taylor was in London working for James Lackington at the famous 'Temple of the Muses' in Finsbury Square. The contrast with his former life could scarcely have been greater. Lackington's 'Temple' was a vast building crammed, as it took pains to advertise, with over half a million books. On the ground floor, which was reputedly large enough to drive a coach and six around, an enormous circular counter was the focus of intense activity, where assistants stood ready to advise, pack up books, and collect payment. Above, circular galleries with shelves full of books rose up to a dome. The whole building, Charles Knight remembered, was a veritable warehouse of knowledge, almost as remarkable in size and interest as 'Saint Paul's or Mrs Salmon's Waxwork'. Lackington himself was a prime example of the self-made man. He had started the business in the humblest of ways, with his private library and a 'bagful of old books, chiefly divinity', worth about five pounds.[7] Five years later, in 1779, he had issued a catalogue of some 12,000 volumes; and in 1781, he was selling 100,000 books annually, at a profit of £4,000. He had succeeded in the simplest of ways – by establishing a rigid system of ready-money selling, by undercutting the prices of his trade rivals, and above all, by believing unshakeably that low prices could be reconciled with substantial profit. From the beginning of his career, indeed, he had acted upon a single conviction that few in the book trade were prepared to countenance. The unprecedented demands for books from all classes of society, he argued, had created a situation where low prices and extensive sales were as profitable to the bookseller as high prices and reduced sales. Such an aggressive disregard for the traditional rules of price-agreements and credit facilities scarcely made him beloved of other publishers and booksellers. But Lackington, shrewdly grasping the economic pressures governing the sales of books, insisted that profit could be made by expanding the reading public as well as by restricting it. He favoured the formation of book clubs and circulating libraries, which others feared. He undercut to sell more copies to more readers with a smaller profit margin. He looked to the poor to buy at reduced prices, and to the rich to sell their libraries *en bloc* rather than piecemeal.

How far Taylor agreed in the end with Lackington's arguments is difficult to say. But the way in which his employer had discerned and stimulated still further the increasing demand for reading material of all kinds could scarcely have escaped his notice. If nothing else, indeed, his introduction to the London book trade made him aware immediately of the immense fluidity that existed in book production. The trade was in the throes of a revolution in reading habits. No longer in the 1800s was it possible to define a clear process by which literature was written and made known to a select and cultivated society. The rapid emergence of a new public who, in Lackington's own phrase, had turned from relating ghost stories on winter evenings to reading *Tom Jones* and *Roderick Random*, had begun to confuse the boundaries of a known audience for literature. Certainly, Lackington himself grossly exaggerated the extent of the new literacy in his contention that 'all ranks and degrees now read'.[8] This was far from the truth. But he did not mistake the nature of the new reading public that was evolving. He had placed his faith, not in a small cultivated cenacle, but in an increasingly amorphous public, whose reading habits cut across traditional barriers of class and culture. By exploding the myths of price-fixing and circulating libraries, he had exploded also the myth that wealth, class, and education clearly defined the readers and patrons of literature. Books were, for him, not the prerogative of a coterie, but a trade; for only as a trade, he believed, could they reach and benefit those 'prodigious numbers in inferior or reduced situations in life'.[9]

If a good deal in Taylor's later career illustrates that he by no means accepted all of Lackington's arguments, he could have had at that time no doubt of their efficacy. He had only to look about him at the galleries and the central counter of the 'Temple' to recognise how prosperous a business Lackington had built. But from a personal point of view, his introduction to the trade in London was not altogether a happy one. The first weeks of his employment went well. He worked a long day, from 8 in the morning until about 8.30 at night, but his talents as a Latinist and bookman and his skill at penmanship were quickly appreciated and put to use. His activity and courtesy too won immediate approval, and Lackington invited him to dine frequently. But the generosity of the firm in its praise was not matched by a similar generosity regarding wages. Taylor, trusting to the house's 'Honor', enquired about the possibility of an increase in salary. Days of polite back-pedalling on the part of Lackington and Kirkman, one of his partners, concluded finally with the promise of a possible Christmas bonus and a possible 'very *important* TRUST',[10] but there could be no increase above the 7/6d. a week he was receiving. Writing home at the end of March 1804, barely four months after his arrival in London, Taylor reported that he had resigned from Lackington's.

However unfortunate such a beginning to his career may have seemed at the time, Taylor derived from his brief stay at the 'Temple' one benefit which was to be of inestimable value to him throughout his life. It was during these months that he first met James Augustus Hessey, his future partner who was later to sustain his efforts on so many occasions when he had almost exhausted himself. Of Hessey's own life before he came to Lackington's little is known. His father had been a quartermaster in the 43rd Foot Regiment from 1773 to 1780, and had fought in the American War of Independence; but he had died in 1786 at a comparatively early age. Hessey himself was born the previous year, on 28 August. As a boy, he had been sent by his guardians to the Grammar School at Burton-upon-Trent, where he gained, in the words of his son James, 'a sound classical education'.[11] Seemingly, like Taylor, he had been attracted by the glamour of London and had left school to become apprenticed to Lackington. When they first met, he was only eighteen, Taylor's junior by four years; yet within a few months, both had become the firmest of friends. In a letter written four years after their first meeting, Taylor painted a verbal portrait of the young Hessey:[12]

James Augustus Hessey is thin, dresses principally in black, his face is round and good-humoured when he does not frown – when he does, *it has the contrary expression.* He is about 22, but retains a boyish appearance about the head. His application is good – his conversation and manners lively. He has a readiness of droll quotation, and humorous allusion – is somewhat witty but had rather be considered a man of strong sense. His enunciation is not very distinct, but rapid, and when he wishes to utter his opinion in a serious manner, he hesitates or stutters a little, as if in doubt what words to select next. . . . He is a great favourite wherever he goes, particularly with young ladies, who like him for his great cheerfulness, and because he sings a little, plays a little, and dances well. . . . His knowledge of the flute qualifies him to play an accompaniment to the piano. . . . In a word, he has wit and accomplishments sufficient to please everybody, and sense enough to make *them* the subordinate part of his character.

During the first months of their friendship, Taylor and Hessey spent much of their leisure time in each other's company, playing duets on the flute and brushing up their Greek together. But by far the greatest influence upon Taylor during his first full year in London was the publishing firm of Vernor & Hood, which he entered only ten days after his resignation from Lackington's. It was a position after his own heart, not only in the responsibility he was required to assume, but also because he found in Thomas Hood, the father of the poet, a generous and kindly master. From the very beginning, he felt at home in the firm, and within weeks of his appointment, he came to regard Hood with a very warm attachment. His behaviour, Taylor reported home, was 'uniformly kind and free':[13]

> I am more than ever attached to Mr. and Mrs. Hood – . . . I can say anything to them, & feel as much at ease, as if with you – Mr. Hood so entirely divests himself of all care when in the midst of his Family & Friends, that he is always playful, & merry – and looks more like a laughing Lad than a Man of business. . . .
> Last Sunday I dined with Mr. & Mrs. Hood at Hampstead – and I was more *at home*, than I have ever been anywhere since I came to Town.

From remarks such as these, which are scattered throughout Taylor's letters of this period, it is clear how greatly the Hoods encouraged his efforts during these early months. He found in them a generous friendship and openness which were offered at the very time he had most need of such companionship. Even with their kindness, though, the sense of solitariness and hopelessness which the city atmosphere created often weakened his spirits. During his first summer in London, he wrote:[14]

> Here I am, Heaven preserve me, in the Midst of a City that cares as much about me as the Man in the Moon does – Such a racket, such a bustle, Coaches, Carts, Cockneys, Cabbages, Carriages, & Codfish – Waggons, Wheelbarrows, Watermen, Wonderful News, Women, and Watchmen, in one eternal clatter tumbling one over another as if London was a great copper Kettle, and they were all boiling together for the D[evi]l's Supper. . . .

And on one evening in March 1805, he returned to his lodgings 'after a close confining Day', and realised that there was 'no one but Strangers about'. The oppression and feverish turmoil of London only served to aggravate his own loneliness. He wrote to James:[15]

9

I have the Headache & lowness of Spirits. . . . I only wish, for the sake of the World, that Mankind was as honest and virtuous as I once imagined – But to see, as I do, daily, thousands fattening on the spoil of thousands – In this great town, as in a great pit full of People, to observe one scrambling over another, kicking, scratching, biting and all Sorts of unfair Tricks practised to raise each Man higher than his Neighbour is absolutely disgusting –

Such low spirits inevitably passed; and indeed, in the light of his future career, this period spent as Hood's assistant was an invaluable apprenticeship. His instruction ranged over every possible aspect of the book trade. He assisted in the production of the several periodicals which the house published. He took copies of each book brought out by the firm to the 'principal people in the trade', received their orders, and thus became known personally to the directors of bookshops and publishing houses.[16] Hood explained the internal organisation of publishing to him and allowed him to witness all the transactions of the house.[17] He met the critic William Gifford who received him 'with the most friendly Regard', and who later promised him the first copyright of any merit which came into his hands.[18] He was soon given the position of reader to the firm, with the responsibility of judging what material was suitable for publication; and when Hood was away from town, he was entrusted with the complete charge of the house, and had about him 'a Levee of Engravers, Designers, & Authors, in imitation of my Master'.[19] And amidst all this, he assisted in publishing the poetry of the firm's most celebrated author, Robert Bloomfield. In early May 1804, he wrote home: 'The Farmer's Boy is now preparing to be transmitted down to posterity with the greatest honours a Book can possibly receive – It will be the second Work stereotyped in England.'[20] Vernor & Hood's decision to print The Farmer's Boy in stereotype amply illustrates, not only the house's progressive spirit, but also the immense readership which Bloomfield then commanded. The plaster-of-Paris method of casting stereotypes had been perfected only two years previously, in 1802. It was a costly method of printing, and only substantial sales could offset the expense of making plates.[21] Yet Bloomfield's popularity was great enough to justify the increased cost. Only a few days after his appointment to the firm, Taylor met the poet at the height of his fame, and one aspect of his celebrity particularly impressed him. With evident astonishment, he wrote home in April: 'We have paid Bloomfield upwards of 4000£ for his 2 little Volumes – It is placed in the Funds and he manages his property with great prudence.

. . . Authors may complain of poverty, but this is paying with a witness – '22

The sum Vernor & Hood had paid for copyright was, of course, far from a unique instance of an author reaping astonishingly high rewards for his work, and Taylor may have known, even before meeting the poet, of previous cases in which the copyright of best-sellers had commanded vast sums – the £2,000 and £3,400 that Smollett and Hume had received for history books, or the £4,500 that William Robertson was given for his history of Charles V. But it seems likely, from his understandable astonishment at the sum paid to Bloomfield, that he had never previously been fully aware of the great financial rewards often involved in the publication of a best-seller. The sale of even a popular book in his father's shop at Retford was a far cry from London, where sales were reckoned in thousands and celebrated authors often received upwards of £1,000 for a single poem. For him to have come face to face with this commercial aspect of publishing so early in his career was an invaluable asset. If Bloomfield's poetry had no other effect upon him, it forced him to recognise that publishing was a trade subject to the same economic laws of supply and demand as any other. High sales in the reading market commanded substantial sums for copyright; poor sales, conversely, a minimal payment. At the very beginning of his apprenticeship, indeed, he had learned from both Lackington and Hood a lesson which provincial bookselling could never have taught with such emphasis. Publishing had to do with sales and demand, finance and economics, as well as with literary worth and excellence. It had, indeed, to reckon with the balance sheet as well as with beauty.

In later years, the question of how closely such high payments for copyright reflected true literary merit was a problem which regularly haunted Taylor's mind; and on many future occasions, he would have reason enough to believe that the relationship between financial reward and literary worth was not a causal but a purely capricious one. But under Hood's guidance, he could for the moment view such difficulties from afar. For the rest of 1804 and throughout 1805, he continued to work as Hood's chief assistant, reading, criticising, and gradually becoming known in the publishing world. To his father and mother he wrote during his first summer in London: 'I am in statu quo, at present, & shall do, most likely, for a long time yet. – But I am always on the alert for seizing any favourable proposition that may be made to me.'23

Eventually, when he had worked for Vernor & Hood for two years, he decided to risk greater independence. Sometime during 1806, Hessey and he formed a partnership as publishers and booksellers and set up in business.[24] In the house at 93 Fleet Street that they had been sharing with two other bachelors, they established a small bookshop. Taylor was the cashier and accountant for the shop, and both were involved in seeking out new customers, not only in London but in the provinces also. They established, too, a small business as binders, and indeed, this aspect of the firm seems to have become one of the more prosperous sides of their trade.[25] In 1810, an advertisement drawn up by Hessey to announce the house's books in general placed a particular emphasis upon the fine appearance of their volumes: 'bound in the most beautiful and splendid manner in calf, russia leather, Morocco, vellum, &c &c . . . many of them ornamented and illustrated with *original Drawings*'.[26] The new firm also began to publish in a small way. By and large, their list during these early years was safe and unadventurous – Headley's *Specimens of Ancient English Poetry*, sermons, domestic homilies, and moral tracts such as William Hussey's *Letters from an Elder to a Younger Brother on the Conduct to be Pursued in Life*. Only new editions of a few established classics, such as Shakespeare, Gibbon, and Goldsmith, pierced the mediocrity of a run-of-the-mill list which was indistinguishable from any other publisher's catalogue of useful, unpretentious books. Business was invariably very uncertain. During the summer of 1809, Hessey reported that trade was continuing as it had done for many months – 'grievously dull':[27]

> I have been dunning every body whom I could dun without much effect – I shall want 100 £ next Week to answer Bills and on Monday I shall scarcely have as many Pence to proceed with. . . .

> . . . from the Experience I have of what our Cares are I am sure I should be miserable indeed had I the serious weight of some of the great Houses in the City on my Shoulders.

Two years later, it was much the same story. Everything, Hessey wrote, was well 'except two evils which beset me, Want of Business and want of Money'.[28] But in spite of the dullness of trade during the summer months, the arrival of visitors in the city for the winter season generally quickened sales and provided the firm with sufficient business to survive. In September 1809, the bookshop in Fleet Street took £267. Eighteen months later, its takings had increased to £360 a month.[29] It was a slow, undramatic development, but the beginnings had been made.

Understandably important though the progress of the new firm was to Taylor and Hessey, the chief emphasis of their correspondence during these early years is upon matters largely unconnected with the difficulties of business. Gradually, their circle of friends was increasing. In March 1811, Taylor wrote to Retford that he had been introduced to Richard Woodhouse, a lawyer who was working with a conveyancer in the Temple. As he had done with Hessey, he supplied his parents with a character sketch of his new acquaintance:[30]

> He is about my own size, but thinner, has red hair, and a florid Complexion – His eyes are deep seated under a straight projecting line which should have eye brows upon it. . . . The character of the face is that of gravity and deep thought, more than genius. . . . He is an excellent Classic, having been last of all at Eton School - has a turn for poetry, by no means contemptible, tho' he thinks meanly enough of it – is abstemious to [a] remarkable degree, of great industry, averse to pleasure (in the London acceptation of the word) – rises early – reads much, and with the strictest attention – Above all things, he is extremely attentive to religious duties, has the highest Veneration for the Scriptures in which [he] delights to read, is of a retired modest behaviour and possesses more real humility than (I was going to say) any one I know; but I certainly think, as much.

From his first meeting with Woodhouse, Taylor was clearly attracted by his quiet and thoughtful manner, and he felt himself 'considerably improved' by his 'conversation and example'. Their talk ranged widely – over books and religion, poetry, the law, and writing – and often, as Taylor confessed, the conversations in Fleet Street continued long into the night, with the result that the circle spent too many hours talking and writing, and not enough taking 'Exercise'.[31] One immediate benefit of their meeting, though, was the formation of the Philological Society, a venture in which both Taylor and Woodhouse were to play leading roles. The purpose of the society, Taylor informed James, was a 'mutual Improvement in the Art of Speaking'. The discussions ranged over many subjects – politics, culture, writing, metaphysics, agriculture – and in several of his letters to James, Taylor reported each debate and indicated the side he had supported:[32]

1. Is England on its Decline? – I said – No.
2. Is good speaking or good Writing the more useful Talent? – J.T. Good Writing
3. Should large Farms be encouraged? *Certainly* not

4. Is a Country preferable to a Town Life? no, exc^t. in Boyhood
& Age
5. Are the Minds of Women inferior by Nature to those of Men?
– In the *reasoning* Powers.

The mind of the society, though, was not always so sternly focused
upon such forensic ability: 'We had a Dinner of the Society last Week
at which I officiated as Vice President – To promote Mirth & Improvement, I sung a Song. . . .'[33] But even with Taylor's singing to stimulate
it, the Philological Society was not destined to revolutionise the
thought of a generation. A year later, Hessey mournfully reported that
the latest meeting had been attended by three members only, and soon
afterwards he wrote its obituary: 'The Philo-logical Society *has been* –
We have now nothing more than to see it decently interred and to pay
its debts honourably – '[34]

Abortive though the society had been, its very existence within
Taylor's circle not only points forward to the way in which he was to
achieve his greatest success in London, but reveals also much of the
way in which his own personality was developing. On an intellectual
level, he had begun to show a strength and fluency in discussion and
argument, in the interchanging of ideas with friends whom he met
often. The enthusiasm of his reports to James illustrates, indeed, how
greatly the variety and comradeship of the society's debate stimulated
him and provided the germ of ideas which he might later explore alone.
Emotionally, too, this kind of close circle was becoming increasingly
necessary to his way of life, giving him a sustenance that he could not
create of himself. Although he remained throughout his life a solitary
in many respects, living closely to himself, he was always to derive his
chief energy not from isolation, which he hated, but from the warmth
and kindliness of an intimate society. The kind of personality which
was developing during these years, indeed, was one which flowered
fully only when inspired by the friendship of others.

The tone and emphasis of many of his letters to James from this
period show clearly this growing reliance upon personal contact for
his well-being. Yet at the deepest level, his need seems to have been not
only to possess close friendships, but to believe implicitly that different
aspects of human experience did connect and relate with each other. In
1806, he wrote to James:[35]

There is a peculiarity in every minute of our lives which fits it to
its place – a Harmony of Events, and Ideas, which (first)
contributes to the progressive Development of our Nature as

Individuals, & (secondly) acts in Conformity, though we cannot see it, with all the other rising varieties of Creation. . . .

Such thoughts, he willingly acknowledged, were 'obscure'; and in their confidence of a final harmony in the scheme of things, they perhaps still clung to an eighteenth-century optimism and clarity of belief. But his deepest concern was that the relationship he perceived between the 'rising varieties of Creation' should not only be recognised on a philosophical level, but also translated into the lives that men led. Knowledge, he came to believe, was of no value intrinsically. Only when it contributed to the betterment of mankind, only in its application and relationship to experience, could it possess any worth. In his Christian belief, similarly, one of his growing concerns was to relate and anchor the Christian ethic in the reality of men's lives:[36]

If we make the View we have as Christians serve as a Test of the relative worth of all our Employments, it will completely answer our Wishes – But who uses his religious knowledge in this Sense? Most people consider Religion & the Business of Life as irreconcilable with each other, and would no more think of making one keep any Proportion with the other, than they would expect to hear how far it is from Christmas Day to Hyde Park Corner.

The key words of these letters – peculiarity, harmony, variety, relative worth, proportion, conformity – illustrate how greatly this idea of the relationship between different aspects of experience had captured his imagination. He came to believe finally that it was rarely possible to evaluate the importance or truth of a particular experience in isolation from its wider context. What became for him one of the foremost virtues was a comprehensiveness of mind which, in its ability to connect and relate, worked towards a deliberate completeness of understanding.

The importance of this way of thinking was in the end much more than the value of a personal philosophy. For within a few years, Taylor was to reveal how closely analogous his literary judgments were to these beliefs. His philosophy constantly emphasised the need to place particular ideas within a broader context, to examine the relationships which existed between specific attitudes and the deep range of experience that lay behind them. Similarly, in his future judgments about literature, he was constantly to argue that true criticism demanded perspective. To be of any value, it could only be of 'that enlarged kind that takes entire Surveys of a Subject'.[37] Past literature must be viewed in the context of the present, and contemporary writing in that of the past. One of the primary tasks of criticism, indeed, was to define the wider literary context in which a particular book was to be placed and subsequently judged. In this attitude, there lay perhaps the first flowering of that breadth of outlook that Trye and Stevenson may have done much to foster in Retford. In it, certainly, there lay one of the chief reasons for Taylor's future success as a publisher of new literature.

During the first years of his life in London, Taylor wrote to James and defined simply one of his chief beliefs:[38]

> had I a friend or brother to whom I wished to communicate an important truth, the result of the best experience I have yet had in the world, it should be this: that is without Charity the Virtues are nothing worth, so the best and noblest powers of the Head & Heart are useless or worse, unless they are made subservient to the welfare, ease & Happiness of Mankind –

But in one respect at least, ideas of love and charity were never to be realised for him. During the early summer of 1811, he spent many weeks holidaying in Claverton, near Bath, on what Hessey was convinced was a matrimonial expedition. A comical letter full of scarcely veiled references was sent from Fleet Street:[39]

> I had quite given you up as lost and had almost, nay had quite, ordered a new suit of Black on the occasion, when I received a Letter from Woodhouse informing me that you are really alive but so changed as scarcely to be known for the same person – your Silence is to me a convincing proof that you are very happy as I who know what Claverton Valley is should not have doubted without such proof –

Both Taylor and Hessey clearly derived much enjoyment from these encounters, and good-humoured advice and warnings of feminine wiles abound in Hessey's letters to his partner during these months. But in May, Taylor wrote and confessed that, with one particularly important relationship, all was not going as well as might be. One of the bachelors with whom Hessey and he shared the house in Fleet Street, Frederick Falkner, was a rival for the lady's affections; and Taylor, perhaps through uncertainty in his own mind about marriage or through fears of inadequate finance to support a wife, allowed Falkner to proceed in his stead.[40] For some time, the disappointment affected him keenly; and over a year later, he wrote a letter which again spoke of the oppressive isolation of London that he hated:[41]

> My Solitude seems more lonely then, when all I see around me are so gay, & apparently happy. There is scarcely a solitary Person to be seen in the Streets. Or if there is one passer by . . . he does not saunter, as if everybody in this great Town was indifferent to him.

Such attacks of depression may well have been made the more acute by thoughts of the companionship which his closest friends now enjoyed. His brother James had married in 1811; and in September 1813, Hessey married Kate Falkner, Frederick's sister. For a time, Taylor continued to live in Fleet Street with Hessey and his wife, but eventually he moved out of town completely and lodged 'at a small neat Inn called "the Spaniards"' overlooking Hampstead Heath. The new environment greatly restored his spirits after the confinement of the city: 'You can't think how pleasant it seems to me to go there after so long a confinement in London. I walk both Morning and Evening and the Distance is at least 5 miles from Fleet Street.'[42]

In other ways, too, his time was becoming increasingly occupied, leaving little opportunity to think upon his own troubles. He was writing a dissertation on the use of Commonplace Books to prefix to the *Literary Diary* that the house published, and collecting material for a book entitled *Grammar made Easy*.[43] He was reading widely, particularly in Spenser, and studying phrenology. But for an understanding of his future success as a publisher, a single aspect of a book he completed during this period is of particular interest. The book was concerned with a subject which never ceased to fascinate him throughout his life – the identity of 'Junius'.

As a piece of literary detective work, a kind of eighteenth-century Mr W. H., the mystery of the Whig letter-writer 'Junius', who had anonymously attacked many members of the government circle during the years 1768-72, had intrigued Taylor for several years.[44] An edition of Junius's letters containing much new material had been published in 1812 and immediately revived public speculation about the identity of the author. Taylor plunged in. At first in a small pamphlet, and later in a volume of some 350 pages, he offered a tightly-knit argument that the letters had been written by Sir Philip Francis. To examine in detail the studied evasiveness of Francis's replies to his theory or the many parallels which he drew between Francis and Junius is unnecessary. With a scholar's thoroughness, he argued dauntingly from every possible viewpoint – biography, dates, political thought, handwriting, personality, historical circumstance, indeed 'every species of inquiry that can be suggested'.[45] But one particular approach he took to the puzzle is particularly interesting – that of linguistic and literary analysis. He collated two descriptions, written entirely independently, which commented upon the general style and tone of the writings of Francis and Junius. The critic of Junius had remarked particularly upon the perspicuity of his language, his 'epigrammatic compression' and the 'ardour and spirit' of his style: 'Rapid, violent, and impetuous, he affirms without reason, and decides without proof; as if he feared that the slow methods of induction and argument would interrupt him in his progress.' The critic of Francis, similarly, noted that in argument 'he lightens rather than reasons on his subject. Vivid flashes from his mind, in rapid succession, illuminate the question, not by formal induction, but by uniform splendour and irresistible corruscation.'

The two critics, as Taylor was quick to point out, were commenting upon two different authors as far as they were concerned; yet the similarity of their conclusions was enough to set him going. He examined the language of speeches and letters more closely, and noticed that both Francis and Junius used on many occasions the curious phrase 'of his side', instead of 'on his side'. Both used the stilted and antique phrase 'so far forth', in place of 'in so far as'; and both habitually wrote 'affectedly' for 'effectively'. He argued further that the occurrence of metaphor offered 'an excellent clue . . . for tracing an anonymous author',[46] and discovered that the metaphors used by Francis and Junius were often remarkably similar. Not only this, but whole phrases were common to both writers.[47] He noted too that instances of personification were equally frequent in their style, and that they often arranged words to form a characteristically antithetical balance. When they inveighed against their opponents, there was a similar rhythm in their language and a similar repetition of key words:[48]

Who attacks the liberty of the press? Lord Mansfield. – Who invades the constitutional power of juries? Lord Mansfield. – What judge ever challenged a juryman but Lord Mansfield? (Junius)

But in the consideration of these offences, who is the offended party? the negro-driver —— Who is the judge of the fact? The driver. Who awards the punishment? The driver. —— Who inflicts it? The driver, with his own hand. (Francis)

By modern standards, Taylor's methods were inevitably unsophisticated, and indeed the final efficacy of his approach is still open to doubt. But in the light of his future career, the importance of *The Identity of Junius* rests not so much in the accuracy of his identification as in this use of linguistic analysis. In the study of the vocabulary and rhythm in the styles of Junius and Francis, in the examination of their use of metaphor, personification, and antithesis, he had revealed not only an interest in language, but a subtle understanding of its usage, and an acuteness of ear to its varying rhythms and structures. In his later association with writers, particularly with John Clare, the importance of this sensitivity to language for an understanding of his author's work was to be clearly illustrated.

Intrigued though Taylor remained by the Junius puzzle throughout his life, neither he nor Hessey was unaware during the months of research for the book that matters of greater moment would soon demand all their attention. The prospect of an end to the twenty-year war against France brought the realisation that their greatest opportunities for expanding the firm were almost upon them, and both had great hopes of a new prosperity in business. In early 1814, Hessey wrote: 'It does seem likely that the prosperous Course of Events abroad will be of great Benefit to *us* and we are bound to take advantage of it and improve the opportunities we may have to the utmost.'[49] Taylor, too, voiced the same optimism: 'Business has been unusually good & promises to continue so . . . we have had a very good year hitherto – Our Trade has gone on gradually improving.'[50] There still remained, of course, serious economic difficulties in the trade, particularly for small publishing firms such as Taylor & Hessey. Stamp duties, which had been raised several times during the war years, were increased again in May 1815 and caused a bitter complaint from Taylor.[51] Two-thirds of the house's outlay in publishing a 500-copy edition would have gone upon the buying of paper, which was taxed at 3*d.* a pound. Printing-house compositors, moreover, earned a wage of 36*s.* a week, the highest-paid skilled workers in London,[52] and consequently the cost of printing new books was high, particularly for a firm which dealt mostly in editions of only 500 or 1,000 copies. But as peace came and commerce again flowed between England and the Continent, the situation became more hopeful. During the latter months of 1816, the price of paper fell from 33*s.* to 28*s.* a ream;[53] bullion was once more coming freely into the country, and the trade in books across the Channel had re-started. There were also more obviously clear reasons for the firm's growing hopefulness. In the summer of 1815, Hessey returned from a visit to Bath with accounts from several booksellers which were 'likely to be attended with much advantage to us'. In early 1816, the house gained some glory by their appointment as booksellers to Prince Leopold. And with peace too came some measure of financial security. A certain Mr Freeman bought a third share of the business, and gave Taylor and Hessey permission to draw £500 from his stock whenever the house was in financial difficulty.[54]

In the larger world of the great publishing houses also, there was an atmosphere of renewed energy and endeavour which helped to foster a sense of buoyancy in the trade. The vast prices paid for copyright, which had amazed Taylor during his first months in London, had become by 1816 a practice common enough to escape notice. For *The Siege of Corinth* and the Third Canto of *Childe Harold*, both published in 1816, John Murray gave Byron 1,000 guineas and £2,000 respectively. A year previously, Sir Walter Scott had received 1,500 guineas for half the copyright of *The Lord of the Isles*, and in 1810, an astonishing £4,000 for *The Lady of the Lake*. So confident indeed were the great houses that poetry would provide an abundant return on the expenses of copyright and publication that it was possible for Longman's to offer the poet Thomas Moore £3,000 for a poem of which they had not read a line. Such vast sums for copyright were not, of course, the result of any philanthropy on the part of publishers. The books answered. Poetry and novels in particular were booming, and selling in thousands. Indeed, there could be no better illustration of the immense attraction new works of this kind held for the reading public than the sale of Byron's *The Corsair* in 1814. On the day of publication alone, the poem sold over 10,000 copies – an event which even John Murray found 'perfectly unprecedented'.

In even more important ways too, the great publishing houses were beginning to exercise an increasing influence upon the promulgation of new literature. Murray, Blackwood, and Constable all sought to make their place of business a centre of literary society, a kind of English Rambouillet salon, where writers dined and talked frequently with men eminent in politics, science, and letters. They advertised new books in conversation, encouraged an interaction of personalities, and promoted a creative context in which men of talent pooled new ideas and experience. Murray's drawing room in Albemarle Street was 'the main centre of literary intercourse' in his part of London; and Archibald Constable, in Cockburn's words, 'drew authors from dens where they would otherwise have starved, and made Edinburgh a literary mart, famous with strangers, and the pride of its own citizens'.[55] No longer in the eyes of many authors was the publisher simply a cipher who transformed manuscript into printed book. In his hospitality to writers, in his generous payment for copyright and encouragement of their work, he had begun to play an increasingly vital role in the fostering of new literature.

Much of this sense of energy and buoyancy in the trade rubbed off upon Taylor & Hessey. Publishable material of all kinds was pouring into the London houses and, as Taylor argued, it seemed that 'Authors [were] in want of Publishers than the latter of Authors'.[56] Against such a prospect of opportunity, he decided in 1816 to put into effect a policy which had for some time been in his mind. In January, he wrote to his mother:[57]

> I think we shall find it better worth our while to publish as many good Books as we can than to keep a general Assortment of other People's Books – If it be proved that my Impression is well founded it will influence our future Proceedings to a certain Extent.

The plan to expand considerably the publishing side of the firm's activities was one quietly made, but the implications of Taylor's decision were to affect literature in a way which could scarcely have been anticipated at the time. Within months, he had begun to conceive of his role, not as the passive publisher of works which were brought to him, but as the active seeker-out of new talent. As he explained to James: '[I] could originate Works, even without any Author bringing his Productions to me. . . . My . . . Plan . . . would be to originate, edit, or propose to others to execute such Works as I conceive would answer.'[58] It was clear that he had begun to think of the publisher's role as a shaping influence in the creation and promulgation of new literature.

For the previous ten years, Taylor and Hessey had served what was in fact an apprenticeship as publishers; and to look back over the early years of their partnership is to recognise how varied their introduction to the trade had been, and how firmly they had laid the foundation for their future success. They had built up a reputation as fair and honest dealers, known and esteemed by the rest of the trade. They had played leading parts in the fostering of a close circle which, in its membership and activities, looked forward to the far more illustrious society of the *London Magazine* years. Both had gained invaluable experience in specialised aspects of the trade – a knowledge of printing and binding, profit and sales, advertising and copyright. But neither of them was unaware that, for all their application, a certain glory had not yet been attained. Their publishing list was still weighed down with safe investments in domestic and religious homilies, in commonplace books, literary diaries, and unmemorable poetry. The books sold, but it was an unexciting list, inspired only by a seemingly invincible mediocrity. In 1814, Hessey wrote to Taylor and caught the mood of the firm with a searching question: 'Miss Edgeworths New Novel is enclosed. Johnsons printed 3000 and could deliver only half what were subscribed for – When shall we pick up a Miss Edgeworth?'[59]

The answer came three years later. Sometime during the first months of 1817, John Hamilton Reynolds, who had met Taylor the previous year during the publication of his poem *The Naiad*, introduced him to a young poet of his acquaintance – John Keats. The introduction marked the beginning of the eight years which Taylor and Hessey often justly remembered as the finest of their lives. By the middle of April, Taylor had decided to publish Keats's poetry. He wrote home to his father quite simply: 'I cannot think he will fail to become a great Poet.'[60]

'A true poet': Taylor and Keats, 1817-21

On the evening of 3 March 1817, a few weeks probably after Taylor and Hessey had first met Keats, the painter Haydon held a party in his studio. The occasion of the celebration was the publication that day of Keats's first volume of poetry. Nearly sixty years later, one of the guests at the gathering, Cowden Clarke, remembered nostalgically the champagne enthusiasm which filled the air that night:[1]

> The first volume of Keats's minor muse was launched amid the cheers and fond anticipations of all his circle. Every one of us expected (and not unreasonably) that it would create a sensation in the literary world; for such a first production (and a considerable portion of it from a minor) has rarely occurred.

The intimate members of the poet's circle hailed the book as the first-fruits of genius. The day before publication, Charles Ollier, who had published the volume with his brother James, forwarded to Keats an advance copy, inscribed with a specially written sonnet which rhapso-dised upon his 'upward daring Soul', his 'eager grasp at immortality', and upon the laurels which would soon be his. Having read the poem 'Sleep and Poetry' which concluded the volume, Haydon too wrote to the poet in a tone of almost Messianic expectancy: 'It is a flash of lightening that will rouse men from their occupations, and keep them trembling for the crash of thunder that *will* follow.'[2]

Reynolds, addressing himself to the world beyond the poet's immedi-ate circle, acknowledged the uncertainty and lack of complete defini-tion in a talent not yet fully matured; but he prophesied that Keats would outshine the greatest poets of his age, and went so far as to compare him with Chaucer and Shakespeare.[3] And in the *Examiner*, Leigh Hunt generously advanced the cause of his protégé, whom he had met the previous October, and celebrated the beauties of 'a fine ear, a fancy and imagination at will, and an intense feeling of external beauty in it's most natural and least expressible simplicity'.[4] Few books in literary history can ever have been published with as much antici-pation.

Yet beyond the infectious partisanship of Keats's circle, in the general judgment of the literary world, there was a more disturbing equivocation. Analysis of the new volume was more dispassionate, and more severe. The *Eclectic Review*, on so many future occasions the most generous and mature critic of several Taylor & Hessey publications, voiced a reasoned criticism of the book. It had been published too soon. By and large, Keats had not yet found a distinctive voice in which to speak. An obvious talent was present, but it seemed a talent that was more a promise of genius than the complete realisation of it. The reviewer, Josiah Conder, believed that he should not have published so soon poetry 'of which a few years hence he will be glad to escape the remembrance. The lash of a critic is the thing the least to be dreaded, as the penalty of premature publication.'5 The criticism was not unjust; for, taken as a whole, the volume was a book of sporadic rather than sustained genius. Apart from one or two of the sonnets and 'Sleep and Poetry', there was not a great deal in it to support Haydon's prediction of a kind of literary Armageddon.

By the end of April, not two months after publication, it was clear that the reading public had endorsed Conder's criticism. As Cowden Clarke later confessed, the literary community seemed determined to ignore the book, and it might well have appeared in Timbuctoo with a far stronger chance of 'fame and approbation'. On 29 April, the Ollier brothers reported to George Keats:6

we think the curiosity is satisfied, and the sale has dropped. By far the greater number of persons who have purchased it from us have found fault with it in such plain terms, that we have in many cases offered to take the book back rather than be annoyed with the ridicule which has, time after time, been showered upon it. In fact, it was only on Saturday last that we were under the mortification of having our opinion of its merits flatly contradicted by a gentleman, who told us he considered it 'no better than a take in'. . . .

The reference in this letter to an actual conversation, the most depressing part of which had stuck in the Olliers' minds, suggests that they were not exaggerating the situation. In spite of enthusiasm and advertisement, the reception of Keats's book amongst the reading public had proved a far severer test than its reception amongst the poet's close circle. And when the initial cheering had died down, it was clear that the volume had passed almost completely unnoticed, and that it was not going to sell.

The situation could scarcely have been worse. To Taylor, the facts must have been clear enough, and many of them spoke against his involvement in Keats's difficulties. The poet was young and virtually unknown; his book as a whole had much merit but hardly a sustained display of genius; and sales had been practically non-existent. For a small house such as Taylor & Hessey, the financial risks of publishing his future work under such circumstances were obvious. Yet within a month, Taylor had decided. On 15 April, he wrote to his father:[7]

> We have agreed for the next Edit. of Keats's Poems, and are to have the Refusal of his future Works. I cannot think he will fail to become a great Poet, though I agree with you in finding much fault with his Dedication &c. These are not likely to appear in any other of his Productions.

Some of the reasons which lay behind this momentous decision are clear enough. His desire to 'publish as many good Books as we can',[8] and to play an increasingly active role in encouraging new literature, were obvious factors. So too may have been the relatively good results that the publishing side of the firm was enjoying during these months, in contrast to the increasingly disastrous losses suffered by its retail trade. But beyond these, it is almost certain that other reasons, of greater moment for the cause of literature, led to his offer to Keats.

In a letter to John Clare three years later, Taylor advocated very briefly the critical approach to literature that he admired before all others:[9]

> I hate Criticism at all times except when it is of that enlarged kind that takes entire Surveys of a Subject, & conceiving old Writers to be new and new ones to be old awards to each his proper Share of Consideration.

How greatly this attitude towards criticism played a direct part in his decision to publish Keats is not altogether easy to tell. Yet it is clear that the breadth and comprehensiveness of outlook reflected in these views reveal him as a publisher particularly receptive to the experiments of new literature. He argued to Clare the necessity of a deliberate completeness of approach in the formation of critical judgments, the need for an enlarged perspective which constantly placed any incidental faults within a wider context. The approach he advocated was one, indeed, in which perspective and an awareness of the broader contexts surrounding any particular work became crucial for a true evaluation of literary merit. And in Keats's case, it is almost certain that such a theory influenced considerably his decision. Whatever uncertainties and weaknesses the poet's first book revealed, Taylor had looked beyond them, and had seen in the volume as a whole certain unique qualities which could not fail to make him a 'great Poet'.

To define in any precise way those qualities which caught his imagination is again not easy. He himself wrote of Keats's work only in the most generalised of terms; and indeed, throughout the few brief years of their association, one looks in vain for that detailed talk about poetry which was later to characterise so strongly his correspondence with John Clare. But one document, never previously published, illustrates how closely Keats and he were in accord in their general thinking about literature. In one of his Commonplace Books, Taylor jotted down some rough notes for a proposed 'Essay on Poetry':[10]

> On the First Order of Poetry: that of the Imagination – the power & extent of it, – Identity – the Language of strong Sensation – Its Universality – Comprehensiveness of all other Qualities – Manner of teaching through the Heart – which is the proper Region of its Govern^m. – naturally dramatic – real to us, because so to him who uses it. – Absorbent of all other Considerations – Only to be understood aright by him who is willing to surrender himself to its Sway. – Greatest of all Things because the Gift of the Creator – Learning injurious to it, if seen, because it belongs to Art – . . . .
>
> The Universalism of this Faculty in entering into inanimate as well as living Objects, & giving a Sentiment to their dead Nature is another Attribute of the true Poet, and one almost peculiar to modern Nations – Hence Sculpture=Poetry
>
> The Reasoning thro' the same Faculty is another Characteristic whereby Truths are taught as if we ourselves discovered them –
>
> So that the true Poet makes every thing, Action, Thinking, Argument, Description, something different, & superior to what it would be in any other Person, by the Force of his Imagination
>
> This is alone the true Poet – the Creator. . . .

Tantalisingly sketchy though these notes are, they demonstrate clearly Taylor's fascination with the nature of the poetic imagination. They reveal also much of his sensitivity to the kind of poetic theory that Keats was to express in future months; and in many later parts of this study dealing with other writers as well as Keats, an attempt will be made to show how closely these views about poetry paralleled the beliefs of the firm's authors. Yet however receptive Taylor was to the imaginative qualities of Keats's poetry, a sympathy in literary beliefs alone could scarcely have induced him to extend to the poet the special kind of understanding which he showed during the first months of their association. Kinship was fostered on a personal level also. In Taylor's own words, he soon came to feel towards Keats a 'strange personal Interest in all that concerns him'.[11] And such interest was soon expressed on a practical level in encouragement and financial support. By the end of April, not only had the firm offered to take from the Olliers all the unsold copies of the first volume and attempt to sell them, but they had also made a firm promise to keep Keats in funds for the first refusal of all his future works.

The sincerity of the promise was soon tested, and it held. On 16 May, Keats wrote to thank the house for their 'liberality in the Shape of manufactu[r]ed rag value £20'. The tone of much of his letter was jaunty and optimistic, but towards the end of it, he suddenly launched into a more disturbing strain:[12]

> I went day by day at my Poem for a Month at the end of which time the other day I found my Brain so overwrought that I had neither Rhyme nor reason in it – so was obliged to give up for a few days – . . . instead of Poetry I have a swimming in my head – And feel all the effects of a Mental Debauch – lowness of Spirits – anxiety to go on without the Power to do so. . . .

However transient such feelings were, they must have brought home to Taylor early how finely the balance lay in Keats's temperament between despair and well-being. Scarcely a month after their agreement, it appeared that he had temporarily written himself to a standstill. As he himself later confessed, his mind was caught at this time in the cross-currents of two kinds of imagination – the boy's and the man's – when the soul was 'in a ferment' and the 'way of life uncertain'. Moving towards the imagination of maturity, he must necessarily pass through 'a space of life' in which there were few fixed points of reference, few structures upon which to build an uncertain philosophy. In poetry, as in life, there existed for him no intellectual or imaginative surety. The creation of his poetry evolved, not from any fixed centre, but from a continual interplay and tension between despair and energy, stasis and exultation.

Over a year later, Hessey had still not fully come to terms with this particular kind of creative restlessness in Keats's temperament:[13]

he is studying closely, recovering his Latin, going to learn Greek, and seems altogether more rational than usual – but he is such a man of fits and starts he is not much to be depended on. Still he thinks of nothing but poetry as his being's end and aim, and sometime or other he will, I doubt not, do something valuable.

The somewhat critical tone of Hessey's judgment sorts oddly with the sympathy that he almost habitually showed towards the firm's authors; but it reveals that he at least was uncertain whether Keats would fully realise his genius. Even for Taylor, who was more generous in his appraisal, these first months may well have seemed a test of faith – faith not only that Keats would now realise his powers, but that his own intuition in deciding to publish his work had not deceived him. Yet the firm's generosity did not dry up. A month after his first request for a loan, the poet wrote again to London. Determining to lose his 'Maidenhead with respect to money Matters as soon as possible', he requested another £30, confident that the firm realised his 'responsibility'.[14] The money was forthcoming; and finally, seven months later, the result of the house's encouragement became evident. In January 1818, Keats took to Fleet Street the first book of his new poem *Endymion*.

Taylor's initial reaction to the poem was evidently very favourable, for to Keats's delight, he suggested publishing the whole poem in quarto if Haydon could be prevailed upon to draw a frontispiece. But as the other three books of *Endymion* were delivered, he seems to have become more uncertain of the poem's merit. In May, his brother James wrote from Bakewell: 'What are your sentiments of Endymion now that it is made a Book of – Does it please you any better than it did at the time I left London?'[15] In his reply, Taylor admitted: 'Endymion does not by any means please me as I had expected.'[16]

The reasons for his disappointment are unclear. Possibly, the almost narcotic mellifluousness of the poem, the lack of a shaping logic to control the accumulation of embellishment upon embellishment, the lack of any underlying pressure or synthesising force, weakened the poem in his eyes. Possibly, too, he was alarmed by the more passionate episodes that Keats had depicted, and became unnecessarily conscious of a seeming indelicacy which might offend the feminine reading public. But he was at the same time clearly unwilling to damn the book as a whole. Much in the poem pleased him, the Hymn to Pan, the episode of Glaucus, and the triumph of Bacchus in particular;[17] and the quality of these passages was more than sufficient to eclipse what he believed were incidental failings. His final judgment was in the poem's favour, and immediately in his letter to James he spoke up for it: 'I can hardly allow others to find Fault with it, because I think they [do] not retain a sufficient Recollection of its Beauties also, & strike a Balance of Opinion in its Favour.'[18]

During February and March of 1818, he supervised the entire process of publication, suggesting possible variants to Keats, emending punctuation, and generally devoting a good deal of time to the book as a labour of love. The task was not easy, for even when the manuscripts were out of his hands, Keats was uncertain whether he had expressed his ideas as well as might be. The shadow of Leigh Hunt was still close upon him, and even when the first book had been set up in print, he began to alter and finally excise some forty lines in an attempt to remove as much as possible of Hunt's stylistic influence. The task of resetting the altered pages certainly cost the firm a good deal in time and money; but there seems to have been already in the minds of both poet and publisher a vague premonition of trouble ahead, an intimation of a more sustained attack by the Reviews upon Leigh Hunt and his satellites. A severe critical reception to *Endymion* was distinctly possible, the more so because Keats, by dedicating his first book to Leigh Hunt, had now become closely associated in the minds of reviewers and public with Hunt and the Cockney School. But in March, these troubles were only a future possibility. Already the present had furnished a problem which demanded all of Taylor's attention.

On 19 March, Keats drafted a preface to *Endymion*. It could scarcely have been composed at a worse time. His brother Tom had just suffered a relapse, and being drawn again into the atmosphere of the sick-room, he poured into the introduction all his frustration with poetry, all his awareness of the poverty and insignificance of individual effort:

In a great nation, the work of an individual is of so little
importance; his pleadings and excuses are so uninteresting; his
'way of life' such a nothing; that a preface seems a sort of
imperti[n]ent bow to strangers who care nothing about it.

The preface struggled along in this tone, following the vagaries of his bitterness. He confessed that *Endymion* was 'an endeavour' rather than 'a thing accomplish'd'. He would have kept it longer from the public, realising its manifest faults, but I really cannot do so: – by repetition my favourite Passages sound vapid in my ears, and I would rather redeem myself with a new Poem – should this one be found of any interest.

And finally, seemingly half-conscious again of some impending attack, he quoted from Marston: 'let it be the Curtesy of my peruser rather to pity my self hindering labours than to malice me.'[19]

It must have been clear to Taylor that so much self-deprecation in a preface, far from being construed as genuine humility and dissatisfaction, would play completely into the hands of the critics. Keats's scarcely veiled references to the London and Edinburgh reviews ('a London drizzle or a Scotch mist'), and his hope that Marston's sentiment would shelter him 'as an umbrella' from any criticism, were not altogether calculated to rouse much sympathy for his cause. Reynolds, acting as mediator, tactfully suggested that he should rewrite the preface. Keats replied: 'Since you all agree that the thing is bad, it must be so'. But unwilling to surrender his position, he continued in a sharper tone and gave voice to a far deeper dissension which he saw arising between himself and the world of letters:[20]

> I have not the slightest feel of humility towards the Public – or
> to anything in existence, – but the eternal Being, the Principle of
> Beauty, – and the Memory of great Men . . . a Preface is written
> to the Public; a thing I cannot help looking upon as an Enemy,
> and which I cannot address without feelings of Hostility . . .
> among Multitudes of Men – I have no feel of stooping, I hate
> the idea of humility to them –
> I never wrote one single Line of Poetry with the least Shadow
> of public thought.
>
> . . . if there is any fault in the preface it is not affectation: but an
> undersong of disrespect to the Public. – if I write another preface.
> it must be done without a thought of those people –

Tom's growing illness may have touched Keats's mind more deeply than can ever be shown; and perhaps the fierce independence and individuality of this letter was a kind of acknowledgment that he was trying to extract from those around him, at the time that his brother seemed to be losing those very qualities. But however personally venial his attack upon the reading public was, Taylor's position was becoming increasingly difficult. For by rewriting the preface in a quieter tone and by omitting the more barbed of the darts he had thrown at the public, Keats did not change his ground. He merely made it appear more reasonable. The growing tension in his relationship with the public was not to be resolved by the alteration of a few words. In under a year, the same quarrel was to arise again even more fiercely, and the task of reconciling the different attitudes of the writer and his public – a theme so deeply woven into Taylor's career – then demanded all his skill as a mediator.

Towards the end of April 1818 *Endymion* was finally published. Receiving his author's copies from the press, Keats wrote to thank Taylor for the particular care he had taken with the book:[21]

> I think I Did very wrong to leave you to all the trouble of Endymion – but I could not help it then. . . . And in proportion to my disgust at the task is my sense of your kindness & anxiety – the book pleased me much – it is very free from faults; and although there are one or two words I should wish replaced, I see in many places an improvement greatly to the purpose – . . . the preface is well without those things you have left out.

Taylor had clearly nursed the volume through the press with more than usual care and attention. Yet the slight troubles of the days preceding publication were soon to be of paltry significance compared with the storm that was approaching; and by the end of the year, both poet and publisher had reason enough to recall Haydon's prediction of thunder and lightning. The tragedy was that he had mistaken both its nature and direction.

Only a few days after the publication of *Endymion*, Taylor seems to have sensed trouble. By some means he heard that William Gifford, editor of the *Quarterly Review* and a kindred soul to Blackwood's *Maga* in his dislike of Cockney poetry, was preparing an article on Leigh Hunt, Shelley, and Keats. On 15 May, he called upon Gifford and appealed for a fair review of *Endymion*. Let the poetry be criticised by all means, but not in a way which dishonestly dragged in personal associations to support an attack:[22]

> I wished him to understand that Keats was a young Man, of great Promise, whom it would be cruel to sacrifice on the sole Account of his Connection with Hunt, a Connection which would doubtless be dissolved by the Difference of their Characters – He heard & assented to all I said, but I fear it is too late to be of much Service, for he pointed to an Article in which they are

noticed, then laying on his Table – & I fear it will not experience any Alteration from my Appeal.

He told James in June: 'If he treats Endymion unfairly I think I shall be tempted to write an answer.'[23] Within three months, though, his worst fears had been realised. On 1 September, the attacks began. The August number of *Maga* denounced what it called the 'calm, settled, imperturbable drivelling idiocy of "Endymion"'. The review showed no mercy. It attacked where Keats was most vulnerable. His youth was incoherently dragged into the argument, and his association with Leigh Hunt, inevitably, provided much ammunition: 'Mr Hunt is a small poet, but he is a clever man. Mr Keats is a still smaller poet, and he is only a boy of pretty abilities, which he has done everything in his power to spoil.' The review concluded with a thrust at Taylor as well as Keats.[24] Implying that the publisher had shown a good deal of foolishness in ever deciding to publish Keats's work at all, it ventured to make 'one small prophecy',

that his bookseller will not a second time venture £50 upon any thing he can write. It is a better and a wiser thing to be a starving apothecary than a starved poet; so back to the shop Mr John, back to the 'plasters, pills, and ointment boxes', &c. But, for Heaven's sake, young Sangrado, be a little more sparing of extenuatives and soporifics in your practice than you have been in your poetry.

Distressing enough though this attack was in itself, it must have been doubly so for Taylor because of the information which had unwittingly been given to Lockhart, the reviewer, by one of his close friends, Benjamin Bailey. In late July, Bailey had dined with Lockhart at the table of Bishop Gleig, and during the evening, Lockhart had begun to attack Keats, abusing him in such vicious terms that Bailey could scarcely keep his temper. In the heat of argument, he began defending Keats by relating his history – his training as surgeon and apothecary and his respectable education – and defended his association with Hunt. The tit-bits of information were precisely what Lockhart needed to ram home his attack.

Bailey clearly realised afterwards that he had played straight into the enemy's hands, for on 29 August, he wrote to Taylor from Carlisle and expressed his fears that *Endymion* would be 'dreadfully cut up in the Edinburgh Magazine'. As a '*man of Genius*', Bailey acknowledged that Keats could and should be defended, and he offered to write an article in the poet's defence were he to be '*grossly* attacked'. But about certain other aspects of the poem he was evidently more uncertain, and his uncertainty exposed again the differences of attitude between Keats and his public which were arising more and more frequently. The attack Bailey feared most was upon the moral integrity of *Endymion*, for it was this question he felt he could not defend. 'There are two great blotches in [the poem] in this respect', he wrote to Taylor:[25]

> The first must offend *every* one of proper feelings; and indelicacy is not to be borne; & I greatly reproach myself that I did not represent this very strongly to [Keats] before it was sent to the Press. . . . The second fault I allude to I think we have noticed – The approaching inclination it has to that abominable principle of *Shelley*'s – that *Sensual Love* is the principle of *things*. . . . If he be attacked on these points, & on the *first* he assuredly will, he is *not* defensible.

To dismiss or even to minimise the seriousness of Bailey's argument is a mistake, for however conservative the views he put forward, they expressed the moral attitudes of vast sections of Keats's potential public. Taylor could refuse to accept this criticism of *Endymion*, but of all men, he could least afford to ignore the implications of it. If the other Reviews were to rest much of their attack upon the supposed indecency of the poem, then many potential readers would accept their judgment, and the book would not sell.

When *Maga*'s attack first appeared, Taylor was out of town. From Fleet Street, Hessey forwarded to him a copy of the magazine:[26]

> I thought you would have been at Retford before this time & I sent thither for you Blackwoods Magazine which contains a cruel attack on poor Keats. . . . It is really time these fellows were put down and I should like very much to see a severe philippick against them in some of our English Magazines –

But the philippics, when they appeared, were not against the critics, but against Keats. The same month as *Maga*'s attack, the June number of the *British Critic* was published. Its review of *Endymion* possessed the single merit of concentrating largely upon the poem itself, without descending to Lockhart's direct attack upon Keats's character and association with Hunt. But the merit was completely eclipsed by the obsessive concern with the sexual impurity that the reviewer claimed to find in the poem.[27] Reading the review, Taylor had reason enough, indeed, to congratulate Bailey on the accuracy of his forecast regarding the moral attacks upon *Endymion*:

> not all the flimsy veil of words in which he would involve immoral images, can atone for their impurity; and we will not disgust our readers by retailing to them the artifices of vicious refinement, by which, under the semblance of 'slippery blisses, twinkling eyes, soft completion of faces, and smooth excess of hands', he would palm upon the unsuspicious and the innocent imaginations better adapted to the stews.

To the discerning, the obsession with impurity might have revealed more of the reviewer's mind than of Keats's; but few seem to have appreciated such subtleties of interpretation. The attack was painful in its persistent childishness; its rhetoric was laboured almost to the point of atrophy; jokes were attempted which never came off, because their conclusions were obvious long before the writer reached them himself. The criticism[28] ended finally with the words:

> We do most solemnly assure our readers that this poem, containing 4074 lines, is printed on very nice hot-pressed paper, and sold for nine shillings, by a very respectable London bookseller. . . .[29] We think it necessary to add that it is all written in rhyme, and, for the most part, (when there are syllables enough) in the heroic couplet.

The end had not yet come. Before the month was over, the *Quarterly Review* published its April issue, and Taylor, if he had not realised it already, saw at last that his appeal to Gifford had gone unheeded. The reviewer of *Endymion*, John Wilson Croker, began by freely confessing the most unpardonable of a critic's sins – that he had not read more than a quarter of the poem. To a man of greater sensibility, such a confession might have seemed the surest way to turn his own invective against himself. But with complete insouciance, Croker lunged on, dismissing the Cockney School for expressing 'the most incongruous ideas in the most uncouth language', attacking Keats's rhymes because it was the mere sound of them and not any concern for their meaning that connected the poet's ramblings; and most pedantic of all, inveighing against his innovations in language, the use of words in ways which corrupted traditional poetic idioms. Inevitably, the old war-cry of Leigh Hunt was raised yet again: 'This author is a copyist of Mr Hunt; but he is more unintelligible, almost as rugged, twice as diffuse, and ten times more tiresome and absurd than his prototype.'[30] And the final paragraph began with Croker's manifest weariness with 'Mr Leigh Hunt and his simple neophyte', and his considered advice to his readers not to buy the book.

At first, the attacks seemed to trouble Keats little. Indeed, from a letter he wrote to Hessey in October,[31] it appeared that he had accepted them with remarkable equanimity:

> Praise or blame has but a momentary effect on the man whose love of beauty in the abstract makes him a severe critic on his own Works. My own domestic criticism has given me pain without comparison beyond what Blackwood or the Quarterly could possibly inflict. and also when I feel I am right, no external praise can give me such a glow as my own solitary reperception & ratification of what is fine.

He acknowledged courageously that whatever weaknesses *Endymion* had revealed, they were crucial to his development as a poet. It would have been of little help had he merely 'stayed upon the green shore, and piped a silly pipe, and took tea & comfortable advice'. The only means by which he could gain greater artistic maturity was by leaping 'headlong into the Sea, and thereby ... become better acquainted with the Soundings, the quicksands, & the rocks'. The only path to follow was one which constantly sustained the autonomy of his particular vision, however uncertain and shapeless that vision was.

> I will write independantly. – I have written independently *without Judgment* – I may write independently & *with judgment* hereafter. – The Genius of Poetry must work out its own salvation in a man: It cannot be matured by law & precept, but by sensation & watchfulness in itself – That which is creative must create itself –

There was much in this letter to encourage Taylor and Hessey. Not only had Keats taken the attacks upon *Endymion* with remarkable resilience, but he had now begun to assert a special kind of exclusiveness about the poetic mind which Taylor in particular always endorsed. Indeed, a comparison of this letter with Taylor's notes in his Commonplace Book illustrates how closely related the literary beliefs of poet and publisher had become. Keats's statement that 'the Genius of Poetry must work out its own salvation in a man: It cannot be matured by law & precept, but by sensation & watchfulness in itself' was firmly echoed in Taylor's argument that imagination, the 'First Order of Poetry', was 'only to be understood aright by him who is willing to surrender himself to its Sway. . . . . Learning injurious to it, if seen, because it belongs to Art – ' Both rejected the relevance of scholarly rules and conscious education to the nurturing of poetic genius. Similarly, Taylor's view that 'the Creator' alone was the true poet clearly reflected Keats's insistence that 'that which is creative must create itself'. For both, creativity, the realisation of new interpretations of experience, was a *sine qua non* of the nature of the poet. Above all, Keats's emphasis upon the imaginative autonomy of the poet, his necessary independence and difference from other men, was an idea which came close to Taylor's own beliefs about the poetic character. For Taylor, poets transmuted 'everything, Action, Thinking, Argument, Description' into 'something different, & superior to what it would be in any other Person'. For him, as for Keats, independence was an inevitable and essential quality of the artist, and 'true Poetic Excitement' an impulse which clearly distinguished the poet from other men.

There could be few better examples of the literary sympathy and understanding that often existed between Taylor and his writers than these comparisons. Indeed, the key words which occur in the statements of both poet and publisher – imagination, creator, independence, genius – demonstrate how close they were in their beliefs about the essential nature of poetry. Yet however firmly Taylor might endorse such views as a reader and critic, as a publisher his position was inevitably more complex. The very nature of his profession compelled him to look, not only towards the writers of the house, but also towards the reading public; and in this Janus-faced role, it was less easy to accept the clearly defined polarities of 'poet' and 'other men' which both Keats and he had supported in the past. No publisher, clearly, could endorse completely the independence and difference of the poet from the rest of mankind, for the financial viability of his firm depended crucially upon a dependence and connection existing between them. Laudable though Keats's autonomy might be in the actual act of creating poetry, in the reading market that independence had to be interpreted and communicated to a public if his books were to sell. Some kind of interaction between poet and reader had to replace the autonomy of the creative act. And when, finally, Taylor turned from poetic theory to see what connection had been forged between *Endymion* and the public, the scene was disturbing.

At the beginning of October 1818, it seemed at first as if the attacks of the Reviews had been almost ineffectual. On the 23rd, Hessey wrote to Taylor with hopeful news:[32]

I have much pleasure in saying that Endymion begins to move at last – 6 Copies have just been ordered by Simpkin & Marshall & one or two have been sold singly in the Shop – there is nothing like making a Stir for it – the papers have said so much about it many persons will doubtless be curious to see what it does contain – & here & there a man of taste may be found to admire its beauties. . . .

For a time, Hessey's diagnosis seemed to be correct. Far from diminishing interest, the attacks had aroused curiosity, and the public was buying the book to discover whether it was indeed as pernicious and morally corrupt as had been stated. But the full influence of the Reviews had not yet been felt. By December, Taylor was clearly becoming aware that the book was not selling well. He wrote to Sir James Mackintosh in Scotland, begging his acceptance of a copy of *Endymion* and hoping that some passages in it would be worth his attention:[33]

Its Faults are numberless, but there are redeeming Beauties in my Opinion, & the Faults are those of real Genius. But whatever this Work is, its Author is a true poet. . . . If he lives, Keats will be the brightest Ornament of the Age.

Spiritually, his faith in Keats's genius had increased rather than diminished, but as he was beginning increasingly to recognise, good sales as well as faith were necessary for the poet's complete well-being. Indeed, the letter to Scotland was very probably an attempt to elicit the active support of the *Edinburgh Review*, in which Mackintosh held a good deal of influence.[34] But it was unsuccessful. The *Edinburgh* remained obstinately silent about *Endymion*, and without its influence to counter the blasts of *Maga* and the *Quarterly*, sales began to fall. In the early spring of 1819, Keats wrote perfunctorily: 'my poem has not at all succeeded.'[35]

It is possible that, even without the attacks of two of the leading Reviews, *Endymion* would not have sold well. It was not a great poem. It lacked organisation and design; and too often, it might have seemed to the reading public, the mythology upon which it rested so heavily was self-enclosed – mellifluously irrelevant to the interests and needs of contemporary society. But it is improbable that these reasons alone could have been sufficient to account for the very poor sales of the book. Hovering in the background, there remained the figures of Croker, Gifford and Lockhart, and the shadows they had cast over the autumn of 1818 were lengthening. Keats realised as much. In December, he wrote hopefully to George and Georgiana: 'it seems to me that Reviews have had their day – that the public have been surfeited – there will soon be some new folly to keep the Parlours in talk – '[36] But barely two months later, at about the time he visited Taylor and Hessey in Fleet Street and very probably saw row upon row of the unsold copies of *Endymion* on their shelves,[37] he wrote again with greater accuracy:[38]

the Reviews have enervated and made indolent mens minds – few think for themselves – These Reviews too are getting more and more powerful, and especially the Quarterly – They are like a superstition which the more it prostrates the Crowd and the longer it continues the more powerful it becomes just in proportion to their increasing weakness – I was in hopes that when people saw, as they must do now, all the trickery and iniquity of these Plagues they would scout them, but no they are like the spectators at the Westminster cock-pit – they like the battle and do not care who wins or who looses [sic].

However greatly his bitterness was now aroused by the attacks of the Reviews, Keats recognised accurately enough the kind of effect they had achieved. In the eyes of the reading public, after battle had been joined both the cause of the attack and its eventual outcome became irrelevant. The conflict captured their imagination; but in the midst of the personal abuse and perverse rhetoric, the book itself was forgotten.

Endymion did not sell. Over three years later, Taylor and Hessey reported to George Keats that, far from breaking even on sales, they were still £110 out of pocket by the book.[39] A few copies were sold upon the appearance of Keats's 1820 volume, but the house was compelled eventually to remainder the poem. Edward Stibbs, a bookseller, bought it for 1½d. a copy, paid 2½d. for the binding, and sold it slowly at 1/6d.[40] The gamble had failed.

In many ways, the year 1818 was a disturbing one for Taylor. Not only did the acrimony of the attacks against Keats understandably depress him, but in business and personal matters too, the year produced more than its share of setbacks. The firm faced an imperative need to consolidate its finances, which were close to insolvency. The bankruptcy of many booksellers in October showed that the trade in books was still distressingly erratic, and such uncertainty in business affected a small publishing house such as Taylor & Hessey more than most. The house in Fleet Street remained in a state of perpetual turmoil, with both Hessey, his wife and children, and Taylor, occupying the premises as a home and as a place of business. His bachelorhood too seems to have become a source of increasing emotional depression, and it is possible during this year that he tried and failed to gain a response from a woman who had also intrigued Keats – Mrs Isabella Jones. Two sonnets he wrote at this time suggest that he was more than usually attracted to her, even though their relationship was one destined to end at arm's length.[41] Yet in the months following the attacks of *Maga* and the *Quarterly*, his time and energy were also being drawn upon increasingly by the gradual expansion of the house, by new publications, discussions with writers, and future policy decisions.

For some months following *Endymion* and its aftermath, he saw Keats rather less frequently. In January 1819, the poet was in Chichester and Bedhampton, and for much of the summer, during his visits to the Isle of Wight with Rice and to Winchester with Charles Brown, Taylor and he met rarely. But on 23 August, he wrote a lengthy letter to him, which suddenly brought into the open again a source of potential conflict between them both. The debate of poet versus public had restarted:[42]

> I feel every confidence that if I choose I may be a popular writer;
> that I will never be; but for all that I will get a livelihood – I
> equally dislike the favour of the public with the love of a woman
> – they are both a cloying treacle to the wings of independence. I
> shall ever consider them (People) as debtors to me for verses, not
> myself to them for admiration – which I can do without. I have
> of late been indulging my spleen by composing a preface *at* them:
> after resolving never to write a preface at all. . . . Just so much as
> I am hu[m]bled by the genius above my grasp, am I exalted and
> look with hate and contempt upon the literary world – A
> Drummer boy who holds out his hand familiarly to a field
> marshall – that Drummer boy with me is the good word and
> favour of the public –

At the time, Taylor was away from London because of illness, and the letter was forwarded to him at Retford. Not only the attack upon the public but the whole tone of Keats's argument evidently disturbed him, for he did not reply to him immediately, but instead sent the letter to Woodhouse, asking for his opinion of it. Possibly, he was uncertain of what kind of pride Keats was speaking when he claimed that 'this Pride and egotism will enable me to write finer things than any thing else could'. He may have been unsure too of the seriousness of this renewed attack upon the reading public. But some part of the letter to Woodhouse must also have indicated his growing impatience with Keats's contempt of the public, for Woodhouse's reply was conciliatory, an attempt to defend the poet from any charge of excessive egotism. In the lawyer's opinion,[43] it was not 'personal pride, but literary pride which his letter shews',

> that disposition which arises out of a Consciousness of superior & improving poetical Powers. . . . Is he wrong to be dissatisfied with the Prospect of a mere 'seat on the Bench of a myriad-aristocracy in Letters'? or to keep aloof from them and their works, – or to dislike the favor of such a 'public', as bepraises the Crabbes, & the Barretts, & the Codruses of the day. – I wonder how he came to stumble upon that deep truth that 'people are debtors to him for his verses & not he to them for admiration.' – Methinks such a conviction on any one's mind is enough to make half a Milton of him.

Woodhouse's generous interpretation had its desired effect. Taylor was reassured that Keats had been voicing a literary, not a personal, pride.

But it was a false truce, for within a month dissension had again arisen, more critically than ever before. On 11 September, Keats was in London and saw Hessey and Woodhouse in Fleet Street. During the conversation, he proposed that the firm should publish immediately another volume of his poetry. Hessey was understandably cautious. Taylor was convalescing out of town, the loss upon *Endymion* was still well over £150,[44] and he himself did not think another book would answer at present. The following morning, Keats breakfasted with Woodhouse and spoke of certain alterations he had made to the ending of *The Eve of St Agnes*. The last three lines had been changed 'to leave on the reader a sense of pettish disgust, by bringing Old Angela in (only) dead stiff & ugly'; and even more radically, the consummation of the love between Porphyro and Madeline, instead of being 'in right honest chaste & sober wise' after their marriage, now took place immediately Madeline had spoken of her love. 'As soon as M. has confessed her love', Woodhouse reported to Taylor, 'P. winds by degrees his arm around her, presses breast to breast, and acts all the acts of a bonâ fide husband, while she fancies she is only playing the part of a Wife in a dream.'[45] The lawyer appreciated that the appeal to the imagination was considerably heightened in the new version, but

I do apprehend it will render the poem unfit for ladies & indeed scarcely to be mentioned to them among the 'things that are'. – He says he does not want ladies to read his poetry: that he writes for men, & that if in the former poem there was an opening for a doubt what took place, it was his fault for not writing clearly & comprehensibly – that he sh^d despise a man who would be such an eunuch in sentiment as to leave a maid, with that Character about her, in such a situation: & sh^d despise himself to write about it &c &c &c – and all this sort of Keats-like rhodomontade.

The position, as Taylor saw it, had now become impossible. If, as Keats claimed, he did not want women to read his poetry, then he had immediately cut away a half at least of his potential public; and for Taylor, the folly of such an attitude as far as sales and public recognition were concerned must have been obvious. From the past experience of the house, both Hessey and he had seen numerous examples of the immense influence that the female reading public wielded over the sales of new books. Only five years previously, in 1814, the advertisement for Ann Taylor's *Practical Hints to Young Females* explicitly defined the kind of readership towards whom the book was directed:[46]

Females in the middle ranks of society, in those especially which include numerous occupations and confined circumstances, are more immediately addressed; and to them many of the following observations assume to be of essential importance.

Within eight months of publication, over 4,000 copies of the book had been sold by the firm. By 1822, it had reached an eleventh edition.

The success of *Practical Hints* was not an isolated example that might have occurred to Taylor. Several other books of the domestic homily variety, directed towards the middle-class female public, had commanded an equally enthusiastic response.[47] Perhaps, in the face of so much accumulating disappointment, Keats was exaggerating this particular attack against female readers. But for Taylor, two hundred miles from London and still unwell, it was clearly becoming increasingly difficult to sympathise with his views. Another thought too may have come to his mind as he read of the alterations to *St Agnes*. Only a year previously, the *British Critic* had obsessively lashed the supposed sexual impurity of *Endymion*. If so much capital had been made from so little provocation, how much greater might be the attack against the far clearer case of sexual licence that Woodhouse had indicated? That such attacks in the past had been blighted and wilfully perverse was, of course, true, but irrelevant. They reflected entrenched attitudes of mind, common to both conservative critics and readers, and the combination was one too powerful for a publisher to dismiss out of hand.

Taylor replied to Woodhouse's letter immediately; and as frequently happens in argument when one side states its case too emphatically, the response was equally emphatic, equally determined:[48]

> This Folly of Keats is the most stupid piece of Folly I can conceive. – He does not bear the ill opinion of the World calmly, & yet he will not allow it to form a good Opinion of him & his Writings. He repented of this Conduct when Endymion was published as much as a Man can repent. . . . Yet he will again challenge the same Neglect or Censure, & again (I pledge my Discernment on it) be vexed at the Reception he has prepared for himself –

This, certainly, was a fair point. Keats, Taylor argued, recognised clearly the hostile reception which the revised version of *St Agnes* would produce; yet he would not compromise with the moral standards of his public. On this occasion, though, Taylor was convinced that compromise was necessary, and he went to some pains to make his opinion felt. He refused to be an accessary in publishing any work which could be read only by men:

> since even on their Minds a bad Effect must follow the Encouragement of those Thoughts which cannot be rased without Impropriety – If it was so natural a process in Keats's Mind to carry on the Train of his Story in the way he has done, that he could not write decently, if he had that Disease of the Mind which renders the Perception too dull to discover Right from Wrong in Matters of Moral Taste, I should object equally then as now to the Sanctioning of the Infirmity by an act of cool Encouragement on my part, but then he would be personally perhaps excusable – As it is, the flying in the Face of all Decency & Discretion is doubly offensive from its being accompanied with so preposterous a Conceit on his part of being able to overcome the best founded Habits of our Nature –

For a moment, Taylor was clearly indulging in a Keats-like 'rhodomontade'; and indeed, the shrill rhetoric of these lines firmly suggests that his objections to the revision of *St Agnes* were a matter of personal opposition to the views Keats had put forward, as well as a question of possible public censure and neglect. But the lines following indicate a possible reason for the unusual sternness of his reply to Keats's argument:

> Had he known truly what the Society and what the Suffrages of
> Women are worth, he would never have thought of depriving
> himself of them. – So far as he is unconsciously silly in this
> Proceeding I am sorry for him, but for the rest I cannot but
> confess to you that it excites in me the Strongest Sentiments of
> Disapprobation.

His continued belief in the worth of women's company makes it clear that successive disappointments had not altered his faith in them. Possibly a remembrance of Isabella Jones or of previous attachments was in his mind as he wrote, and the contrast between them and Keats's theoretical dismissal of women readers was too galling to stifle the indignation he felt. Youth could afford to make such judgments; but at thirty-eight the perspective has changed, and the heart has become perhaps less ingenuous and more inflexibly serious in its desires. All this is no more than a hint; but Keats's criticism seems to have touched Taylor in a particularly vulnerable place, for his final reply was unusually stern. If the poet would not agree to leave the scene between Porphyro and Madeline as it had stood originally, then

> I must be content to admire his Poems with some other Imprint,
> & in so doing I can reap as much Delight from the Perusal of
> them as if they were our own property, without having the
> disquieting Consideration attached to them of our approving, by
> the 'Imprimatur', those Parts which are unfit for publication.

At first sight, the debate over *The Eve of St Agnes* may now appear an unnecessary difference of opinion, that might quickly have been resolved by goodwill and concessions from both sides. But as on many other occasions in Taylor's career, this seemingly trifling disagreement was in fact the focus of a far wider and more diffuse struggle, which was not susceptible to so easy a resolution. From Keats's alterations had arisen the problems of how far any poet or publisher should compromise with the generally accepted standards of taste in the reading public, of how greatly public voices such as the *British Critic* might influence the reception of supposedly indecent literature, and how justified any publisher was in making concessions to public morality for the sake of sales. Each of these questions revealed in turn the complex pressures of finance, sales, public attitudes, and critical opinion which influenced the promulgation of new literature. No clearer illustration of the complexity could be given, indeed, than the ambivalent position Taylor adopted towards Keats's alterations. Both before and after the dissension, he looked steadily towards the poet and firmly endorsed his belief in the creative autonomy of the writer. Yet on this one occasion, he looked just as steadily towards the reading public and clearly echoed its moral standards. Here, as on so many other occasions in his career, he was at the centre of the tensions between the writer and his public, the unsteady fulcrum of a literary see-saw.

In a letter to Haydon of the previous year, Keats expressed an argument which crystallised the essential difficulty that Taylor faced now and throughout his career: 'I never expect to get anything by my books: and moreover I wish to avoid publishing – I admire Human Nature but I do not like *Men*. I should like to compose things honourable to Man – but not fingerable over by *Men*.'⁴⁹ There lies behind this statement of belief, as behind many similar affirmations from contemporary writers, a high courage and integrity in asserting tenaciously the visionary idealism of the poet, and his concern with only the noblest qualities in mankind. Yet the independence of outlook that this belief necessarily involved held several dangers. Too easily, the affirmation of the poet's autonomy or difference from other men was carried beyond the actual act of creating poetry into the reading market itself. The poet became independent of other men, not only in his creativity, but also in the selling and interpreting of his work to the public. He continued to dislike '*Men*' at that very point in the diffusion of literature where connection and interaction were most crucial. For Keats at least, the result of such independence was ingenuous as well as potentially tragic. By asserting that his poetry was ideally composed for an abstraction labelled Human Nature, but not for a reading public, he attempted to divorce the creation of literature from its promulgation in the market. Yet, as Taylor knew only too well, it was impossible for any publisher, even the most visionary, to support this divorce. The books of his house were read not by 'Man' or by 'Human Nature', but precisely by those hundreds of readers who fingered; and indeed, unless they did thumb through the books he brought out, he could not survive. To abstract the economic reality of a reading public and transform it into a philosophy of human nature with which his authors might be reconciled was clearly impossible. The reality of the public, however philistine and myopic, had in the end to be faced.

Finally, Keats allowed the original version of *St Agnes* to stand, and the disagreement was forgotten. Yet this autumn of 1819 was a disturbed time. Increasingly the focus of their association, which had once centred so firmly upon the glory of new poetry, was shifting towards more urgent personal crises. In November, Taylor tried to revive Keats's enthusiasm. He invited him to dinner and enquired particularly about the progress of his writing. Two days later, though, the poet wrote to him and announced his decision not to publish any of the poems he had ready.[50] It was a far cry from his visit to Fleet Street two months previously, when he had suggested to Hessey that the firm might publish another volume immediately. But despite his seeming lack of enthusiasm, Taylor decided in December to bring out a second book of his poetry, to include *Lamia, Isabella,* and the original version of *The Eve of St Agnes.* It was a decision of some courage, for the house was still out of pocket by *Endymion,* and at the time there was no sign that the leading Reviews were finally turning towards an appreciation of his poetry. But by late April 1820, Taylor had in his hands the completed manuscripts for the new volume. The previous September, he had been somewhat uncertain of the quality of *Lamia:*[51]

> I did not enter so well into it as to be qualified to criticise, but whether it be a want of Taste for such Subjects as Fairy Tales, or that I do not perceive true Poetry except it is in Conjunction with good Sentiment, I cannot tell, but it did not promise to please me –

But now, able to judge the poems as a whole in their context, he gave the volume far greater unqualified praise than he had ever granted *Endymion. Lamia* in particular seems to have caught his attention much more than six months previously,[52] and *Isabella* had always pleased him. Hessey too gave warm praise to the new poems. Writing to Clare,[53] he anticipated that

> the simplicity of Isabella will please you much – Hyperion is full of the most sublime poetical Images and the small Poems delight me very much. . . .
> For my own part I think no single volume of Poems ever gave me more real delight on the whole than I have received from this. I shall feel anxious to hear your opinion of it.

Finally, at the end of June, Taylor wrote to his father announcing the impending publication of the new volume. His letter demonstrated clearly that, despite disappointment and dissension, his faith in Keats's genius had rather increased than diminished. He now believed quite simply that he was the greatest poet of his age:[54]

Next week Keats's new Volume of Poems will be published, & if it does not sell well, I think nothing will ever sell again. I am sure of this that for poetic Genius there is not his equal living & I would compare him against any one with either Milton or Shakespeare for Beauties.

The expectancy of the days preceding publication was echoed by Richard Woodhouse. Even before the volume had appeared, he reported, some 160 copies had been subscribed for.[55] Yet for Keats himself, in spite of reasonably good spirits, the book was coming out 'with very low hopes'. 'This shall be my last trial', he promised Charles Brown, 'not succeeding, I shall try what I can do in the apothecary line.'[56] His illness was becoming increasingly evident, and causing serious concern. Sweltering in Bath in a sudden heat-wave of early summer, Taylor wrote to Hessey:[57]

The Illness of our poor Friend Keats gives me real Concern. I am much afraid of his Health & feel the greatest Anxiety lest he should add one more & the best of all to the ill fated Men of Genius who have been gifted with Talents the Admiration of the World, & the Bane of all Praise to the Possessor. The Book looks every thing that I could wish, & at 7/6 is cheap in my Opinion.

At the beginning of July, *Lamia, Isabella, Eve of St Agnes and other poems* was published. But if the book pleased Taylor, all was not well with it in Keats's eyes. Without consulting him, Taylor and Woodhouse had prefixed to the volume an 'Advertisement' which explained the reason for the inclusion of the uncompleted poem *Hyperion*:

If any apology be thought necessary for the appearance of the unfinished poem of HYPERION, the publishers beg to state that they alone are responsible, as it was printed at their particular request, and contrary to the wish of the author. The poem was intended to have been of equal length with ENDYMION, but the reception given to that work discouraged the author from proceeding.

There can be no doubt that Taylor and Woodhouse had inserted the advertisement with the best of intentions. If the Reviews had made so much capital out of the completed *Endymion*, how much more might they make of an unfinished poem? But Keats was angry. In an advance copy, he crossed out the entire advertisement, scrawling above it 'I had no part in this; I was ill at the time.' To the statement that the reception given to *Endymion* had discouraged him from finishing *Hyperion*, he

wrote in retort, 'This is a lie.' It was the climax of many disappointments. From the very beginning, he had not wished to include *Hyperion*
in the volume because of its fragmentary state. But Taylor had insisted.
Yet as far as the Reviews at least were concerned, Taylor had judged
rightly, for the unfinished *Hyperion* received more praise than any other
poem in the book.[58] In general, many critics seemed to be moving
towards an appreciation of Keats's genius. Gold's *London Magazine*
concluded[59] that the poetry in the new volume could not fail to make
any reader

> pause on the extraordinary powers of the human, on the
> wonderful destinies of man, and yet think there exists such gross
> stupidity, nay so deplorable a want of taste, amongst the bulk of
> English readers, as not to discover in Mr. Keats powers and
> acquirements that dazzle while they instruct, and astonish while
> they delight.

And in August and October, two years too late, the *Edinburgh Review*
finally broke its silence and joined in singing the praises of both
Endymion and the 1820 volume.[60] Of *Endymion*, it said:

> We are very much inclined indeed to add that we do not know
> any book which we would sooner employ as a test to ascertain
> whether any one had in him a native relish for poetry, and a
> genuine sensibility to its intrinsic charm.

For Taylor, this encomium most of all must have appeared as the
supreme irony. Recognition of Keats's poetry, slowly and painfully
extracted, had been given at last by a leading Review, but to all intents
and purposes, it was now too late. Had the *Edinburgh* spoken up two
years earlier to counter the blasts of *Maga* and the *Quarterly*, Keats
might have enjoyed more fully the acclaim which was rightly his; but
now it seemed almost as if no difference existed between praise and
censure; both were eclipsed by the increasing seriousness of his illness.
The same month as the *Edinburgh Review*'s recognition, he wrote to
Taylor:[61]

> My Chest is in so nervous a State, that any thing extra such as
> speaking to an unaccostomed Person or writing a Note half
> suffocates me. This Journey to Italy wakes me at daylight every
> morning and haunts me horribly. I shall endeavour to go though
> it be with the sensation of marching up against a Batterry. The
> first spep [sic] towards it is to know the expense of a Journey and

a years residence: which if you will ascertain for me and let me know early you will greatly serve me. I have more to say but must desist for every line I write encreases the tightness of the Chest, and I have many more to do. I am convinced that this sort of thing does not continue for nothing – if you can come with any of our friends do.

It was, perhaps, during the last few months in which he knew Keats that Taylor's sympathy towards him was shown most completely. Keats's illness seems, indeed, to have acted upon him as a catalyst, giving him renewed energy to complete tasks which the poet could not now complete, and defend ideas of justice and fair dealing which he no longer had the strength to tackle. To Clare he wrote privately:[62]

We have had some trouble to get through 500 copies of his work, though it is highly spoken of in the periodical works, but what is most against him, it has been thought necessary in the leading Review, the Quarterly, to damn his [Poetry] for imputed political Opinions – Damn them who could act in so cruel a way to a young man of undoubted Genius. I hate Criticism at all times except when it is of that enlarged kind that takes entire Surveys of a Subject, and conceiving old Writers to be new and new ones to be old awards to each his proper Share of Consideration. Besides in Poetry I think Praise should be given where it is due, and that Silence is sufficient Dispraise – I hate that Irish Mode of pummelling a poor Fellow when he is down, and Poets especially who never seek to hurt others. To fall foul on them because they cannot give so much pleasure as they wish is to behave worse than Dogs do to each other.

These lines illustrate yet again, not only the generosity of his attitude towards new literature, but also that comprehensiveness of mind which had almost invariably characterised his opinions of Keats's poetry. The critics, he implicitly argued, had magnified incidental weaknesses in Keats's work and presented those faults as the complete picture. Their narrow-minded dogmatism had subverted the enlarged perspective with which they should have judged his poetry. And there had been in their criticisms too a strain of wilful, personal vindictiveness which had allowed of no compromise, and which had deliberately confused the poetry itself with the personality of the poet.

With such thoughts in his mind, it was evident that Taylor was working up for a defence of Keats as vigorous as the attacks upon him, and the opportunity to express his views was not long in arriving. On 31 August, he received a call from William Blackwood, and it was obvious as soon as they met that there would be a heated argument. Taylor was not in a happy mood. He had heard the previous evening that Keats had again 'ruptured a Vessel in the Lungs & now lies in a dangerous State'.[63] Blackwood attempted to forestall any vituperation by saying that *Maga* was now disposed to speak favourably of the poet's work; but this was an ingenuous attempt to skate on firmer ice, as Taylor was quick to point out. His argument with the Reviews had never been about mere criticism of Keats's poetry, but about the dishonest way in which they had dragged in personal animosities to bolster their attacks. 'Why', he asked Blackwood, 'did they attack him personally?'[64] Blackwood denied that they had.

> No? did not they speak of him in ridicule as Johnny Keats, describe his Appearance while addressing a Sonnet Ailsa Crag, and compare him as a Friesland Hen to Shelley as a Bird of Paradise; besides what can you say to that cold blooded Passage where they say they will take Care he shall never get 50 £ again for a Vol. of his Poems – what had he done to cause such Attacks as these?

Blackwood feebly attempted to explain that 'it was all a Joke':

> the writer meant nothing more than to be witty. He certainly thought there was much Affectation in his Poetry, and he expressed his Opinion only – It was done in the fair Spirit of Criticism. . . .

Taylor retorted, 'It was done in the Spirit of the Devil, Mr Blackwood.' He was on unshakeable ground. It was in vain for Blackwood to argue, as he did, that a poet challenged public opinion by publishing a book at all, for the disproportion between the youthful uncertainty of Keats's challenge and the acrimony with which it had been counterattacked was glaringly obvious. Taylor insisted that to attack at all, even for a truly bad poet, was unnecessary. Neglect and the failure of their hopes were more than sufficient punishment. His final thrust was unanswerable:

> Mr Blackwood, Why should not the Manners of Gentlemen continue to regulate their Conduct when they are writing of each other as much as when they are in Conversation. – No man

would insult Mr Keats in this Manner in his Company, and what is the difference between writing & speaking of a person except that the written Attack is the more base from being made anonymously & therefore at no personal Risk.

He concluded finally:

> I feel Regard for Mr Keats as a Man of real Genius a Gentleman, nay more as one of *the gentlest of human Beings*. He does not resent these Things himself, he merely says of his Opponents 'They don't know me.' Now this Mildness makes those who are his Friends feel the more warmly when they see him ill used. But this Feeling is not confined to them. I am happy to say that the public Interest is awakened to a Sense of the Injustice which has been done him, and that the Attempts to ruin him will have in the End a contrary Effect.

Soon afterwards, Blackwood left, 'evidently cooler than he entered'.[65] Taylor was pretty sure that he would never call on him again.

Taylor's optimism that public interest in Keats's cause was growing was refreshing, but scarcely justified by the facts. In spite of Blackwood's statement that *Maga* would speak favourably for the new volume, by no stretch of the imagination could it be said to do so. It conceded that, had Keats allowed his talents to mature under better guidance, he 'might have done very considerable things'; but as it was, 'he bids fair to sink himself entirely beneath such a mass of affectation, conceit, and Cockney pedantry, as I never expected to see heaped together by any body, except the Great Founder of the School.'[66]

But with *Lamia*, it was not the Reviews that were destined to cripple the book's sales, but scandal – and its appearance demonstrated yet another of the pressures so often brought to bear upon the firm's publishing. On 4 June 1820, Caroline of Brunswick landed in England in a determined attempt, as she put it, to secure her rights or blow the King off his throne. For much of the summer, it seemed that George IV's attempt to pass the Bill of Pains and Penalties through Parliament would end in revolution. For weeks the streets of London were in uproar, paraded day after day by thousands of Caroline's supporters. A battalion of the Guards mutinied; the Duke of Bedford was convinced that the British monarchy was at an end; and round the House of Lords, Wellington supervised the erection of barricades to protect ministers as they alternately deliberated and dozed. Passion, scandal, and intrigue in high places became the focus of conversation from the back-street alleys to the aristrocrat's drawing room;[67] and inevitably, the quarrel between George and Caroline brought forth a mass of pamphlets and articles of every political persuasion, which sold in their thousands. In August 1820, Charles Phillips published his tract *The Queen's Case Stated*. By the end of the year, it had reached an astonishing twenty-second edition. R. M. Bacon, the editor of the *Norwich Mercury*, confessed to his readers, 'We feel it will be in vain to attempt to engage attention upon any subject but the proceedings against the QUEEN.'[68] And Leigh Hunt accurately reported to Shelley, 'You may look upon the British public, at present, as constantly occupied in reading trials for adultery.'[69] Scandal had captured the interest of the entire city, and beneath the volume of pamphlets and tracts which poured from the presses, Keats's book could scarcely avoid being quietly buried. Taylor wrote in August: 'Trade is bad everywhere, but I hope when this investigation is over we shall have quiet Times again, when People will have Leisure to buy what they may want.'[70] But by the time some semblance of stability had been restored, Keats was dead. Over three months later, in late November, the firm's trade was still being disrupted by the crisis. 'We are all in a bustle about the Queen's business', Hessey wrote to Clare, 'which has almost put a stop to all other business.'[71]

For both Taylor and Hessey, the implications of the fate of *Lamia* were unavoidable. More even than the attacks from the Reviews, the impact and immediacy of political uproar had turned the minds of potential readers away from Keats's poetry towards matters which had caught their imagination more deeply. Again, a serious gulf had arisen between the poet and his public – a gulf in which the public had not, as before, blindly followed the opinions of the Reviews, but more distressingly, had largely ceased to notice him at all. It was a subtle turn of the screw, but neither partner could afford to ignore the wider lesson of this summer. A society haphazardly steering its way from potential revolution towards some kind of political stability has not always time consciously to foster its own literary heritage.

Lamia did not sell. In November, Hessey attempted to revive interest by printing some advertisements for the volume, believing that the public would 'want to read now the trial with its long details is over'.[72] But the public, if they were now reading, were not reading Keats. Nearly two years later, Taylor reported to Clare that 'the real Admirers of Poetry are left alone in the List of Purchasers, & their numbers are very few. Of Keats's poems there have never yet been 500 sold.'[73] In

October 1828, eight years after its publication, he was still advertising the first edition of *Lamia*.[74]

For both Keats and Taylor, 1820 had been a year of mixed blessings. Keats had gained some recognition at last, but his condition was now critical. Ill health, indeed, had dogged both of them for many months, perhaps making each at times more stern in his demands of the other than if both had been well. But even these troubles were eclipsed in August by a more pressing need – Keats's lack of money for his journey to Italy. It was clear that, after numerous loans which had not yet been repaid, he could not afford to pay for the journey out of his own pocket; and there seemed only one solution – that Taylor and Hessey should advance him as much money as was necessary. Yet the strain which such a prospect would place on the firm's finances was immediately obvious to both partners, for throughout the year, the house had been sailing dangerously close to insolvency. From April onwards, Taylor's letters to his brother James had requested loan after loan to help the firm over its difficulties:[75]

> I think we had better have a little Money from Mr G. G. for we are a good deal straitened just now. . . .

> I think we had better have the £500 so you will do the needful if you please without further hearing. . . .

> From our returns being £1000 less this year (in cash) than last and from our payment of capital we feel a good deal straitened for money. . . .

> We are (at 93) in Want of some Change, for my partner has communicated to me this morning that we have nothing in our Coffers, and by Wednesday next our payments . . . recommence –

Yet despite the serious state of the house's finances, there could be no doubt whether or not the necessary money should be advanced to Keats. Sometime in early August, Taylor wrote again to James and asked for another large loan. James immediately sent to Fleet Street 'three Bills value Five hundred pounds'. It was a heaven-sent gift. Leaving Hessey to acknowledge James's letter, Taylor rushed to Hampstead on the morning of 18 August and announced that the finances for the journey were now assured. Undoubtedly aware that neither James nor he might be repaid for many months, he gave Keats what was necessary.[76]

As a direct result of James's generosity, Taylor was able on 11 September to write Keats a letter which disposed of all his debts to the firm.[77] Although the house was still some £250 out of pocket by *Endymion* and *Lamia*, he bought the copyright of the two books for £100 each. Subtracting the poet's debts of £70, this left Keats with £130, to which the firm added another £50, 'to take you to Italy'; and an understanding was made that more would be forthcoming should the need arise. Taylor repeated to Keats that the house would publish his poetry entirely at their own risk ('if it does not answer, the Loss is ours: whatever succeeds we deem the Profit wholly yours'), and trying to raise Keats's spirits as he had done many times in the past, he concluded:

> You will do well to publish again as soon as you have the power
> to produce anything, and the Success you may rely upon it will
> in every Instance increase. I hope yet to see you as rich and
> renowned as you deserve to be. – Meantime wishing you a
> pleasant Voyage, perfect Health, and all Happiness, I remain,
>   My dear Keats
>   Your faithful Friend
>   John Taylor

On 17 September, Taylor was at the wharf at Tower Dock from which Keats was to sail in the *Maria Crowther* with his companion Joseph Severn. Together with Haslam and Woodhouse, he sailed with him as far as Gravesend where they disembarked and said their final farewells. What his emotions were, it is almost impossible to say, for knowing the seriousness of Keats's condition, there must have been deep in his mind a fearful suspicion that he would never see him again alive. He promised him that he would write to his sister Fanny, and give an account of the departure. Woodhouse took a lock of the poet's hair, and Taylor gave him as a parting gift an old Greek and Latin Testament, inscribed simply 'John Keats, from his friend John Taylor'. Then the boat moved away from Gravesend and was lost to sight.

In the months that followed, Taylor continued to help Keats's cause. Despite another attack of ill-health, he had collected by February 1821 another £150 from the poet's well-wishers to pay for further expenses. But without the actual presence of Keats himself in his circle, knowing of his condition only through letters which took nearly a month to arrive, his hope now became strangely passive. The poet remained in his mind, possibly remembered at times with something of the appalling intensity which Charles Brown described.[78] Hessey, in a letter to

Severn, spoke of 'the uneasiness which he feels, and the depression of spirits which he suffers, whenever he hears or speaks of poor Keats'.[79] But as the New Year came in, whatever hope he had of Keats's survival gradually died. On Christmas Eve of 1820, Severn wrote to him and reported that Keats was spitting cupfuls of blood. The poet had sent a message to his publisher:[80]

> 'Tell Taylor I shall soon be in a second Edition – in sheets – and cold press' – he desired me tell you some time since – that he would have written you – but felt he could not say anything – it gave him pain –

Towards the end of January, Severn wrote again:[81]

> – his suffering now is beyond description. . . .
>
> . . . he could not read your letter when it came – altho' he opened it – . . . I trembled when he looked at your name – but he wept most bitterly – and gave the letter to me –

Both Taylor and Hessey replied in February to Severn – Hessey with long, religious, and yet deeply felt letters in which he begged him to try and persuade Keats to pray for divine forgiveness. For Taylor too, Keats's dying drew his mind towards the eternal peace which God had promised. He urged Severn to try to convince the poet of the reality of a God who could and would relieve him in his extremity, and he prayed that Keats would be blessed with 'Peace, his Peace that nothing earthly can take away'.[82] But in his mind, the poet had already died. On 17 February, he wrote to his father:[83]

> My poor Friend Keats is by this Time dead – a Letter came to-day from Mr Severn his Companion dated 3 weeks ago, in which he says that Dr [Clark] thought Keats could not live a fortnight longer.

On 9 March, he reported to Clare that Keats was still alive, though very weak. Then finally, on 18 March, a note came from Charles Brown, enclosing a letter from Severn of 27 February:[84]

> Read the enclosed – it is all over. I leave to you the care of inserting his death in the papers, – word it as *you* please, – you will do it better than I can, – in fact I can't do it.

After the news had come, Taylor carried out the various small duties which remained. Obituaries were inserted in newspapers and magazines, *Maga* included, and from Italy Severn sent him Keats's death mask which he kept with him until his own death over forty years later. But with Keats now dead, the circle of intimate friends who had gathered about him in the past began to break up, and its former enthusiasm suddenly turned sour. With the best of intentions, Taylor decided at the end of March to write a memoir of him, hoping whilst his disappointments and death were still fresh in the public mind to show him in his true light – as the greatest poet of his generation. But Taylor's 'indecorous haste' angered Leigh Hunt, Dilke, and particularly Charles Brown, who considered the whole plan a mere 'bookseller's job', and the more to be condemned because it had been publicly announced 'even before Mrs Brawne's family and myself had got our mourning'.[85] Certainly, Taylor had laid himself open to this interpretation, and Brown was more than justified in criticising the timing of the announcement. But his subsequent machinations were less than generous. Leigh Hunt eventually demanded that Taylor should agree to submit his memoir to Brown for approval before he himself would give any help in the way of correspondence and reminiscence; and Brown himself, in the heat of the argument, wrote of the publisher:[86]

> I confess I could not trust [Taylor] entirely; now and then he is a mere bookseller – somewhat vain of his talents, and consequently self-willed. My anxiety for poor Keats's fame compelled me to make this request; for, in my opinion, Taylor neither comprehended him nor his poetry. I shall always be the first to acknowledge Taylor's kindness to Keats; but towards me his conduct has been ungracious and even unmannerly. . . . I fear Taylor may do Keats an injustice – not knowingly, but from the want of knowing his character.

It was a harsh judgment, and largely untrue. To argue in particular that Taylor had not understood Keats's poetry when, of all men, he had most repeatedly emphasised the uniqueness and genius of his work, was a manifest distortion of the truth. Perhaps, indeed, the most convincing reply that could have been given to Brown's criticism was contained in a letter which Taylor wrote to Clare at the end of March:[87]

> The Life of poor Keats is ended at last; he died at the Age of 25. He used to say he should effect nothing on which he would rest his Fame till he was 30, and all his Hopes are over at 25. But he has left enough though he did not think so – and if his Biographer cannot do him justice, the Advocate is in Fault, and not the

Cause. Poor fellow! Perhaps your feeling will produce some lines to his memory. One of the very few Poets of this Day is gone.

In one sense, this last sentence was the final crystallisation of all his thoughts about Keats. Beyond the dissensions and difficulties which the publishing of his work had involved, he remained convinced that he had been one of the very few poets of his generation. One comparison which he drew at this time between Keats and another poet, Henry Milman, illustrates yet again the sureness of his judgment. In May 1820, the *Quarterly Review* had promised to Milman, the author of *The Fall of Jerusalem*, 'without extravagant encomium . . . whatever immortality the English language can bestow'.[88] This absurd praise of a completely unmemorable poem, coming as it did from a Review which had consistently belittled Keats's achievement, provoked a contrast too sharp and galling to avoid comment. In the same letter to Clare, Taylor wrote:[89]

I have not read with any attention Milman's Poem but from what I saw of it I concluded that it wanted the true Gift of Poetry, the Inspiration, and that it possessed every other kind of excellence. But that Want is the Devil, in things pretending to be Poetry. Education never *made* a Poet, though it may help a Man much who is one. I wish we had fewer of these Fellows who dress themselves up as the Sons of Apollo, and by dint of Words and the Repetition of certain Greek and Latin Lines, gain Possession of the Poet's Fame to the Exclusion of the rightful Heir.

These lines echo again one of the chief themes of his notes in the Commonplace Book – the uncommonness and difference of genius, and the distinction which had always to be insisted upon between mere scholarship and true poetic inspiration. To the very end of his association with Keats, he himself recognised that distinction. In the poet's own epitaph, he was aware of the uniqueness of the mind that had composed such a line:[90]

we are told that Keats desired to have this line put upon his Tombstone 'Here lies one whose Name was writ on Water'. If I had seen this Inscription on a Stone in a Country Churchyard I should have felt that it recorded the death of a Poet, or at least of an uncommon Man.

And such uncommonness possessed a particular kind of integrity which should not be destroyed. In August, he wrote to Severn about the inscription for Keats's tomb, and suggested that the poet's own epitaph would be quite sufficient – but the line should stand alone without embellishment:[91]

> It is very simple and affecting, and tells so much of the Story that none need be told. Neither Name nor Date is requisite. These will be given in his Life by his Biographer. So, unless something else is determined on, let this Line stand alone. I foresee that it will be as clear an Indication to Posterity as the plainest everyday Inscription that one may find in Westminster Abbey.

Perhaps, in these thoughts about Keats's epitaph, the essential directness of Taylor's belief in him is finally crystallised. Beyond the complexities of the debates between poet and reading public, political crisis and the cause of literature which he faced as the publisher of *Endymion* and *Lamia*, there constantly emerges the decisive simplicity and clarity of his faith in Keats's genius. During the months of 1818 when the sustained invective of the most powerful Reviews had been turned upon *Endymion*, and even during the quarrel about *The Eve of St Agnes*, one searches in vain for any wavering of this faith, for any indication that he then believed Keats's talent was less than he had once thought. The dissensions, serious and unresolved though some of them were, never betrayed him from the steady belief that Keats was, quite simply, the finest poet of his age. That belief, as has been seen, was shown in many ways – in talk and encouragement, hospitality and loans – but a single sentence from a letter to his father[92] seems to reveal it more decisively than any other: 'I am sure of this that for poetic Genius there is not his equal living & I would compare him against any one with either Milton or Shakespeare for Beauties.'

The years of expansion, 1817-20:
Leigh Hunt, Hazlitt, Cary, and the Reviews

When Keats died in 1821, he had known Taylor and Hessey for barely four years. Compared with many of Taylor's other friendships – with his brother James, with Hessey, and John Clare – it was a brief enough association. Yet in retrospect, this very brevity only serves to concentrate the work which he did on the poet's behalf. So insistently indeed does the figure of Keats touch upon his life during these years that it is often difficult to see them apart. In 1814, ruefully meditating upon the latest success of Maria Edgeworth, Hessey had asked, 'When shall we pick up a Miss Edgeworth?' By 1821, the question had been so abundantly answered with Keats's name that he often stands at the very centre of the firm's achievements. For the four years of their association with him, and even indeed for the whole of their career in the trade, he becomes something of a presiding genius, the focus through which their progress as publishers is most clearly seen and evaluated.

Certainly, a judgment upon Taylor & Hessey's work from this viewpoint would in many ways be just. Much of any publisher's success must finally be gauged from his ability to sustain his writers' efforts, and his willingness to look beyond temporary difficulties and dissensions in a desire to publish the best of contemporary literature. And yet, as has been seen with Keats, Taylor's task did not simply involve the encouraging of an individual writer's genius. The publishing of *Endymion* and *Lamia* probed far broader issues – the impact of political crisis upon literature, the influence of contemporary critical and moral values, and the effect of public attack upon sales and recognition. Taylor's role in his association with Keats was not restricted to the fostering of his talent, important though this was. A vital part of his success as a publisher depended also upon his understanding of the wider pressures – moral, political, social, and economic – which affected the promulgation of literature.

In the face of so many ill-defined and often conflicting interests, his position was often unenviable; and indeed, what remains one of the most remarkable aspects of his whole career is that he did not fail in his main purpose more often. On one occasion, though, he did; and the failure emphasised again the lesson of both *Endymion* and *Lamia* – how easily a new work might be dismissed for reasons quite extraneous to its literary merit.

In September 1816, at the very time that Taylor had resolved to expand the publishing side of the firm, Leigh Hunt sent him a collection of manuscripts and printed extracts with the suggestion that he might compile and publish a volume from them. It was an assorted batch of material, containing 'The Letters of Harry Brown', political satires in verse which had already been printed in the *Examiner*, the poem 'Hero and Leander' and 'the MS "Lives"'. Taylor promised an early decision, and on 20 September he replied to Hunt's proposal.[1] He had read the poems carefully, but he did not think it would 'answer our purpose to publish them', and

as the letters were printed in the Examiner and Taunton Courier they have been seen by and are still in the possession of many of those who were the likeliest to become purchasers – and nos. 4 & 5, tho' proper for a newspaper, are not well adapted for a Volume which we should hope would live longer than such Topics and such Men are likely to be remembered –

The last few words of this criticism are particularly interesting, for they reveal not only the reason for the rejection of 'The Letters', but also one of the chief policies that the firm was to follow throughout its career. Taylor, clearly, was determined to publish, not books of only topical and temporary interest, but works which would outlive the age in which they had been written. Yet not all of Hunt's suggestion was rejected. Taylor thought highly of the poem 'Hero and Leander', and proposed that when Hunt could send enough other material to fill a volume, the firm should publish the poem. And, as a token of their good faith, the house advanced him, before February of the following year, twenty guineas in part-payment for the new poems.

At the time, Taylor was evidently eager to publish Hunt's work, for even the bitter attacks to which the poet had been subjected by the *Quarterly* in 1816 seem to have made no impression upon his decision. But by March 1817, it had already become clear that the association between them had lost some of its initial glitter. On 22 February, the house wrote to Hunt saying they would be glad to receive the manuscript poems 'according to the Plan first agreed on'. But Hunt had evidently no poems to send. He wished instead to annul the contract, and Shelley, acting as his agent, visited Taylor and Hessey to discuss terms. The result was almost inevitable – a complete disagreement or misunderstanding over the terms of the annulment which dragged on for over a year. Shelley understood from the conversation that the firm would be willing to cancel the contract upon the repayment of the £20, or they would take this sum from the profits on the second edition of Hunt's *The Story of Rimini*, to be published by them in association with R. Triphook. Taylor understood something entirely different. The twenty guineas, not pounds, which the house had advanced was to be repaid immediately. On 2 April, the firm wrote again to Hunt:

> We have not heard from you since we consented to annul the Bargain for your poems on condition of being repaid the sum for which we had bought them. We mention the circumstance for fear there should be some mistake, as Mr. Shelley assured us the money would be returned immediately – if we are still to consider the Copyright ours, we shall be glad to receive the Ms as soon as possible that we may publish without Delay –

The courtesy of this note is evidence that Taylor & Hessey were unwilling to give Hunt up without some attempt at reconciliation. But the poet delayed. He did not answer the firm's letter until two months later, and then reported that he had told Triphook to include the house's name on the title-page of *Rimini*, 'according to your acceptance of my offer on that subject'.

For nearly a year, strangely, the matter rested there. But in early 1818, the disagreement blew up again, and any courtesy that remained was now a thin façade for indignant anger. On 17 March, Hessey wrote to Taylor that Hunt had finally sent the twenty guineas with interest: 'Miss Kent came with it, and she says Mr. Shelley never told Hunt that the money was to be paid for immediately, but that we were to hold the Rimini & their produces as a sort of security –' Hessey included with his note a copy of part of a letter from Shelley to Hunt. Shelley was ready to swear, 'if necessary in a Court of Justice', that the firm had told him they would surrender the copyright for £20 or would accept the profits from *Rimini* until the sum was repaid.

Without Shelley's reference to a court of law, it seems probable that the association between Hunt and Taylor would merely have died quietly. But Taylor, never more angered than when it seemed his own honesty and integrity had been impeached, wrote Hunt a final letter, which catalogued the stages of their quarrel in a cool, staccato tone. He repeated that, in his first conversation with Shelley, he had agreed to annul the contract, provided Hunt returned the loan of twenty guineas immediately, and he added that Shelley had spoken 'in strong terms of our liberality'. But the proposition that the firm should be paid out of the profits of *Rimini* 'was not only never mentioned, but there was not opportunity or need for proposing it – '.

Hunt did not reply. 'Hero and Leander', the poem which Taylor had agreed to publish, did not appear until 1819, when the Ollier brothers brought it out in a volume with 'Bacchus and Ariadne' and 'The Feast of the Poets'. Another casualty of the disagreement too was *An Epistle to Lord Byron and other Poems*, which was advertised as in the press upon the end pages of Taylor's *Junius*, but which was never published by the firm. Hunt did not sever relations with the house entirely, but his siding with Brown and Dilke against Taylor in the argument over Keats's biography revealed a clear distancing between the two men. In the end, the firm was never to publish a single line of his work.

In retrospect, the association between Taylor and Hunt appears as a curious interlude in the steady progress the firm was making as Keats's new publishers; and at first sight, it is tempting to argue how little extra patience and understanding would have been needed to have restored the good relations between them both. If Taylor had been more content to bide his time with Hunt, as he did with Keats, the unwritten poems might well have been composed, and the book published. Perhaps, too, if Hunt had entered into direct negotiations with the firm about the annulment, instead of allowing Shelley and Elizabeth Kent to act as well-meaning agents of misunderstanding, the outcome of their association would not have been so clouded in recrimination. But to suggest these hypotheses only serves to demonstrate again the fundamental uncertainty of that process by which new literature comes to be published. The lesson which Hunt's book taught is an invaluable one: that new works may be cast aside for the least, as well as the greatest, of reasons. His poetry remained unpublished by the firm, not for any reason to do with its intrinsic merit, nor for any dramatic dissension in literary principles or beliefs, nor indeed for any fear of public attack, but because far more mundane matters persistently interrupted any fostering of sympathy. Delays, money, and misunderstanding assumed too great an importance; and beneath the unnecessary stumbling block of twenty guineas and the profits of *Rimini*, the poetry itself was finally buried, so far as the house of Taylor & Hessey was concerned.

If, from 1816 to 1818, money had greatly contributed to the quarrel between the firm and Hunt, it threatened also during these years an association of far greater importance – that of Taylor and Hessey themselves. In spite of the atmosphere of buoyancy in the Trade at the end of the war against France, the firm continued throughout this period to face serious financial difficulties. In August 1816, Taylor wrote his father a letter which revealed for the first time the gravity of their situation:[2]

> by my apparent Arrangements with Hessey, it will ultimately come to pass, I think, that I shall take up my Abode in Fleet Street. . . . he will go to Bath, & leave me in Possession of all that is good or bad in Fleet Street – Not that he seems at all desirous of quitting the Concern, but he feels that it cannot support us both. . . . Perhaps even now we may not separate, but I do not otherwise know how to go on with the Business. . . . We have not Money to carry it over the End of the Year or none of these Plans would be necessary.

Chief amongst the problems which the firm faced was the retail side of business. Far more subject to the fluctuations of trade than the publishing concern, it had during the ten years from 1807 to 1816 lost nearly £3,000; and even the small but steady profit made by the publishing side could not offset such a substantial loss each year. For some time, each partner had supervised the part of the business best suited to him: Taylor had taken the publishing, Hessey the retail. But the expenses which Hessey had to bear as the father of an increasingly large family made it impossible that he should ever gain a profit from the shop in Fleet Street. By September, though, no firm decision had yet been made about what might be done for the best. 'We shall probably jog on as usual', Taylor wrote, 'endeavouring to make the most of the Business by personal Attention on our own parts, & diminishing the Expenses by both living in the same House.'[3]

For almost a year, the firm jogged on. But in the summer of 1817, scarcely two months after the house's courageous decision to publish Keats, Taylor wrote to his brother James with a piece of news that might have been comical had it not been so catastrophic: the firm's total profit for the previous year had been precisely £2. The retail side had lost £318, the publishing had gained £320.[4] Only by borrowing

Statement of Accounts
Bakewell MSS   John Taylor to James Taylor jun.   23 October 1817

Retail

	Half Profit	Taylor's expenses	Loss	Gain	Hessey's expenses	Loss
April 1807–June 1808	410. 3.6	595.14.11	185.11.4 [sic]		549. 0.3	138.16.8 [sic]
to June 1809	420.13.2	472. 2.10	51. 9.8		557.15.0	137. 1.9½
to June 1810	495. 0.6	479.14.9½		15. 6.6 [sic]	528.15.2	33.14.8
to June 1811	447.17.9½	545.17.0½	97.19.3		600.17.7½	152.19.10
to June 1812	501.16.5	487. 7.3		14. 9.2	501.18.9½	0. 2.4
to June 1813	671.14.4	641. 3.8½		30.10.7½	680. 0.8½	8. 6.4½
to Dec. 1815	1198.13.8	1149. 6.7		49. 7.1	2087.14.9	889. 1.1
to Dec. 1816	302. 3.11	744. 3.8	441.19.9		1142.15.6	840.11.7
			=loss of 669.6.7½ [sic]			=loss of 2200.14.4

Publishing

April to December 1815 leaves each of us a Profit of   83.13.5
to December 1817   „   „   „   „   167. 4.0

Taylor's capital +570   250.17.5   H's cap. +1500   250.17.5

820.17.5   1750.17.5
− 669. 6.7   − 2200.14.4

Profit 151.10.10   Loss 449.16.11

from friends such as Freeman (the owner of a third of the shares since 1816), and by drawing upon their own capital, had they managed to survive at all. Throughout the summer, in an atmosphere of growing crisis, letters full of involved calculations were sent to Bakewell and Retford asking for advice and help. Finally, on 23 October, Taylor wrote to James with a statement of accounts which clearly showed that the firm was almost bankrupt. It revealed that only by drawing upon the whole of his capital had Taylor made a profit at all, and Hessey, having drawn upon a capital of £1,500, had still lost nearly £450 (see p. 63). Taylor added the inevitable conclusion:

> considering that no Exertions, nor any Savings of mine could stand against so heavy an Expenditure, & that sooner or later my property must also, if it was ever so great, be involved with that of Hessey, I proposed to him (as the only Chance remaining) either to take the Retail Business, or the Publishing, & let each do the best he could for himself. . . . I was willing to give him his Choice, being ready to take either – It was not possible to state anything fairer: at the same Time I know that it was almost Hobson's Choice to H.: for he cannot live upon the publishing Concern, with his Family. Yet what could I do more? . . . When I consider the long Acquaintance which has subsisted between us, his many estimable Qualities, and the little Babes that are dependent upon him for support, I feel the strongest Wish to see him placed in the most secure and comfortable Situation our Circumstances will allow –

By the end of November, Hessey had proposed that the partnership should consider itself dissolved as from the previous Christmas.[5] Taylor was to take the publishing concern, and Hessey the shop in Fleet Street.

If the firm's dilatoriness in reaching written, binding agreements was on several later occasions a major source of contention between them and their authors, it was on this occasion the source of their salvation. Christmas passed, and there was still no dissolution. At the end of January 1818, Taylor reported that Hessey was stock-taking: 'I have Reason to think from his great Cheerfulness, and the Amount of Business done, that he is perfectly content.'[6] By March, there had still been no firm decision. Taylor listed the many advantages which both would gain from ending the partnership; yet too easily, with that characteristic balancing of alternatives, he pictured the other side of the coin:[7]

an Unwillingness to make positive Changes – to leave a Friend
with whom I looked to be associated for the Remainder of my
Life . . . and a Fear lest my quitting the Retail Business might
take away some of the Friends by whom it has been supported
(which Woodhouse thinks would be the Case) all these pull so
hard on the other hand as almost to make me stand stock still.

By the summer of 1818, it was clear that talk of dissolution, although
it was to be discussed for several years, never again threatened to
become a reality before the best of the firm's work was done. The retail
business was still losing heavily, but Taylor discerned some signs of a
slow improvement; and the publishing side was 'a really good Concern,
& capable of doing much more than the Retail'.[8] Within six months,
an enthusiasm too long missing from his letters returned: 'Our Business has been unusually good since Christmas, and from all I see & hear,
the Town is likely to have a very great Season this Year.'[9]

The fear of bankruptcy and of a dissolution of partnership was
temporarily allayed. But throughout the firm's greatest years, understandably eclipsed by the publishing of Keats and Hazlitt, Clare and
De Quincey, the house's financial insecurity remained as a persistent
pressure upon their work. Indeed, it was the insecurity, the fluctuations
in the annual returns for bookselling and publishing, which constituted
Taylor & Hessey's chief difficulty. Against a background of continual
poor sales and profits, they could with great effort have economised
and tightened unnecessary spending. But no pattern of sales or expendi-
ture remained the same for any considerable period. Within months,
even weeks, sales had fluctuated wildly, and any plan, of either austerity
or expansion, had to be suddenly reversed. At the beginning of 1818,
Taylor wrote that the retail business in London was 'recovering its
former Energy. . . . Trade has been much better with us for the last 4 or
5 Months, and it now bids fair to realise the Views which we lately
feared were vanished for ever.'[10] But nine months later, he wrote to his
father, 'At no Time have so many [Booksellers] been insolvent.'[11] He
reeled off a list of men whose businesses had failed: Rest Fenner, Black
& Son, Williams, Scholey, Nowill & Burch. Three months later again,
business had been 'unusually good', and the City was expected to enjoy
'a very good Season this Year'.[12] Against such a background of
perpetual economic fluctuations, the firm juggled uncertainly with
profit and loss, expanding a little with an eye upon the future economies
that invariably followed. In financial terms, indeed, the whole of their
career was a gamble; and in the end, perhaps, the partnership survived as

long as it did only because Taylor and Hessey gambled better than most.

If nothing else, the financial crisis of 1817 and 1818 must have brought home to Taylor in a particularly immediate way the lessons suggested much earlier in his career by Lackington's flourishing business and Vernor & Hood's payment of £4,000 to Robert Bloomfield: that literature was now a trade and books a commodity subject to the same economic laws as any other, that the publisher who ignored the market and the growing financial power of the reading public invited certain bankruptcy. Indeed, two of his remarks from this period illustrate well his continuing awareness of the economic pressures upon publishing, and the implications of those pressures in terms of the taste of the reading public. In 1819, he wrote to James and reported that Lord Liverpool's administration had determined to stamp out the glut of political pamphlets flooding the market by imposing a stamp duty of fourpence upon all tracts containing more than two sheets. The plan, to him, demonstrated nothing but the abiding ignorance of the Government:[13]

> If by this means they were to succeed, which they will not, in putting a Stop to these political Papers, at what a Price would they effect it! – The Bookseller's Committee told them to their evident surprise, that Howard & Evans of Long Lane now sell as many of Miss Hannah More's, & other religious & moral Tracts as would pay a Duty at that Rate of 25,000 £ a year. And this is nothing to the immense Number of cheap Works of that kind in Circulation, which actually employ no less than 10,000 Persons in carrying them through the Country.

Four years previously, he had jotted down in a Commonplace Book three figures which illustrated another aspect of the same story:[14]

> Philips (Sir Richard) told me yesterday that in the Course of last yr ending Mid^r he sold off
> 30000 Goldsmiths Grammar of Geography
> 10000 Blair's Class Book
> 75000 Mavor's Spelling

He added no comment to either of these statements, but with the financial insecurity of the firm a continual worry during these years, he could scarcely have failed to have been impressed with such vast sales. The figures reflected clearly, not only the economic influence of the reading public, but even more importantly, the prevailing interests and taste of that public. Each year, Howard & Evans were selling a million and a half pamphlets of a moral or religious nature, illustrating how deeply religious debate captured the minds of many readers. In 1815, one bookseller alone had sold 75,000 copies of a spelling book within a year, emphasising similarly how greatly the ability to read was sought, and how much it was to any publisher's advantage to provide the field of remaining illiteracy with the basic tools of learning. Faced with the implications of these and many other figures, Taylor & Hessey took the hint they afforded; and in common with every publisher, they compromised with the demands of the public and thereby ensured the survival of the house until the best of its work was done. Indeed, if the firm's chief glory during its greatest years was always to be the publishing of works of genius, its financial salvation was the publishing of uninspired mediocrity.

To examine at great length the house's staple diet of religious and moral works which invariably answered the public demand is unnecessary. But a few of them illustrate, if nothing else, how impossible it was for either partner to ignore those books which firmly reflected the interests of the reading public. Harvey Marriott's *Catechism*, published by them in 1813, went through an edition of 1,000 copies in under six months, and a second edition of 2,000 copies was immediately printed. A selection of sermons by the Rev. E. Robson, likewise, went through nearly two editions in 1818. A year later, when the first edition of Alfred Buckland's *Letters on the Importance, Duty and Advantages of Early Rising* had been sold, Taylor wrote to the author offering 100 guineas for the sole copyright. So confident was Buckland of his position that he demanded £500. 'I wish I had written on this subject,' Taylor confessed, 'anything of the kind is sure to sell.'[15] He was not mistaken. Within the year, nearly three editions of the book had been sold.

But by far the greatest successes of the firm during these years were the books of Mrs Ann Taylor and Miss Jane Taylor of Ongar. The title of the first of their works to be published by the house (Ann Taylor's *Maternal Solicitude for a Daughter's Best Interests*) evokes the genteel, dutifully moral way of life their books depicted, and the solid middle-class world which read them. But however uninspired as literature, they sold on a scale which was never to be repeated for the firm. Taylor & Hessey bought the copyright of *Maternal Solicitude* for sixty guineas, with the guarantee of a further ten guineas on the third and any subsequent edition of 1,000 copies.[16] It was probably the most profitable investment they ever made. The book was published on 22 September 1813 in an edition of 750 copies. Within three months, another edition of 1,000 had been called for; by July 1814, a third; and by January 1815, a fourth edition of 1,250 copies. Ten years later, the work had reached a twelfth edition. The story of their other books was the same. During 1815, 4,000 copies of Ann Taylor's *Practical Hints to Young Females* were sold in a mere eight months; and 3,000 copies of Jane Taylor's *Display, a Tale for Young People* went off in seven months in the same year. Many of the Reviews, particularly the *Eclectic*, the *British Critic* and the *Monthly*, gave the books high praise, and their opinion was endorsed by the public. By 1830, three of their works had reached a twelfth edition, another a tenth, one a seventh, and later books fourth and fifth editions.[17] Indeed, there could be no clearer indication of the immense popularity of their works than the profit the firm made upon them. In 1826, the average annual return that the books had brought in was estimated at £814 – a total profit during the twelve years from 1814 of over £10,000.[18] Five years later, in 1831, when their selling capacity must almost have been exhausted, Taylor was still able to sell the copyright and remaining stock for £600.[19]

These details of good sales and profits were obviously figures to cheer the hearts of Taylor and Hessey. But perhaps neither of them was unaware in later years of two comparisons which darkened the picture. During the early 1820s, as the seventh and eighth editions of the Taylors' books came from the press, the first edition of *Endymion* was remaindered for fourpence a copy. And in 1828, as several of these works reached their eleventh and twelfth editions, Taylor was still advertising the first edition of *Lamia*.

If there was a moral to be drawn from this comparison, it was as well that Taylor and Hessey did not draw it. To have lingered long upon the sales and profits that the Taylors' works had achieved might only too easily have attracted them in a direction far removed from Keats, De Quincey, and Clare. But both partners continued to retain a steady view of the firm's chief policy. The house would consider enduring talent first, and the balance-sheet afterwards. Gradually, this order of priorities attracted new writers. By 1818, indeed, the firm's liberal spirit, its invariable fair-mindedness and constant enterprise, had become well known in the Trade. And with recognition came, in the early months of that year, a critic whose talent Taylor greatly admired. By the summer, the house had published a collection of essays by William Hazlitt.

How and when Taylor and Hessey were first introduced to Hazlitt is unknown; but certainly by January 1818, when he was delivering his lectures on the English Poets at the Surrey Institution, they had heard much about him, and had probably already met him. Shortly after the lectures concluded, an agreement was reached between them, by which the firm was to publish the second edition of his *Characters of Shakespear's Plays* and the first of *Lectures on the English Poets*.

At first, there was every reason for Taylor to rejoice at the agreement with Hazlitt. Not only had the house gained some prestige by becoming his publishers, but in terms of sales also, the future appeared promising. The first edition of *Shakespear's Plays*, published by the Ollier brothers in 1817, had been sold in under a year, and there seemed no immediate reason why the second edition and the new volumes of lectures should not gain a similar success. Even the shadow of *Maga* and the *Quarterly*, ghosts which were regularly haunting the firm during these months, seems to have done nothing to affect Taylor's optimism. On 4 June, he wrote to Bakewell about 'the critical Heart of Mr Gifford. . . . As for Hazlitt, he may say what he will of him – they are old Enemies of each other. But the Lectures on the English Poets which we have just published by Hazlitt, is a book of extraordinary ability.'[20]

Yet, however greatly Taylor admired the new work, he was certainly unaware at the time how deeply the old enmity between Hazlitt and the reviewers would cut into his world. The awakening was not long delayed. A few days only after he had written to James, the January number of the *Quarterly* appeared. Its review of *Shakespear's Plays* was bitterly hostile.[21] It attacked Hazlitt's 'sedition' and 'senseless and wicked sophistry', and concluded that

> The few specimens which we have selected of his ethics and his criticism are more than sufficient to prove that Mr Hazlitt's knowledge of Shakespeare and the English language are on a par with the purity of his morals and the depth of his understanding.

The article was the fuse for the most concentrated period of hostility between Hazlitt and the Reviews. The *Quarterly* later continued in its July number with an attack upon *The English Poets* and Hazlitt's lack of 'accurate reasoning, just observation, and precise, or even intelligible, language'. And to add more deadly fuel to the fire, the August number of Blackwood's *Maga* turned from its previous equivocation about the essayist to the most vicious of personal attacks. From the generosity of Patmore's evaluation that he was 'among the best, if not the very best, living critic of our national literature', which had appeared in an earlier number,[22] the Review turned suddenly to a sustained attack upon the critical and personal vices of 'pimpled Hazlitt'. The August number bitterly attacked his supposed mediocrity, his ignorance and unoriginality. 'Truth and falsehood' were 'indifferent' to him, and his lectures were pure 'coxcomb'. Through the pages of 'Hazlitt Cross-Questioned' and 'On Shakespeare's Sonnets', Wilson the reviewer dealt out slander upon slander, equalled in viciousness only by the attack Keats was receiving from Lockhart in the same number.

At the time of *Maga*'s attack, Taylor was out of town; but soon after the review had appeared, Hazlitt called upon Hessey and appeared 'very much moved' at what had happened. Keats dined with them both in Fleet Street and noticed the bitter silence which surrounded the subject.[23] After consulting about what might be done for the best, Hazlitt and Hessey eventually resolved to 'remain quiet and let [things] take their Course'.[24] But for Hazlitt himself, such an acquiescence was asking too much of his patience. He had already answered the *Quarterly*'s attack in the *Examiner* of 15 June, with a character-sketch of 'The Editor of the Quarterly Review'. The article slashed at Gifford as a 'cat's-paw', as 'the invisible link, that connects literature with the police'. And now, in response to *Maga*'s attack, he wrote 'A Reply to Z' which was sent to the *Edinburgh Review*,[25] instituted a claim for libel against *Maga*, retained Francis Jeffrey as counsel, and demanded damages of £2,000. Eventually, the case was dropped, but Hazlitt had still one last blow to deliver. In March of the following year, there finally appeared the *Letter to William Gifford, Esq.* With a white-hot fury which even he rarely equalled, his words burned across the page. The months of accumulated resentment and bitterness, and the attacks upon him as the third-rate pimpled critic of loose morals, produced a counter-attack of unsurpassed irony and invective. For more than forty pages, he tore Gifford apart with the most persistent fury. The *Quarterly* was damned as the 'receptacle for the scum and sediment of all the prejudice, bigotry, ill-will, ignorance and rancour, afloat in the kingdom'. Its editor was a liar, the head of a literary police, a man 'grown old in the service of corruption'. With a brilliant incisiveness of language, he taunted Gifford, 'To crawl and lick the dust is all they expect of you, and all you can do' and 'They know that if you cease to be a tool, you cease to be anything'. In the end, the letter did not silence Gifford, but he felt the diamond brilliance of Hazlitt's anger too deeply ever to contemplate such sustained invective again. It was a muted voice which answered the essayist's charges over six months later. The old energy had gone. Perhaps he was aware that, after the *Letter*, any retort could not fail to be an anti-climax.

To follow in detail the sporadic yet complex manoeuvres of attack and counter-attack which Hazlitt, Gifford, and *Maga* pursued for many years is unnecessary.[26] But the reaction of Taylor and Hessey to the acrimony in which they had become involved is of obvious importance. To a very great extent, they stood by Hazlitt; and indeed, perhaps the strongest testimony of their continued faith in him was their publishing in April 1819 the *Lectures on the English Comic Writers*, for which he probably received twice the sum of the *English Poets* copyright.[27] Yet despite the firm's continued support in the form of discussions and loans, despite the encouraging news that Hazlitt too was eager to press on with new works, there were hints of some uneasiness which momentarily clouded the good relations. On the last day of 1818, a year in which Taylor had witnessed too much hostility and bitterness to allow of much optimism for the coming year, he wrote to his father:[28]

> The New Monthly Magazine contains another outrageous
> Attack on Hazlitt. – I am sick of all this Scurrility, and must
> give up the Writer, unless he can protect himself & his Reputation
> better. – It is unpleasant to my Feelings to read such Articles
> anywhere & on any person, but of course still more so when we
> publish their Works.

Certainly, Taylor's temporary reaction in this letter to Hazlitt's part in the hostility was less than generous; but it is clear that he had growing cause to feel distressed by the attacks that the firm's authors had suffered during the year. Nor, indeed, had severe criticism been confined to Keats and Hazlitt. He himself had come under bitter attack for the publication of *The Identity of Junius*. In 1817, he reported that both the *British Critic* and the *Monthly Review* had damned the book, and with some justice complained of the editorship of these Reviews:[29]

> The British Critic is an absurd intolerant Blockhead, but he is
> writing for Promotion, as the last Editor, Reanch, succeeded so
> well by the same Means – It is almost enough to make one turn
> Dissenter to see such Time-Servers in the highest Places of our
> Establishment – but bad Men are everywhere.

A year later, the *British Critic* had given up the chase; but the *Monthly Review*, in its third article upon *Junius*, continued the attack and publicly accused Taylor of deceit in bringing out the second edition of the book at a price of 12/-. Feeling 'more dull & dispirited than usual', Taylor wrote to his father:[30]

This state of uneasy Feeling has not been diminished by looking over the Magazines – they are so full of Revilings of one Side against another that it is sickening to read them – You may perhaps think that I am personally affected by some of these when I tell you that Junius is again attacked in the Monthly Review; but I assure you that I think this is not the Case, for the Attack is so obviously illfounded that I must be silly indeed to let it interest me. . . . You may judge of the Falsehood of his Assertion, when he affirms that the first Pamphlet which they reprobated as dear at 5/- has now had a Portrait forefixed to it & the *'Vendors modestly'* charge for it now no less than 12/-. In this it is plain that the Writer never saw the Volume itself – but it was reviewed in a former No & then as evidently by a Person who had never read it. Such are the Leaders of the public Mind.

On Taylor's own account, there was clearly no great love lost between the Reviews and him; and very possibly about this time, he noted in one of his Commonplace Books a quotation which revealed his estimation of the whole tribe of critics: 'By a Critic was originally understood a good Judge; but now, with us, it signifies no more than unmerciful Faultfinder; two steps above a Fool, & a great many below a Wise Man.'[31] But by the end of 1818, it was obvious that the most notorious of the Reviews had set out to vilify and destroy two writers, Keats and Hazlitt, whom he believed were among the greatest of the age. Perhaps, to the philosophic mind, viewing attack *sub specie aeternitatis*, it was clear that such polemic could never in the end achieve a complete destruction. By some alchemy, future generations would eventually rescue *Lamia*, *Endymion*, and Hazlitt's *Lectures* from the neglect and failure which had originally surrounded them. But, as Taylor might have justifiably retorted to such a belief, a publisher lives by the moment as well as for the future. No house survives upon the potential recognition of its writers. And for Taylor & Hessey at least, the attacks of the Reviews succeeded in the only way that was important at the time. The reading public consigned Hazlitt, as it consigned Keats, to the virtual anonymity of remaindered authors. Hazlitt wrote later that, before the *Quarterly's* review of *Shakespear's Plays*, the volume had raced through nearly two editions within three months. After the attack appeared, the house never sold another copy of the book.[32]

For the second time in his career, Taylor had seen the crippling effect of public attack upon the sales of the firm's books, and he may well have tried during these months, as did Keats and Hazlitt, to define the reasons for the pervasive influence of the Reviews. One explanation at least for the success of the attacks against both poet and essayist was obvious: the firm had at its command no medium through which the reading public might hear any defence. Throughout this time, the house did of course attempt to collect what support it could. Taylor, as has been seen, applied to the *Edinburgh Review* for its help, and tried to argue Keats's case to Gifford. The liberal editor of the *Champion*, John Scott, was enlisted and very probably wrote the protest against the attacks on Keats which appeared in the *Morning Chronicle* in October 1818. Hessey too defended another of the firm's writers who had been damned by the *Quarterly*, Morris Birkbeck, in a letter to *The Times* of 23 October.[33] Yet despite these efforts, it was clear that the firm was answering the attacks with one arm tied behind its back. Not only were Taylor and Hessey largely lost in the world of cheap showmanship and arbitrary bitterness which *Maga* and the *Quarterly* revelled in, but they also lacked the means by which their case might be forcibly presented to the public. The odd letter to the newspapers, the odd conversation in defence of Keats or Hazlitt, could clearly never produce that sustained impact upon the public mind that a regularly appearing Review was able to command. To rout the critics, it was not simply necessary to be more brilliantly critical than they. Hazlitt had achieved this in his *Letter to William Gifford*, but it had not helped his books to sell. The defence had to be repeated time and again through a medium which stood constantly in the public eye.

The great Reviews were such a medium. In terms both of circulation and of regular appearance, their power was obvious. On even a conservative estimate, the sales achieved by each number of *Maga* and the *Quarterly* in their hey-day were fifteen or twenty times greater than those attained by *Lamia* or *Shakespear's Plays*. In January 1818, a few months before the attacks began, John Murray wrote to James Hogg that the *Quarterly* was selling 12,000 copies of each issue, and he confidently predicted an increase to 14,000 by the summer of that year.[34] And by 1820, *Maga*, if its own figures could be trusted, was selling a little below 17,000 copies each month.[35] Even more importantly, the regular appearance of these Reviews ensured a continuity of readership. It allowed them to sustain an attack over a period of time, without the constraining thought that what they had to say could be said once, and once only. The crucial difference between a new book and a Review, indeed, was precisely that the writer of a book could not automatically rely upon further editions in which he might qualify his original argument or answer his detractors. He was not granted the continuity of argument which the Reviews enjoyed. Only too frequently, a book stood or fell by the thoughts within the cover of its first edition.

These two factors of extensive sales and regular appearance clearly contributed much to the substantial influence over the public achieved by *Maga* and the *Quarterly*. Yet by themselves, they seem insufficient to account for the power wielded by the greatest of the Reviews, for high sales were of course as much a result of their influence as the reason for it. One wider reason for the effectiveness of their propaganda, however, was suggested by a correspondent to the *London Magazine* in 1820. The subject of the article was the attack upon *Endymion* by the *Quarterly*:[36]

> Almost anywhere else it would have been harmless, and unworthy of particular notice; but *there* it cannot fail to gain a certain degree of credit from the company which it keeps. It would be foolish to doubt or deny the extensive effect which such an article is likely to produce, appearing as it does in a work which is read by tens of thousands, nine-tenths of whom are not able to judge for themselves, and half the other tenth of which will not take the trouble of doing so.

The final words of this criticism are particularly interesting, for they echo a view of the reading public which both Keats and Hazlitt voiced also. Keats, as has been seen, saw the public as essentially passive and gullible. Their minds were 'enervated' and 'indolent'. They looked to the Reviews as to a 'superstition', blindly accepting the tablets of stone handed down by Croker or Gifford without ever troubling to form independent judgments. Hazlitt went further. He argued that it was not simply ingenuousness but a particular kind of moral cowardice in the public that had allowed the Reviews to influence sales so greatly. Writing of the attacks upon his *Shakespear's Plays*, he claimed that 'The public, enlightened as they are, must have known the meaning of that attack as well as those who made it. It was not ignorance then, but cowardice, that led them to give up their own opinion'.[37]

However greatly the bitterness of both Keats and Hazlitt had been aroused by the effectiveness of such attacks, their views certainly spoke a part of the truth. Large sections of the reading public did regard the great Reviews as 'a kind of Delphic Oracle, and Voice of the Inspired', as Carlyle wrote of the *Edinburgh*.[38] Certainly too, *Maga* and the

Quarterly in their criticisms had exploited levels of showmanship and personality which it was difficult for any public to ignore. Mud was slung freely, and it was impossible for most readers to turn to a serious consideration of the books involved against such a background of personal abuse and brilliantly perverse rhetoric. Then, as at other times, personality spoke louder than poetry, and heroes and villains louder than reasonable men. But beyond these factors, the chief Reviews all voiced at one time or another in their career a single argument which was almost certainly the principal reason for their influence – an argument which, in the end, came into direct conflict with Taylor's own thinking about the nature and purpose of literature.

In its crudest form, the emphasis which, whether formulated or unformulated, invariably guided the Reviews in their criticism of new books was the inflexible belief that literature was part of an integrated social fabric. It was created from, and should thereby reflect, the general patterns of moral and political allegiance which society as a whole had adopted. It could not contract out from that allegiance, nor expand its function by erecting new structures of belief. When it did, when it explored experience which held only an imaginative and individual truth, it was to be damned. At most, it was an interpreter of existing forms of belief, not a catalyst of change.

Many articles in the chief Reviews demonstrate how greatly this prevailing argument provided a comprehensive pattern of evaluation for all types of literature. Allegiance to existing social and moral beliefs became the yardstick of criticism; and only too frequently, a judgment upon the intrinsic artistic merit of a new work was coloured by a rigorous examination of the religious commitment and political sympathies that the volume revealed. Two Reviews, indeed, stated their approach quite unambiguously. In an article upon Leigh Hunt, the *New Monthly Review* for September 1818 asked what was evidently thought a pertinent question about literature: 'How can so contemptible a being as the Editor of the Examiner newspaper, presume to talk of poetical capabilities when the germ of all true poetry is religion and patriotism?' And Blackwood's *Maga*, in another article attacking Hunt,[39] argued:

The two great elements of all dignified poetry, religious feeling, and patriotic feeling, have no place in his mind. His religion is a poor tame dilution of the blasphemies of the *Encyclopaedie* – his patriotism a crude, vague, ineffectual and sour Jacobinism. He is without reverence either for God or man.

Religion and patriotism – the words echo as a critical war-cry through page after page of the fiercest attacks by the Reviews upon contemporary writers. It was not without reason that Andrew Lang once described John Wilson Croker as an 'Anglican berserk';[40] nor indeed that Croker himself argued, 'Party is much the strongest passion of an Englishman's mind. Friendship, love, even avarice, give way before it.'[41] For the twin themes of religious and political conservatism were the critical beacons of both *Maga* and the *Quarterly*. With the sanctity of exaggerated truth, Peacock brilliantly exposed the religious inflexibility of the *Quarterly* in his satire *Melincourt*, when Messrs Killthedead, Paperstamp, Antijack, and Feathernest continually interrupt the conversation with cries of 'The Church is in danger! the church is in danger!' And Croker's belief in the supremacy of party loyalties in an Englishman's mind reveals how deeply entangled one Review at least was with political conviction – how difficult it became to divorce criticism of literature from the scarcely muted patriotic hysteria which lay in the background. As Taylor laconically remarked in 1818, 'I think the *loyal* Critics (as they would be thought) are by far the most brutal & inveterate Abusers at present.'[42]

Religion and political loyalty were inviolable. It is clear how deeply such argument attracted the conservative minds in a society confusedly steering its way from rick-burning towards some sort of social stability. The aristocracy had an evident vested interest in the Tory Reviews' affirmation that literature could not contract out from collective morality and political allegiance, for such an assertion placed a tight rein upon imaginative heresies which might further disrupt existing structures of moral and patriotic belief. Similarly, the middle classes, of whom Francis Jeffrey estimated in 1812 'not less than two hundred thousand persons . . . read for amusement and instruction',[43] were gradually achieving an economic and political emancipation from both the upper and the working classes, which depended likewise upon some form of stable structure within society as a whole. *Maga* and the *Quarterly* voiced their interests. They relied upon conservative canons of morality and national loyalty as a firm basis for criticism of literature. A man could not be a good poet and a bad patriot. Only by endorsing the existing beliefs of the literate community could literature of worth be written.

This indelible connection between literature and political and moral allegiance, insisted upon by Tory reviewers, was at least qualified by one leading Review – the *Edinburgh*. In December 1808, its editor Francis Jeffrey voiced an opinion which was to guide much, though not all, of its criticism during these years:[44]

no party politics, and nothing but exemplary moderation and impartiality on all politics. I have allowed too much mischief to be done from my mere indifference and love of sport; but it would be inexcusable to spoil the powerful instrument we have got hold of, for the sake of teazing and playing tricks.

The liberalism of Jeffrey's desire to divorce the criticism of literature from political bias was refreshing; yet even he insisted that writers could not explore areas of experience which held only a personal validity. For him, as for the Tory Reviews, literature should reflect the mind of society, but it could not enlarge that mind, still less disturb it. As soon as a writer began to create for others, Jeffrey argued,[45] he became a public servant with the duty to construct only

such objects as are the *natural* signs and *inseparable* concomitants of emotions, of which the greater part of mankind are susceptible; and his taste will *then* deserve to be called bad and false, if he obtrude upon the public, as beautiful, objects that are not likely to be associated in common minds with any interesting impressions.

For him, the objects presented in a work of art were impotent unless they focussed an inevitable chain of emotional reaction between writer and reader. The writer's apprehension of a beautiful object must generate unforcedly an emotional reaction to that object which most readers were capable of experiencing. If the equation did not hold, his taste deserved to be condemned.

The *Edinburgh's* belief in this firm relationship between writer and reader in imaginative reaction was revealed no more clearly in the practical business of criticism than in John Wilson's review of the fourth Canto of *Childe Harold*.[46] The strength and genius of Byron's poetry, Wilson argued, was derived precisely from the close association between the poet's own imagination and 'the public mind':

He lives in a sort of sympathy with the public mind – sometimes wholly distinct from it – sometimes acting in opposition to it – sometimes blending with it, – but at all times, – in all his thoughts and actions having a reference to the public mind. . . . The existence he paints is – now. . . . It is his to speak of all those great political events which have been objects of such passionate sympathy to the nation . . . it is a living speaker standing up before us, and ruling our minds. . . . His travels were not, at first, the self-impelled act of a mind severing itself in lonely roaming from all participation with the society to which it belonged, but rather obeying the general motion of the mind of that society.

The closeness of this relationship between Byron and his public was not exaggerated. As Bulwer Lytton later argued, the first two Cantos of *Childe Harold*, in their satiety, discontent, and restless melancholy, 'touched the most sensitive chord in the public heart – they expressed what every one felt.'[47] And to read the accounts by Charles Knight or John Clare or Lytton of the emotions of the common people as Byron's funeral cortège passed through the streets of London, is to realise how deeply the man himself and his poetry had reflected the restless disillusionment of ordinary people.[48] Yet the key phrases of Wilson's argument – 'sympathy with the public mind', 'reference to the public mind', 'obeying the general motion of the mind of that society' – demonstrate again a conception of the writer as a reflector of experience rather than an explorer of it. It is unlikely that even the *Edinburgh*, for all its liberalism, would have endorsed the argument that it is in the very nature of literature to explore at times areas of human experience divorced from ordinary understanding. Indeed, the abiding concerns of contemporary writers to examine the nature of inspiration and imagination, soliloquy and individual vision, were not in the end the concerns of the great Reviews. For the most liberal, literature had to connect with the feelings of the public mind; for the most dogmatic, it was obliged to reflect the existing structures of moral and political allegiance which society as a whole had adopted. For both, its field lay exclusively in the 'general motion of the mind of that society'.

It seems probable that, in this general argument, the chief reason for the influence of the leading Reviews is to be found. By endorsing the need for a stable, and even static, relationship between literature and society, they themselves became one of the principal agents by which that relationship was established and supported. With individual aristocratic patronage almost dead, their power was, indeed, that they had become the voice for the public patronage of literature.

In several obvious ways, Taylor's position as a publisher often revealed similar objectives to the Reviews. Like them, he was concerned to establish a firm relationship between writers and the reading public. Like them too, he looked towards 'the public mind' to discover its interests and general movement. Yet in his thinking about the nature of literature, the differences between him and the Reviews appear far more substantial and striking than the similarities, for only rarely during the firm's greatest years did he endorse their belief that writers should, before all else, mirror the general moral and political attitudes of their public. There can be no doubt that he bowed to moral convention in the case of *The Eve of St Agnes*, as he was to bow on several later occasions to religious and political pressures in the case of Clare and Landor. Yet at the same time, he consistently affirmed the difference of the writer from the rest of mankind, the presence in literature of an imaginative logic which did and should not necessarily correspond with the movement of an ordinary reader's mind. 'True Poetic Excitement' was, he believed, an impulse which clearly distinguished the poet from ordinary men; and in his Commonplace Book, as has been seen, the theme of imagination as that creative force which differentiated the writer and his public was persistently emphasised. It is very unlikely that he would have supported, even in part, Jeffrey's basis for criticism, still less of course the arguments of *Maga* and the *Quarterly*. What appears from his scattered notes and remarks about literature is, indeed, a consistent belief in the imaginative autonomy of the writer. It was, finally, more valuable that an author should explore the working of his own imagination than possibly compromise that exploration by a constant reference to the 'public mind' of his society.

In the end, it was, perhaps, because Hazlitt found in these beliefs some echo of his own thoughts that his association with Taylor lasted as long as it did. Yet the final glimpse of their relationship is not altogether a happy one. One disappointment is that, during 1818 and 1819 when they were in contact with each other most frequently, Taylor did not write of the particular qualities in Hazlitt's work which most attracted him. Over six years later, he did define them – but by that time, the fruitfulness of the old friendship had been forgotten, and a quarrel had arisen between Taylor and Walter Savage Landor, in which Hazlitt had taken Landor's part. In the heat of debate, Taylor's words were too greatly coloured by the unjust treatment he felt he had received from both Hazlitt and Landor, and he was not able to speak dispassionately of the essayist's work:⁴⁹

I wish [Landor] had not pledged himself to this high opinion of Hazlitt as a Writer – it will remain in Existence when he would desire it be annihilated & forgotten – and with all my admiration of H's Style which is generally vigorous & happy, I cannot but think that Landor himself will confess ere long that he has much overrated it. Hazlitt's Power is great chiefly because it is highly concentrated. Were he to spread himself abroad on all subjects

as Landor does it would shew no Strength: this is apparent from
the laxity of its Nerve on those Subjects which he is not familiar
with, & from his proneness to repeat himself on those which he
has studied. – He owes more to the Intensity of his Feeling than
to his intellectual Greatness – his Expressions are powerful in
proportion to the Strength of his Impressions; and these are of
limited Range having little or no Sympathy with what is truly
noble – What there is good in him may be said to be of the
Devil.

The last few lines of this criticism in particular were too greatly dis-
torted by Taylor's feeling of injustice to speak any truth. He had
retreated behind a veil of shrill rhetoric and exaggeration. Yet it cannot
be forgotten that, in friendlier times, he had once called a collection of
Hazlitt's essays 'a Work of extraordinary Ability'; and that even amidst
the hostility of 1825, hints remained of the old understanding. Only
three days before writing the criticism, he had spoken of Hazlitt to
Julius Hare as an 'inoffensive & much injured Man'.[50] And even in his
prejudiced evaluation of the essayist's work, there were indications too
that the argument had not altogether blinded him to his distinctive
genius. He justly spoke of the acute concentration of his style and the
'Intensity of his Feeling' as keys to his work, and rightly argued the
close relationship between 'the Strength of his Impressions' and the
vitality of his style. These isolated points were, unfortunately, never
developed; but if they did not state, they at least pointed towards,
important aspects of Hazlitt's work. As Taylor partly suggested, the
centre of much of his work which was published by the firm was not
so much his intellect as his own perspicuity and enthusiasm – an
enthusiasm revealed most brilliantly when it flashed and splintered in
an isolated phrase, in a spontaneous reaction to a single event which had
moved him. In De Quincey's words, 'the atmosphere that moulds . . .
the dynamic forces that combine' were only on occasions to be found
in his writing. More often, and particularly in the moving eloquence of
his later excursions into autobiography, he had forced the world
through the troubled centre of his own crystal, and could see it only in
that light.

Sometime during October 1817, when Hazlitt was only a name to
Taylor and Hessey, and Leigh Hunt still a somewhat perplexing reality,
there was a meeting on the sands of Littlehampton which eventually
brought two more poets to Fleet Street. Samuel Taylor Coleridge,

taking the sea air, was attracted one day by the sound of a man reciting Homer to his son. After several silent encounters, Coleridge introduced himself. 'Sir, yours is a face I *should* know: I am Samuel Taylor Coleridge.' Thus was Henry Francis Cary, the translator of Dante's *Divine Comedy*, introduced to the poet whom he had known was visiting the district, but whom he had never dared to approach. The walk ended with Coleridge dining at Cary's table, and with him taking away that night the tiny volumes of the second edition of Dante, which Cary had published at his own expense three years earlier. As the translator wrote in a later and more sumptuous edition, this small book, measuring about three by four inches only, 'was printed in so small a character as to deter a numerous class of readers from perusing it'. But the following day, when the two men again met, it was clear that Coleridge had burned some midnight oil in reading much of the translation, for he was able to recite whole pages from it. Before leaving Littlehampton, he had not only encouraged Cary with his high opinion of the work, but had promised to give active assistance in promoting its sale.[51]

On his return to London, he sounded out opinions regarding publishers for a possible new edition, and all his acquaintanceship seem to have pointed the way to 93 Fleet Street. Alexander Chalmers, 'a veteran in the literary Market', told him that Taylor and Hessey were 'men that *give* respect as well as receive it'. Another friend, Coleridge reported to Cary, 'infallible in worldly knowledge', had been pleased to see the firm's name in one of his prospectuses; they were very honest and honourable men.[52] The poet himself considered Taylor and Hessey 'men of high estimation as Tradesmen', and in January 1818 he proposed that they might publish a new edition of the translation. Within a month he was able to report to Cary:[53]

I have received together with the Dante that I had lent them
such a handsome, friendly Letter from Taylor and Hessey,
expressing their wish to be the publishers of such a work, and
their desire in any manner to be serviceable to the Author – that
I cannot delay expressing a strong wish, that you might be able
to think of some friend who could pick out the books at your
Lodgings.

Despite the fact that, when they were first approached, the minuscule 1814 edition had lapsed into complete obscurity, over a thousand copies remaining unsold, Taylor and Hessey were evidently eager to act as Cary's publishers. Taylor, indeed, was convinced of the lasting merit of the translation:[54]

> The only clever Work, likely to live a long Time, which interests us at present, is the New Edition of Cary's Dante. Sir James Mackintosh, in a Letter he wrote me, said it was the finest Translation in the Language since the Time of Fairfax's Tasso, & I am as certain it is superior to that.

On 11 May, Coleridge, Cary, Taylor, and Hessey gathered in Coleridge's rooms at Highgate; and an agreement was signed by which the firm purchased the remainder of the 1814 edition, to be sent out under their imprint, for £109, and paid £125 for the right to publish a new edition of 750 copies.[55] Compared with the £60 for a thousand copies and ten guineas for subsequent editions which the house had paid Ann and Jane Taylor, the sum that Cary received was high; and indeed, he was well satisfied with the terms of the agreement. Even more pleasing during the months that followed was the close interest which Taylor took in preparing the translation for the press. For the rest of the year and on into the following spring, letters came from Fleet Street with discussions upon the size of type to be used for the edition, assistance in the form of rare books for the introduction, and detailed criticisms on points in the translation, aiming at a more perspicuous and tighter rendering. In December, Taylor wrote quoting some verses where he felt the metre needed mending. He did not truly think them defective, but an old ghost laboured at the back of his mind:[56]

> the Quarterly Reviewer has no Feeling for such [lines] as:
> 1.33 Who hath so hardily entered this Realm.
> 2.68 To the waters of Peace, that flow diffus'd.
> 3.72 Doth more & better Execution &c &c.
> Precedents for all these are plentiful in Milton, but were he alive now, can you conceive any thing more ridiculous than the rough handling he would get from Mr *Gifford*, on account of his verse & his Politics?

But though he felt a little anxiety about these small instances of metrical freedom, he was more confident in approving Cary's use of archaic words in the translation. Here, of course, he was on firmer ground. His interest in language had continued to mature throughout his years in London, and he now argued that the importance of the subject could scarcely be over-estimated:[57]

It appears to me that the Principle of the Investigation [into Language] is one of the most important of all that have engaged the Attention of Men, & the Consequences of it to the Illustration of Antiquities, History, Manners, & Religion are such as I had scarcely foreseen. – The Inconvenience of it to me is the plunging me into such various and abstruse Disquisitions that I cannot find Time for the Lengths everywhere [?] that I ought to do. One Word leads on to another till in fact all things are drawn into the Vortex.

Yet from the philological vortex, Taylor managed to draw up a few pieces of information to aid Cary; and finally, on 15 July 1819, he was able to announce to his father: 'I have at length got through the task of correcting Dante and the poem will be ready for sale next Week.'[58]

The whole year taken to prepare the edition was a characteristically leisurely amount of time for the firm, but when the translation appeared in three octavo volumes at 36s., there could have been little doubt that the delay had been worthwhile. The edition was a fine one. Cary's original 'Life of Dante' had been expanded to almost twice its former length; an index was included; extensive notes had been provided at the foot of the page; and not the least of the improvements, the translation could now be read without eye-strain. Taylor had decided upon a type at least twice as large as that of the 1814 edition, and with generous margins and line-spacing, the appearance of the book itself finally did Cary's translation justice. By the end of 1821, the 1,750 copies of the 1814 and 1819 editions had been completely sold, and Cary had also received a further forty guineas for an additional sale of 250 copies. Perhaps, if Taylor and Hessey needed reassurance that the world of poetry readers had not altogether died, the sale of Cary's Dante provided that assurance. Against the background of the attacks upon Keats and Hazlitt, the book brought honour and contemporary acclaim when the firm had reason enough to despair of ever hearing such praise for their enterprise. And even more than this, both partners had gained in Cary a sincere and modest friend who was not to leave their society before demonstrating further his wide reading and enthusiasm for European literature.

So frequently during these years was the energy and endeavour of the firm clouded with attack and misfortune that it is salutary for a brief moment to see Taylor and Hessey away from the front line of battle. The society which they had gathered about themselves in the old

Philological days had become by 1820 an important part of their lives, a means of relaxation from the seriousness of their main purpose. Richard Woodhouse was still the closest of friends, a fluent talker who whiled away many an evening in conversation and reading. Keats's friend, John Hamilton Reynolds, gave to the group also a charming irreverence which often punctured the ponderous dignity that sometimes surrounded the philological Taylor and the metaphysical Coleridge. His wit and sense of humour were a constant delight to the circle. In April 1819, an announcement of the forthcoming publication of Wordsworth's poem *Peter Bell* inspired him to one of his quickest and most comic pastiches. He composed his version of Wordsworth in five hours, and, with the willing conspiracy of Taylor, the burlesque was printed and published in record time. Coleridge murmured a few words of imperturbable logic and vague amusement with the prank. Assured by Taylor that there had been no 'base breach of trust', he found that it was doubtless all very droll. But if his smile at the joke was never far from a stifled yawn, the book at least caught the public imagination for a few weeks. It was seen by Lamb 'in every bookseller's window in London', and by the following year, had run through three editions.

With Keats and Hazlitt frequent visitors to Fleet Street, with Cary's modesty and Coleridge's brilliant conversation ('He talked on for ever; and you wished him to talk on for ever', as Hazlitt wrote), with Woodhouse as a discerning and able consultant who often raised Taylor's spirits when the future seemed bleak, with Reynolds the witty iconoclast and William Hilton quietly painting miniatures for the group, Taylor and Hessey revelled in their company. For Taylor, the society was certainly a remembrance of the comfort and hospitality he had enjoyed at the Hoods' during his first years in London, and an intimation perhaps of the early *London Magazine* days, when Hood, Lamb, and Cary were to vie as the most outrageous punster in evenings blurred with venison and wine. London was no longer the detested 'great copper Kettle' of his early years. The noise was still there, but it had become the noise of companionship.

Even with such a sympathetic circle willing to while away his time, though, Taylor was not allowed to lose sight of his main purpose. A few weeks before Cary's edition of Dante was published in 1819, he received a parcel from his cousin in Stamford, Edward Drury:[59]

I now beg your inspection of the poems I mentioned some short time ago in a letter to Mr. Hessey. They are written by a labouring man in this neighbourhood, who seems to have a strange taste for poetry, and if *his* compositions are poetry, there cannot be a stronger proof of the art being a *gift*, as it is called.

The 'labouring man' was John Clare. Less than two months after receiving the first manuscripts, Taylor had decided to publish Clare's poetry; and by the end of the year, the firm had pledged itself to friends of the poet 'to give £100 to Clare, whether the Work succeeded or not'. In addition, they would act as his advisers 'without Emolument or Advantage, on all future Occasions, let who would be his Publishers'.[60] It was a worthy beginning to a friendship which, despite arguments and dissension, was one of the finest of Taylor's life.

{ 4 }

Taylor and Clare: 1819-37

Of all the relationships which existed between Taylor and the writers he published, his association with John Clare was in many ways the most important. Important not only because his own beliefs about the nature of poetry were revealed more clearly in his letters to him than to any other writer, but also because their friendship produced a sustained interaction of ideas which directly influenced the writing of Clare's poetry. The difference between his association with Clare and, for example, with Keats, is a marked one. In the case of Keats, as has been suggested, many of Taylor's theories about the primacy of imagination or the importance of a creative autonomy clearly echoed the poet's own beliefs. Yet these ideas, crucial though they may have been in fostering a literary and personal sympathy between them both, influenced the actual act of composition only on the rarest occasions. Apart from isolated instances, one searches in vain for the crossings out, those expansions and modifications to a first draft, which clearly indicate Taylor's presence and advice during the writing of a poem. In the practical business of composing poetry, this kind of interaction between poet and publisher was not present.

But with Clare it was. Relying far more than Keats had ever done upon Taylor's skill as editor and adviser, Clare brought him far closer to the actual making of poetry than he had ever been before. In his capacity as philologist, transcriber, censor, and critic to the poet, he became closely involved with the complex ways in which imagination affected the writing of poetry. He was faced with questions of poetic language and structure which demanded practical solutions: the substitution of this word for that, the rejection of one stanza in favour of another. He became concerned with problems of poetic form and the necessity for a firm, imaginative logic which controlled the incidental details of a poem. And in addition to all this, there were too the more mundane tasks of deciphering and transcribing manuscripts, selecting and editing poems. With no other writer, indeed, was he to come so close to the sweat of creating literature.

The beginnings of this interaction become evident as soon as he received Clare's first manuscripts from Edward Drury. Without doubt, there was much in these early poems to intrigue him. The poetry was sprinkled liberally with dialect words, which obviously would have appealed to the philologist in him; but yet at the same time, Clare was clearly not a dialect poet in the tradition of Burns, for he relied on it far less. In his almost instinctive dialogue with the natural world, he sometimes wrote regardless of poetic form and structure; yet at times also, as in the poem 'What is Life?', there was a nervous, astringent intellect at work, which controlled the accumulation of detailed vignettes of observation. At the heart of these early poems, there was indeed a certain perplexity. Self-consciousness worked uneasily against a direct and innocent apprehension of the external world. The world of maturity, which sought to analyse and define experience, was brought to bear upon an instinctive and total receptiveness to the world of nature.

There can be little doubt that this seeming lack of a realised centre in Clare's poetry would have intrigued Taylor. As his earlier researches into the Junius mystery have already demonstrated, he delighted in organising material which appeared at first sight allusive or muddled in its nature. There was always, indeed, something of a detective mentality in his character, which was fascinated by the prospect of discovering the key that elucidated a complex problem. And very probably, Clare's manuscripts, misspelt and inchoate as they sometimes were, presented a similar challenge. The fascination lay not only in organising the material for publication, but in discovering that key which would unlock the centre of his poetry and his particular vision.

Important though the presence of this challenge was, however, it is unlikely that this alone could have induced Taylor to publish Clare's work. Beneath the problems of editing and organising the manuscripts, there seem also to have been more substantial qualities in the poetry that particularly attracted him. To define those qualities in any categorical way is not easy, for unfortunately, he never wrote at the time of his initial reactions to Clare's poems. But only a year before his first reading of the manuscripts, he composed a sonnet, never previously published in full, which firmly suggests one reason at least for his attraction.[1] In it, he attempted to define a particular aspect of artistic expression which he believed essential in any work of art: whether the form chosen happened to be chiefly visual, as in sculpture and painting, or predominantly auditory, as in music and poetry:

On Simplicity

When Earth half form'd lay dark & still, God said
  Let there be Light! and at that Word the Sun,
  The Moon, the Stars their radiant Course begun.
Simplicity is strength; whether display'd
In Language, or by the creative aid
  Of Colour, or when Sounds melodious run
  Their Changes, or in Statues slowly won
From their cold Homes, as if of Man afraid.
  Behold the Theseus, easy in powerful Grace;—
  Their artless Dignity of Form and Face,
Who bade the false Tongue stiffen;—
List the Lyre of earliest Times, or how the Winds inspire
  One only String;—and think how deadly ran
  These Words in David's Ear 'Thou art the Man'.—

The sonnet is fairly commonplace verse, though its climax is carefully
wrought, and the monosyllabic directness of 'Thou art the Man'
reinforces well the assertion 'Simplicity is strength'. But the theme of
the poem is of particular importance, for it is very possible that Taylor's
emphasis upon simplicity in artistic expression informed much of his
early admiration for Clare's poetry. His argument in the sonnet was
the strength to be gained from a style which conveyed a direct and
immediate impact upon the listener or viewer of art. The language of
the prophet Nathan, which revealed David's sin to him, directly
exposed his guilt. It stated the fact in the simplest way possible, in four
words of monosyllabic directness, without concessive clauses or the
slightest modification of a complete accusation. The language had been
stripped bare of complexity. In its brevity and precision, it had gained
a strength and immediate force which had burned into David's mind.

It would, of course, be too much to assert categorically that the chief
reason for Taylor's attraction to Clare's work was his awareness of the
fundamental directness of the poet's observation, the final simplicity
and strength of his vision. Yet it is more than likely that a firm connection did exist in his mind between the theme of his sonnet and
Clare's poetry in general. Most especially does this seem probable
because of his own interest in language, for it was precisely from
Clare's use of dialect words that his poetry gained the directness and
precision of style that Taylor had advocated in his poem.

One of the most sustained examples of this kind of linguistic strength
is to be found in Clare's poem 'The Flight of Birds':[2]

The crow goes flopping on from wood to wood,
The wild duck wherries to the distant flood,
The starnels hurry o'er in merry crowds,
And overhead whew by like hasty clouds;
The wild duck from the meadow-water plies
And dashes up the water as he flies;
The pigeon suthers by on rapid wing,
The lark mounts upward at the call of spring. . . .
Whizz goes the pewit o'er the ploughman's team,
With many a whew and whirl and sudden scream;
And lightly fluttering to the tree just by,
In chattering journeys whirls the noisy pie. . . .

There is in these lines a distinctive kind of tension which is echoed throughout Clare's early poetry, a tautness and sharpness of expression which comes from the positioning of the dialect word within the framework of a less verbally evocative diction. In the passage, each dialect or onomatopoeic word falls generally in the middle of the line ('flopping', 'wherries', 'whew', 'suthers', 'whirl'), acting as a kind of caesura to arrest the attention, and providing a kernel around which each line is built. Even more importantly, the strength of such lines derives from an outlook which has its eye constantly fixed upon the natural world. Clare's use of onomatopoeic words points, indeed, to that direct and uncomplicated apprehension of sound, in which an echoic word is used because it most closely recreates the natural sound of bird in flight. The 'whizz' of peewits and the 'whewing' of starlings is heard and transferred directly to the page, without modification or colouring.

Taylor himself never stated explicitly the firm connection which existed between Clare's use of dialect and the strength and simplicity of his expression; yet it is clear that the whole question of the poet's language fascinated him. A large part of the introduction he wrote to his first volume, indeed, centred upon an examination of the wider issues raised by this use of dialect speech:[3]

[Clare] employs the language under his command with great effect, in those unusual and unprecedented combinations of words which must be made, even by the learned, when they attempt to describe perfectly something which they have never seen or heard expressed before. And in this respect CLARE's deficiencies are the cause of many beauties, – for though he must, of course, innovate, that he may succeed in his purpose, yet he does it according to

that rational mode of procedure, by which all languages have
been formed and perfected. Thus he frequently makes verbs of
substantives, as in the lines,

> 'Dark and darker *glooms* the sky'—
> 'To *pint* it just at my desire'—

Or of adjectives, as in the following,

> 'Spring's pencil *pinks* thee in thy flushy stain.'

. . . there is no innovation in such cases as these. Inseparably
connected with the use of speech is the privilege to abbreviate;
and those new ideas, which in one age are obliged to be
communicated paraphrastically, have generally in the next some
definite term assigned them: so legitimate, however, is the
process of this, by reason of certain laws of analogy which are
inherent in the mind of man, and universally attended to in the
formation of new words, that no confusion can arise; for the word thus
introduced into a language always contains its meaning in its
derivation and composition, except it be mere cant as is not
meant to live beyond the day. . . .

As Taylor justly and perceptively argued, Clare's use of dialect or of
unusual combinations of words was not so much an innovation in
language as the realisation of the potential resources that language had
always contained. He saw too that the poet's use of dialect had helped
to create a brevity and clarity of expression. Instead of conveying the
sound of birds in flight by means of clumsy periphrasis, Clare had
abbreviated his expression by using a clear and definite term known to
him. But in the introduction, Taylor's final concern was to do more
than merely justify the use of such language to the reading public. He
suggested also the nature of the linguistic tradition from which the
poet's dialect had sprung:[4]

a very great number of those words which are generally called
new, are, in fact, some of the oldest in our language: many of
them are extant in the works of our earliest authors; and still a
great number float on the popular voice, preserved only by
tradition, till the same things to which they were originally
applied again attract notice. . . . Many of the provincial
expressions, to which CLARE has been forced to have recourse,
are of this description, forming part of a large number which
may be called the unwritten language of England. They were
once, perhaps, as current throughout the land, and are still many

of them as well-sounding and significant, as any that are sanctioned by the press.

In his awareness of the unbroken oral tradition upon which Clare's use of dialect was based, Taylor had undoubtedly pointed out an important reason for the strength of the poet's language. Clare's dialect derived much of its sharpness from a direct apprehension of the natural world; but it derived as much power, if not more, from a centuries-old continuity of meaning expressed in living speech, not the written word. And as Taylor almost certainly recognised, by unconsciously accepting this kind of language to speak of 'the same thing to which [it was] originally applied', Clare had gained a strength and precision of style which any poet might have reason to envy.

Throughout the autumn of 1819, Taylor, Hessey, and Drury prepared for the publication of the new book. Taylor was occupied in writing his introduction and in compiling the glossary of dialect words which was to be appended to the volume. And in Stamford, Drury began an extensive campaign to advertise the book in local newspapers: 'I want to prepare the public here, to raise the expectation of the little book, by a series of advertisements, and would wish to begin at least 3 months before publishing.'⁵ But then abruptly, in the midst of correspondence and arrangements passing between Helpstone, Stamford, and London, a sudden clouding of the light:⁶

> It is to be greatly feared that [Clare] will be afflicted with insanity if his talent continues to be forced as it has been these 4 months past; he has no other mode of easing the fever that oppresses him after a tremendous fit of rhyming except by getting tipsy . . . next morning a stupor with headache and pains across the chest afflicts him very severely . . . you will easily suppose how true is my account when I assure you he has rhymed and written for 3 days and 3 nights without hardly eating or sleeping.

But hints such as these, dropped almost negligently and certainly with no intimation of Clare's final tragedy, were understandably eclipsed by the activity of the days preceding publication. On 16 January 1820, the first edition of *Poems Descriptive of Rural Life and Scenery* finally appeared. The very next day, a hasty letter from Drury in Stamford spoke of an unprecedented sale:⁷

> I shall want more of Clare's Poems before you can send them, having at shop-shut only 1 copy left. Send another 25 p. Coach

if you can conveniently do so, *immediately*. About fifty more, by Waggon will satisfy the town & neighbourhood which seem disposed to buy freely.

A few days later:[8]

> Despatch a dozen more of Clare's Poems by an early coach, for I have only two left. . . .
> Send 12 copies by return Coach – I have *not one* left.
> Send 50 or 100 by Way. . . .

By 8 March, not two months after publication, 1,000 copies of the book had been sold, and Taylor was already preparing another edition of 2,000 copies.[9] By 25 May, a third edition had been printed,[10] and by the following year, a fourth. The book had answered abundantly. The public in both city and countryside was flocking to buy it. Clare had become the darling of the London literary scene.

Even these halcyon days of the summer of 1820, however, were not altogether without their difficulties. Almost as soon as the book was published, indeed, considerations quite extraneous to its literary merit began to cloud the great success it had achieved with the public. Not only had there arisen a vexed disagreement between Taylor and Drury about money paid to Clare, profits, and copyright agreements; but also Clare's patron, Lord Radstock, who had begun in 1819 a subscription list to allow the poet a steady yearly income, had voiced decided objections to several passages in the first edition. Two poems, 'My Mary' and 'Dolly's Mistake', stood condemned as 'indelicate' for too earthy a description of rustic wooing habits; and even more objectionable to Radstock were lines in 'Dawnings of Genius' and 'Helpstone', which lashed out upon the evils of wealth and position:[11]

> The rough rude ploughman, off his fallow-grounds
> (That necessary tool of wealth and pride,). . . .

> Accursed Wealth! o'er-bounding human laws,
> Of every evil thou remain'st the cause:
> Victims of want, those wretches such as me,
> Too truly lay their wretchedness to thee:
> Thou art the bar that keeps from being fed,
> And thine our loss of labour and of bread;
> Thou art the cause that levels every tree,
> And woods bow down to clear a way for thee.

By the beginning of May, the rumblings had become persistent. Mrs Emmerson, the kindly and humane nuisance who acted as Clare's worldly-wise fairy godmother throughout his early career, wrote to him pointing out that Radstock was both 'an ornament and blessing to mankind', and reported him as having said: 'Tell Clare if he still has a recollection of what I have done, and am still doing for him, he must give me unquestionable *proofs* of being that Man I would have him to be – he must *expunge – expunge!*'[12] Immediately, Clare wrote to Taylor, in a tone which shifted quickly from tolerant weariness with the whole matter to a less benign annoyance:[13]

> Being very much bothered latley I must trouble you to leave out the 8 lines in 'Helpstone' beginning 'Accursed wealth' and two under 'When ease and plenty' – and one in 'Dawnings of Genius' 'That necessary tool' leave it out and put —— to fill up the blank this will let em see I do it as negligent as possible D—n that canting way of being forced to please I say – I cant abide it and one day or other I will show my Independence more strongly than ever   you know who's the promoter of the scheme I dare say –

As far as the disagreement over profits and copyright was concerned, Drury was eventually pacified with an agreement which gave him a quarter profit on all Clare's published poetry; but it was clear by the summer that Radstock presented a more formidable opposition. He was fighting for higher stakes, for a proprietary interest in Clare which might often touch great generosity, but which expected in return for that generosity the undisputed right to censor freely. By September, he had played his trump card. If the lines attacking wealth and position that he objected to were not omitted from the fourth edition, he would publicly disown Clare.[14] Increasing pressure too was being applied by several of the firm's friends as well as Clare's for the cancellation of the offending verses in future editions. Seeing the almost unanimous objection to the radical lines, and increasingly concerned lest the sale of the book should be injured by his holding out, Taylor decided finally to omit them. He remained convinced of the needlessness of the omissions for the reasons Radstock had given, but since 'so decided a Set' was clearly to be made against Clare if they were not, 'let them be expunged and welcome. . . . When the Follies of the Day are past with all the Fears they have engendered we can restore the Poems according to the Earlier Editions.'[15]

But, as Taylor realised, the outcome of this particular surrender was inevitable. Having acquiesced in the censorship of a few lines, pressure was soon put upon him to omit further radical sentiments. By the end of the year, Radstock, having been given an inch, was taking a yard. Taylor wrote to Clare:[16]

> in The Peasant Boy, Lord R. has put his Mark 'This is radical Slang' against 2 of the best Stanzas, viz. 107 'There once were homes etc' and 108 'O England, boasted land of liberty.' Are these to be omitted also? If so, others will be offensive next.

Throughout his letters concerned with the dispute, Taylor's arguments were eminently reasonable, and indeed, even after giving in to pressure about the lines in 'Helpstone', he felt strongly they should be retained.[17] But by the end of 1820, with the additional omissions that Radstock required, his patience had become exhausted, and the struggle between patron and publisher, no longer veiled in strained politeness, came into the open. In December, Radstock invited him to dine, and was refused. He then wrote urging that a written agreement should be drawn up between Taylor and Clare. Taylor replied that the benefits Clare was receiving from the house were, in fact, far more substantial than if they had been under a written obligation to the poet. Radstock countered:[18]

> You talk of suspending your 'present labours, as not coming within the province of a publisher' – In this, I shall only observe – that had Clare's poems appeared without an *Introduction* and no Lord Radstock had stepped forth in support of the work, my own opinion is, that a second edition of the poems would not yet have showed itself – That your labours were great respecting the little vol. in question, I most willingly allow – but that you were amply remunerated I am equally convinced.

To an ear as sensitive to language as Taylor's, the finely wrought cadence of this last sentence may well have been the final insult. He replied:[19]

> The observations contained in your Lordship's last letter have materially altered the complexion of our correspondence – I will write to Clare to know whether we are to treat with him, or your Lordship, for the Copyright of his next Volume; and upon his answer will depend whether I shall again have the honour of addressing your Lordship.

In retrospect, the details of the disagreement between Taylor and Radstock are only of slight interest. The quarrel was to be prolonged, in patterns which shifted from contrived tolerance to openly expressed anger, until Radstock's death in 1825. But beyond the varied and often subtle pressures brought to bear by both sides, it is possible to discern the broader implications of the conflict. Most obviously, Radstock's demands that certain radical and 'indelicate' lines in Clare's poetry should be expunged was a clear indication of moral and political pressures censoring freedom of expression in literature. He had judged the offending lines in much the same way that the most inflexibly conservative of the Reviews might have done – with an eye more upon their moral and political allegiance than upon their intrinsic literary merit. Clare, indeed, had waved the same red rag before him as Leigh Hunt had before *Maga*. But the presence of censorship is less remarkable than the extent of the influence he wielded during these months. The pressures put upon Taylor to omit any hint of radicalism clearly demonstrate that the power of aristocratic patronage in determining the subject matter of literature was not completely destroyed, even in 1820. Certainly, such power was more diffused and indirect in its influence than it had been in the early eighteenth century. Clare did not depend upon Radstock for economic support as he might well have done in 1720. But the moral influence of aristocratic patronage was still a force to be reckoned with, as Taylor had been compelled to recognise. The trump card Radstock had played in the quarrel was not a withdrawal of his financial support for Clare – this might easily have been countered – but the threat of a public denunciation of the poet for his radicalism. And as Taylor knew, such moral thunderings would not go unnoticed.

Yet however greatly Radstock's interference temporarily clouded the success of *Poems Descriptive*, it was clear in the end that he was fighting a losing battle, and Clare's own reactions to the quarrel revealed why. Although the poet was confident that Taylor would remain 'polite to those whom you may find impossible to please rather than make me the looser', he acknowledged that finally he must cast his hopes on one side or the other:[20]

> when it can no longer be endured I shall be happy to confess I prefer T & H to the multitude – but when vanity even if it was on a signpost sees her name & tittle tattle generously recorded good bye patronage & with a welcome I say

Gradually, during the years following, he moved away from Radstock and Mrs Emmerson and towards Taylor for the different kinds of sustenance he needed. Intent on the same fame and immortality as he later saw as Byron's achievement, he realised increasingly that Radstock's dilettantism, however influential over a part of the London literary scene, could not in the end secure him that fame. Poetry was no longer the business of the gifted amateur, and not for much longer would its composition be controlled, even sporadically, by well-read dabblers in literature such as Radstock. The task of encouraging and promulgating the work of new writers was now a profession, not a hobby. It demanded, not simply an instinctive understanding of what was good literature, but a specialised knowledge of the Trade, of the reading market, of economics and sales. It demanded that practical experience of how and when to introduce poetry to the public, and of the influence that contemporary values exercised upon the minds of readers. And, as Clare finally realised, it was Taylor and Hessey, not Radstock, who had this kind of experience.

The lesson that this knowledge was important was learned the hard way. Understandably, after the large sale of *Poems Descriptive*, Clare was eager to repeat his success. The book had sold well over 3,000 copies within a year, and he was anxious to sustain public enthusiasm with a new volume. But Taylor was more cautious, and began to delay. In June 1821, Mrs Emmerson remonstrated:[21]

> the *procrastination* is most *shameful* – every family of consequence who patronised your 1st volume will in another Month be out of Town – What can be the motive of your Publishers they alone can say – but the *interest* of the *Author* is most certainly neglected.

Taylor was conscious that he was partly at fault, and he apologised to Clare. But with some justice, one reason for the delay might also have been laid at Clare's door – to his own enthusiasm and impatience with correcting and rewriting first drafts. As sonnet and lyric and countryside sketches poured forth from Helpstone, he began to rely increasingly on Taylor to transform rambling and untidy manuscripts into poetry ready for publication. His faith in Taylor's talent as an editor was implicit, but at times the very implicitness of this faith resulted in the publisher doing his own job for him. From the very beginning, Taylor was uneasy about the responsibility he had been given:[22]

> I have been in general dissatisfied with my Corrections, & may possibly restore many of the passages as they stood in the original, so freely express your opinion of all of them . . .

your Corrections have invariably been approved . . .
Have I altered them for the better?

Yet together with the uncertainty, there was also a slight tiredness for a
task, never truly the responsibility of any publisher, which was becoming increasingly uncongenial: 'if I could have found any one who
would [have] taken the Editing off my Hands, so as to have done it to
my Mind, I would gladly have given them 100 £.'[23]
  Certainly, the state of Clare's manuscripts exculpated Taylor in part
for the delay. But beyond this, it is clear that a more serious problem
was worrying both Hessey and him. The poetry which Clare had sent
for the second volume was good, but in many respects it was a mere
repetition of what had already appeared in *Poems Descriptive* – and here,
as both recognised, there lay a danger. Even before the first edition of
the 1820 volume had been published, Taylor had pointed out to Clare
one of the chief perils of authorship:[24]

> In Authorship you will find, *if* you succeed now, that greater
> things will be expected from the next work, & so on successively.
> . . . Bloomfield lost what I fear he will never recover, by failing
> in his last Work, the Banks of the Wye.

Hessey too argued the same point to Edward Drury:[25]

> Clare you know has a reputation to *support*, and what he publishes
> in future must not only not be inferior, it should be beyond his
> former Efforts. Selection & Caution are therefore quite requisite.

But Clare, not able to 'pass five minutes without jingling his poetic
bells',[26] was understandably forgetful of this advice during the months
of his success. Continually, as manuscripts flowed from Helpstone to
London, Taylor urged him increasingly to be more severe in his own
criticism of his poetry, to take more time over composition, to write
fewer and better poems:[27]

> let me beg of you to be more patient in the attempt to write,
> whatever you may do with Respect to reading. Your best pieces
> are those which you were the longest Time over, & to succeed in
> others you must not hurry.

But in his early years, this was not Clare's way. He could not constrain
the original impulse that the natural world had provided by correcting
first drafts, crossing out immediate responses, and forcing poetic form
upon his experience. To allow conscious deliberation to colour that

experience was to destroy the instinctive dialogue he held with Nature. Yet, as Taylor saw, if he did not consciously work towards some kind of discipline and sense of form in his work, he would produce too many poems that were rushed and repetitive – and the fate of such poetry in the reading market was only too clear. But in spite of the firm's caution, Clare, Radstock, and Mrs Emmerson continued to press for the immediate publication of a second volume, and towards the end of September, almost five months after the original date proposed for publication, *The Village Minstrel* appeared.

Although, by December, the book had sold 800 copies, its relative failure in the eyes of the public soon became apparent. Clare, too late, condemned the sixty sonnets in the volume as 'poor stuff', and revealed his dissatisfaction with the long title poem: 'I . . . often feel sorry that I did not withold it a little longer for revision the reason why I dislike it is that it does not describe the feelings of a ryhming peasant strongly or localy enough.'[28] Much of this was an understandable denigration of talent in the face of disappointment; but part of it spoke the truth. For *The Village Minstrel*, if it had in places equalled, had not exceeded, expectation. Taylor had advised Clare that 'greater things' would be expected of him after an initial success, and had urged him to take time over composition only so that he might not repeat himself. For in the end, it was perhaps only by struggling with his material, only by exploring rather than describing his experience, that the poet could ever gain the more substantial recognition he desired – 'the quiet progress of a name gaining its ground by gentle degrees in the world's esteem', wherein lay 'the best living shadow of fame to follow'.[29] However attracted the reading public had been in 1820 by his descriptions of rural life, it was soon apparent that their interest in detailed vignettes of the countryside had been satisfied, and that he needed to move on to other things. As Hessey argued to him,[30] there was a need now for something more than

> the Morning & the Noon & the Evening & the Summer & the Winter, & the Sheep & Cattle & Poultry & Pigs & Milking Maids & Foddering Boys . . . the world will now expect something more than these; let them come in incidentally, but they must be subordinate to higher objects.

In the years following, Clare was to explore increasingly those fields of experience open, in Hessey's words, to 'the poet and Man of Mind'. His direct perception of beauty in the natural world was never to be destroyed, but it was to be tightened and focused more finely. A deeper synthesis, a more insistent sense of form and structure, was to inform his whole work.

In November 1821, the *London Magazine* contained a letter written by Taylor entitled 'A Visit to John Clare' and addressed to readers of the magazine. In the letter, Taylor returned again to the subject of Clare's language; and as in his introduction to *Poems Descriptive*, he took the opportunity of a public forum to defend vigorously the poet's use of dialect...[31]

> some of [Clare's] friends object, in my opinion most unreasonably, to this choice of words: one wishes that he would *Thresh* and not *thump* the corn, another does not like his eliding the first syllable of some of his words, as "pproaching' &c. Everyone seems to think that the words or phrases which are in common use in his native place ... ought to be reckoned the true and entire 'world of words' for all Englishmen; and so each disallows by turns almost every expression which has not received the sanction of the court. At that rate, Spenser and Shakespeare ought to be proscribed, and Clare may be well content to endure their fate.

But Taylor's chief theme was now more than mere defence. He was concerned to examine the basic imaginative reasons which lay behind Clare's use of provincial speech. The very fact that the poet did not follow contemporary poetic idiom, he argued, firmly indicated his literary originality:

> in reality, Clare is highly commendable for not *affecting* a language, and it is a proof of the originality of his genius. Style at second-hand is unfelt, unnatural, and common-place, a parrot-like repetition of words, whose individual weight is never esteemed, – a cluster-language framed and cast into set forms, in the most approved models, and adapted for all occasions, – an expedient, in fact, to give an appearance of thinking, without 'the insupportable fatigue of thought'. It suits the age, for we abound with machinery, invented to supercede man's labour; and it is in repute, for it 'is adapted to the meanest capacities'; but there never was a great poet, or grand original thinker in prose, who did not compose his phraseology for himself; words must be placed in order with great care, and put into combinations which have been unknown before, if the *things* which he is solicitous to express, have not been discovered and expressed before. In poetry,

especially, you may estimate the originality of the thoughts by that of the language; but this is a canon to which our approved critics will not subscribe: they allow of no phrase which has not received the sanction of authority, no expression for which, in the sense used, you cannot plead a precedent. They would fetter the English poet as they circumscribe the maker of Latin verses, and yet they complain that our modern poets want originality!

There could be few better examples of Taylor's perception and intelligence as a critic than these two passages. His attack upon stale, mechanical poetic idiom, indulged in by the scholarly poetasters of a generation to disguise their lack of originality, reveals yet again his receptiveness to the experiments of new literature. Suspicious of outdated linguistic traditions which stultified innovation in poetic language, he argued convincingly that such traditions inevitably emasculated language; words became constricted within formalised patterns, and thereby lost in power and richness. Yet his concern in the article was more than an attack upon dead idiom as such. Implicitly, he was attacking too the kind of contemporary criticism which did not move beyond the words of a poem to explore the complex amalgam of thought and emotion that language expressed. Many years previously, he had written to James: 'words themselves are but the means, or medium by which we become acquainted with *Things*, viz. the Substance.'[32] Now, with Clare, he was clearly attempting to discover the kind of 'substance' which lay behind the poet's use of dialect words. He saw that his use of rustic speech was not simply the patois of a countryman who lacked the more extensive and elegant vocabulary of the cultured writer. If he had discarded 'a cluster-language framed and cast into set forms', and had worked for a different combination of words, it was because, at the deepest level, he was striving to express what amounted to a new way of thinking about the natural world. His rejection of previous poetic idioms to describe nature was proof, as Taylor justly argued, not simply of the originality of his language, but also of the originality of his thought: 'words must be placed in . . . combinations which have been unknown before, if the *things* which he is solicitous to express, have not been discovered or expressed before.'

The kind of originality which Clare revealed in his early poetry has already been partly suggested. In his direct and almost primitive perception of the natural world, he found in Nature not a means of exemplifying thoughts which had come to him independently of the external world, but a way of thinking in itself. The objects of the countryside and his relationship with them made up the totality of his thought. The centre of his poetry lay, not in thought or reflection, but in the tangible objects of the natural world – in the violets and brooks, the birds and cottages around Helpstone. They remained the anchor of his vision from which he never took his eyes. The chain between cause and result, Nature and poem, was immediate and overwhelming. The sound of birds in flight was heard and described, and the description founded completely upon the hearing. There was not yet an extension of the original external impulse towards the vaguer recesses of mind and imagination, towards that distillation of observation which did not record fact, but reinterpreted it.

But even though this direct apprehension of the natural world was at the centre of much of Clare's early poetry, Taylor seems to have been aware too, even at this time, of another impulse at work, which had begun to change the poet's clarity and directness of observation. In the same letter to the *London Magazine*, he commented at some length upon a poem which had attracted much attention in *The Village Minstrel*, 'The Last of March – written at Lolham Brigs'. In the poem, Clare had described a part of the undistinguished fen countryside around Helpstone:[33]

> Here 'neath the shelving bank's retreat
>   The horse-blob swells its golden ball;
> Nor fear the lady-smocks to meet
>   The snows that round their blossoms fall;
>   Here by the arch's ancient wall
> The antique eldern buds anew;
>   Again the bulrush sprouting tall
> The water wrinkles, rippling through . . .
>
> Yon bullocks low their liberty,
>   The young grass cropping to their fill;
> And colts, from straw-yards neighing free,
>   Spring's opening promise joy at will:
>   Along the bank, beside the rill
> The happy lambkins bleat and run,
>   Then weary, 'neath a sheltering hill
> Drop basking in the gleaming sun.

In the letter, Taylor recounted how, with Clare, he had visited the exact scene that the poet had described. He could not but notice the remarkable difference between reality and poem:[34]

after well considering the scene, I could not help looking at my companion with surprise: to me, the triumph of genius seemed never more conspicuous, than in the construction of so interesting a poem out of such commonplace materials. With your own eyes you see nothing but a dull line of ponds, or rather one continued marsh, over which a succession of arches carries the narrow highway: look again, with the poem in your mind, and the wand of a necromancer seems to have been employed in conjuring up a host of beautiful accompaniments, making the whole waste populous with life, and shedding all around the rich lustre of a grand and appropriate sentiment. Imagination has, in my opinion, done wonders here, and especially in the concluding verse, which contains as lovely a groupe as ever was called into life by the best 'makers' of any age or country.

It is very possible to explain this difference between fact and poem by seeing in the lines a projection of Clare's own sense of happiness into an unremarkable landscape.[35] But Taylor's emphasis upon imagination and 'sentiment' suggests too that other pressures had been present in the creating of the poem. The chain of immediacy and tangibility between Clare's poetry and the natural world, which his use of dialect had originally suggested, was slowly breaking. Another force had come into play – the complex arrangement and colouring of the original object in the alembic of his imagination. No matter that here it was happiness which changed unloveliness into beauty. The result was still a distortion of fact, a colouring of the poet's almost scientific accuracy of description. Writing to Taylor, Clare himself pointed out what had happened. He had been inspired to write the poem, not by the scene which lay before him, but by the reflections of an 'old croney', which had burned into his mind:[36]

as we warmed with our beer he reflected on the age of the brigs and remarked what scores had past over them that was now in the dust   pointed to sprouting cowslips as a promise of spring & his observations struck me so forcibly that I could not get it out of my head & made most of the poem before I got home

The poem had been born, not so much from an instinctive dialogue with nature, but rather from conscious reflection; and that consciousness had been extended into the poem itself. Working against the dialogue, there ran a more disturbed awareness, reflecting upon the irrevocable transience of human life:[37]

These walls the work of Roman hands!
  How may conjecturing Fancy pore,
As lonely here one calmly stands,
  On paths that age has trampled o'er.
The builders' names are known no more;
No spot on earth their memory bears;
  And crowds, reflecting thus before,
Have since found graves as dark as theirs.

During the years that followed, with much of that slow insistence that marks a disintegration exquisitely achieved, this primitive opposition between unselfconsciousness and the gradual imposition of thought and reflection was to extend itself in ever more entangled patterns through Clare's poetry. It was revealed as a struggle between tangibility and dream in 'A Daydream of Summer', a long poem in which he sought in imagination his childhood sweetheart Mary Joyce, and discovered tragically that his very consciousness of the quest destroyed the imaginary presence of Mary herself. It was to be demonstrated much later in a growing obsession with the nature of personal identity, and with time that destroyed youth – obsessions which both fragmented the union with nature he had at first experienced. It was shown too in the writing of such poems as 'The Dream', in which he recognised clearly that the forces of consciousness and reflection could destroy the union he held with the natural world: 'I mustn't do no more terrible things yet   they stir me up to such a pitch that leaves a disrelish for my old accustomd wanderings after nature – '[38]

Certainly, Taylor, at the time of writing his letter to the *London*, could not have been aware of the full implications of this new force in Clare's poetry. The tension between the poet's dialogue with nature and a more conscious, sombre monologue within his own imagination was not clearly defined at the time. And even in the later years of their association, the conflict became too diffused, too deeply submerged beyond exposition and explanation, to allow a comprehensive analysis of what was happening. Clare's mind moved in the end beyond words. Yet if Taylor did not point explicitly to the full meaning of this tension in his poetry, he at least pointed out that it existed, and that, slowly, it was changing the kind of poetry he was writing. It was no mean achievement of literary understanding to have seen that much.

On 1 August, Taylor wrote to Clare with a plan for a new book.[39]

I shall be very agreeable to the Publication of another Volume this coming Winter. . . . Talking the other Day with Hessey, it occurred to me that a good Title for another Work would be 'The Shepherd's Calendar' – a Name which Spenser took for a Poem or rather Collection of Poems of his – It might be like his divided into Months, & under each might be given a descriptive Poem & a Narrative Poem.

Yet however encouraging Taylor's letters might have been to Clare in their evident desire to suggest ideas for a new volume, the poet's health was not improving. Rather, his letters to the firm caught at the growing sense of unreason which was increasingly affecting him. 'The blue devils', he wrote to Hessey, were his 'constant Companions'; his 'insides' felt 'sinking & dead', and there was a sensation in his head 'as if cold water was creeping all about'.[40] But Clare was not alone in his misfortunes. There were illnesses too in London. Taylor had suffered a severe bilious attack which had confined him to his bed for several days during the early summer of 1822. In March 1823 and also during the autumn of that year, he was again ill from over-work. In the autumn of 1824, he was away from London, yet again recuperating from illness. Against such a background of sickness and enforced recuperation, it was clear that he would have to rely heavily upon outside help if Clare's new volume was to be published without delay. By the summer of 1824, he had in his hands the majority of poems for the book, and in August, Harry Stoe Van Dyk, a friend of Radstock and Mrs Emmerson, offered to copy out the manuscripts fairly. Taylor willingly accepted. But, as had happened with *The Village Minstrel*, delays began to arise. Van Dyk was too occupied with other business to concentrate fully on the task, and he had to confess to Clare three months later:[41]

I am so much employed with different things that I get on shamefully slow in copying out your poems: in fact I truly regret for your sake that I made the offer to Mr. T. as another with plenty of time on his hands might have done them & I could have looked over them afterwards.

To add to Clare's growing vexation at the delay, Van Dyk had cut and added to the original manuscripts:[42]

I have taken liberties with yr. text in *omissions* which I hope you will pardon for I feel that it is a very delicate task & one on which I often doubt my own capability of judging. Here & there

I have ventured a line also and have thus secured a pilfered
passage to posterity.

But such omissions and pilfered passages were not calculated to improve
either Clare's poetry or the relationship between himself and Taylor.
By March 1825, their friendship was at a critical stage. Taylor wrote to
Helpstone in a tone which revealed clearly the tiredness and mental
fatigue that had been building up for some time:[43]

> The fact is this, my Heart has not been in the Business from my
> Conviction that I could not make up such a Volume from the
> whole Collection . . . as would surpass the others or equal them
> in the Estimation of the public – and you were too ill to make
> perfect those parts which I should have found it necessary to cut
> away. Not but that I think there are many Poems of as great
> Merit as any you have written, & in some places perhaps greater;
> but the whole Collection would I felt be regarded as inferior.
> However I will do my best and if the Result is not so successful
> as I could wish you must not hold me responsible.

He offered to part with the poems, if Clare so wished, and to place
them in the hands of anyone whom the poet thought more likely to do
them justice, arguing 'it is better to terminate the Connection at once
than to continue it in Distrust'. But perhaps Clare was aware that none
of his friends save Taylor had that patience and understanding which
could make of his often disorganised drafts poetry ready for publication, for by the end of May, the quarrel had worked itself out. Taylor
cemented their former friendship, and acknowledged that he had been
largely to blame for the delay:[44]

> I am very sorry to have hurt your Feelings by any thing I have
> said or done or omitted to do. Putting myself in your Situation
> I dare say I should have complained as you did – and yet I could
> think that if you were in mine you wo'd see that I was less
> blameable than I seemed to be. However I am willing to confess
> that I have been in fault, and now that I can begin to see my
> Way through the first Difficulties I trust that the rest of the Road
> will not present similar Instances of Obstruction. As for
> quarrelling, I am sure that it ought to be far from you & me,
> for I could never say one Word to give you Pain which would
> not re-act with tenfold Fury on myself – and you, I am sure,
> desire not to speak harsh things to me. Let these differences now
> be forgotten.

There can be little doubt that a large part of the delay in publishing Clare's third volume was due to Taylor.[45] But to condemn him out of hand for his procrastination, or to argue that he was growing increasingly apathetic towards Clare's poetry, as has been suggested, is a distortion of the truth. The delays were not altogether without cause. Not only was he very seriously ill in August 1825 with an attack of brain-fever, but Clare's own manuscripts had begun to present increasingly difficult problems of deciphering and organisation. In January 1826, Taylor wrote to Helpstone in scarcely concealed annoyance at the charges of unreasonable delay, and explained precisely why the book had not yet been published:[46]

> I must now as frankly tell you, that for the principal part of the Delay & the present total Stop again, you are alone responsible. Look at the Vol. of MS. Poems which I now send you, & shew it where you will, & let any of your Friends say whether they can even read it. I can find *no one* here who can perform the Task besides myself. Copying it therefore is a Farce for not three Words in a Line on the average are put down right, & the number omitted by those whom I have got to transcribe it are so great, that it is easier for me at once to sit down & write it fairly out myself. But suppose I attempt to do this: here I encounter another Difficulty:– the Poems are not only slovenly written, but as slovenly *composed*, & to make good Poems out of some of them is a greater Difficulty than I ever had to engage with in your former Works, – while in others it is a complete Impossibility.

The criticism was certainly justified, for the particular manuscript in question which Clare had sent lacked even an elementary organisation of material.[47] Not only was his hand difficult and at times almost impossible to read, but he had shown little care for the reader, ignorant of how he intended the poetry to be finally presented. One fragment entitled 'The Mole Catcher', the first draft of which was scored through, continued in its second version for eighteen lines, and then ended abruptly, without explanation, with the words: 'I leave them as a father does his son   Keats Feb: 1824.' And the first version of 'July', which ran to over five hundred lines, was suddenly broken up by the interpolation of an entirely different poem entitled 'A Village Evening', which left the original poem without any conclusion.[48] Clare, indeed, was only too conscious how disconnected his material was. On page 73 of the manuscript, he had written to Taylor: 'I have sent this rough book   tis all I have got of the Calendar here & if I should get better you may send me it back to finish   if not you must make the best of it.'

But the state of the manuscripts was not the only difficulty. Even when they had been deciphered and organised, the sheer length of the title poem alone posed a serious problem. If all the poetry Clare had sent was to be included in the volume, Taylor argued, the book would be too long:[49]

> I have been reckoning the number of Lines and Pages which the present Plan of our new Volume gives us and I find that we shall have about twice as much Matter as we require – 20 pages to each Month will make a Vol. of 240 pages, which alone is a large quantity – . . . I am as you see at a loss what to do, but let me have your opinion, & in the meantime I will consider further of the matter: perhaps between us we may hit on the best plan.

It is difficult to be sure of the precise reasons why Taylor considered the proposed edition too long. Certainly, economic factors may have weighed heavily on his mind. The two volumes of *The Village Minstrel* published in 1821 had contained some 420 pages; yet the book had not answered, and even as late as in 1829, he was to be left with nearly £300 worth of unsold copies on his hands. With some justice, he may have felt that the risks were too great in throwing caution to the winds again with *The Shepherd's Calendar*. Possibly, too, he may have thought that, on artistic grounds, the book needed to be shortened – that in parts of the long title poem, Clare was again repeating himself with an accumulation of thumb-nail sketches of the countryside. But whatever his reasons for trying to abbreviate the poetry, the result was clear enough. By the time the book was ready for publication, he had cut away a third of the title poem, and considerably reduced the length of other poems. His own word for the operation was 'slashing'.

It is in his editing of *The Shepherd's Calendar* that many of Taylor's ideas about literature, previously expressed in only a theoretical vein, are translated into practice, into the specific task of substituting this word for that, of rejecting one stanza in favour of another. Yet it is for his editing of this volume too that he has been most severely attacked in recent years by Clare's own supporters. It is argued that he reduced the title poem to a bare torso of what Clare had written, that he consistently emasculated the strength of the poet's language by excising many dialect words, and that he adhered too closely to the prudishness of his age by censoring many passages which spoke of sensual pleasures and radical political attitudes – that, in short, *The Shepherd's Calendar* as published was a travesty of Clare's wishes and intentions.[50] It is, of course, impossible to deny that these arguments have some basis in truth. But only too frequently, the truth that has been presented has been too overtly slanted; evidence that might modify any strong criticism of Taylor has been ignored or omitted; complexity has been simplified.

No better illustration of the kind of simplification that has occurred could be given than one particular attack against Taylor for his suppression of dialect words. Whilst acknowledging his earlier support for Clare's rusticisms, two critics in particular argue[51] that by 1826 his attitude had changed, and that in *The Shepherd's Calendar*,

> almost all Clare's 'provincialisms' were replaced by words acceptable to London literary taste.

> The very grain of Clare's language was smoothed and planed away by Taylor in his insistence on the need to 'purify the dialect of the tribe'.

Ten examples are quoted from the published version, in which Taylor, either through misreading or deliberate policy, clearly did reduce the force and sharpness of Clare's dialect by substituting more commonplace and more immediately comprehensible expressions. Yet to seize upon these alterations without examining what he did not excise is, equally clearly, a distortion of his position regarding the poet's language. A comparison of Clare's original manuscripts with the 1827 edition reveals, indeed, precisely how many provincialisms and 'unusual combinations of words' were allowed to stand. In the title poem alone, Taylor retained:

> icy spars . . . shoots crizzling (p. 3)[52]
> running night . . . grizzles (p. 4)
> the water . . . crizzled o'er (p. 9)
> as silence sliveth upon sleep (p. 13)
> Some . . . go whisking on (p. 13)
> [in Clare's MS. 'wisking on']
> mong mossy stulps (p. 24)
> Frost . . . numbs it into ice (p. 26)
> icicles . . . eke their icy tails (p. 26)
> The foddering boy forgets his song . . .

And croodling shepherds bend along
Crouching to the whizzing storms (p. 26)
swopping white birds (p. 27)
elting soil (p. 27)
Teazing twitch (p. 29)
Nauntly crow (p. 29)
[in Clare's MS. 'nauntling crow']
the solitary crane . . . cranking (p. 31)
love-teazed maidens . . . slive (p. 34)
the snowdrop hings (p. 34)
teazing weeds (p. 42)
the nooky church (p. 43)
[in Clare's MS. 'nookey']
The . . . hen banes belted pod (p. 52)
crimpling feet (p. 52)
in snugger rest (p. 55)
the restless heat seems twittering by (p. 65)
the ruddy child . . . poddles (p. 69)
the moiling day (p. 69)
younker (pp. 69 & 75)
morts of threats (p. 69)
shockers follow (p. 71)
chimbled grasses (p. 71)
the restless hogs . . . crump adown (p. 74)
Each burring wheel (p. 76)
the plopping guns (p. 84)
[in Clare's MS. 'ploping']
the crimpt brakes (p. 86)
quawking crows (p. 86)
[in Clare's MS. 'qawking']
ekes his speed (p. 91)
snow is besom'd from the door (p. 93)
[in Clare's MS. 'beesomd']
the crumping snow (p. 94)

As these examples demonstrate, far from consistently suppressing
Clare's dialect words in the interests of propriety or comprehensibility,
on many occasions Taylor retained his earlier perception of the importance of such language to Clare's work, and he did support frequently
his use of provincialisms. If there is a charge to be made against him,
clearly, it should be on the grounds of inconsistency, not that he insisted

upon planing away 'the very grain of Clare's language'. This is a simplification of the facts.

There can be no doubt that this inconsistency or uncertainty of attitude characterises much of Taylor's editing of *The Shepherd's Calendar*. It is to be found, not only in his suppression and endorsement of dialect words, but also in his attitude towards Clare's radicalism and supposed 'indelicacies'. The examples of his censorship of radical sentiments and hints of sensuality have been forcefully presented. Scattered throughout the poet's original manuscripts had been references to the evils of enclosure and to injustices meted out to the poor, which were deleted by him and appeared nowhere in the 1827 volume. The ending of 'June', which touched too closely upon the distinction between rich and poor,[53] was excised:

> As proud distinction makes a wider space
> Between the genteel and the vulgar race
> Then must they fade as pride oer custom showers
> Its blighting mildew on her feeble flowers.

In 'May' and 'October' too, Clare's criticism of enclosure, a sorrow intensified for him by the contrast between the present and those past years when no 'tyrant justice [rode] to interfere', was cut out, with the result that 'May' presented a false sense of joy and well-being. His depiction of love also, too earthy in its accuracy, was expunged by Taylor. The maiden 'in her unpin'd gown', 'wi heaving breast', was not to be found by those who read the published version of 'August'; and 'her white breasts hankerchief' in 'May' was discreetly altered to the more delicate and tasteful 'bosom's handkerchief' for publication. But yet again, although Taylor may justly be criticised for such excisions, the justice of the criticism is seriously put in question when the evidence of what he did not censor is omitted. Although he unquestionably expunged many of Clare's radical opinions, he also retained lines which qualify the argument that his prudishness consistently stultified the vigour of the poet's depiction of love. In the second version of 'July', there occur the lines, retained for publication, describing 'the milking maiden':[54]

> And red lips never paled with sighs
> And flowing hair and laughing eyes
> That oer full many a heart prevailed
> And swelling bosom loosly veiled
> White as the love it harbours there
> Unsullied with the taints of care

In the 'swelling bosom loosly veiled' was a suggestiveness surely equal to 'the heaving breast' which was expunged in 'August'.

If, then, the retention of these lines and of many of Clare's dialect words puts into question the strict justice of the attacks which have been made against Taylor, the problem yet remains of what kind of attitude his editing of the book reveals. Undoubtedly, he was inconsistent in his practice. Provincialisms and 'indelicacies' were both censored and allowed to stand. Yet, as on so many other occasions in his career, this kind of ambivalence reveals not only the uncertainty of his own mind, but also the broader pressures which influenced him as a publisher. As editor and publisher of *The Shepherd's Calendar*, indeed, he stood as the arbitrator between two worlds – Clare's, sexually realistic, radical in politics, uneducated in the niceties of correct punctuation, spelling, and grammar, and the largely middle-class world which bought his poetry, sexually romantic or squeamish, conservative in political attitude, attentive to the correct and acceptable use of language. The shades of Lord Radstock, Mrs Emmerson, and the many others who had voiced decided objections to Clare's first volume, continued to force him to tread a tight-rope between moral and political fastidiousness and the healthy outspokenness of Clare's poetry. He was the unfortunate mediator who was attacked both for allowing radical and 'indelicate' sentiments to remain, and for expunging them.

As early as 1820, Hessey had written to Clare pointing out the very real difficulties that Taylor faced as the publisher of his work. Of the cancellations which had been made to the second edition of *Poems Descriptive* he remarked:[55]

[Taylor] perceived that objections were continually made to them [the 'indelicacies'] & that the sale of the Volume would eventually be materially injured & therefore he determined on leaving them out. Whether it be false or true delicacy which raises the objection to these pieces it is perhaps hardly worth while to enquire. If we are satisfied that in the Society which we frequent certain subjects must not be even alluded to, we must either conform to the rules of that Society or quit it. An author in like manner is expected to concede something to the tone of moral feeling of the Age in which he lives, and if he expects or wishes his works to be popular, to afford amusement or convey instruction, he must avoid such subjects as are sure to excite a Prejudice against him & to prevent his works from being generally

read. And, after all, there is no hardship in all this. There is
plenty of room for a man of Genius, of Delicacy, of Taste, to
exercise himself in, without touching upon such things as are by
common consent now avoided in all good Society as repugnant
to good Taste and real Delicacy.

Certainly, Hessey's argument was not without some strong traces of
conservatism, and in his belief that writers must expect to concede
something to the 'tone of moral feeling of the age', he was partly
echoing the great Reviews' conception of literature as a reflection of
contemporary experience, rather than an exploration of new structures
of thought and attitude. But he did define acutely the problem which
Taylor and he faced. Clare might justifiably write supposedly radical
or indelicate poetry, but it was the firm who had to tone down such
opinions; for it was only by some concession to contemporary values
that his poetry would sell and earn the fame he himself desired. As
Hessey implicitly argued, it was no matter that the conservative beliefs
of large sections of the reading public were built upon castles of sand,
which would eventually crumble. What was important for the house
was that such delicacy of taste and such fear of radical sentiments
existed in society, and demonstrably affected the sales of books. Leigh
Hunt had been attacked for his 'crude, vague, ineffectual, and sour
Jacobinism', Shelley for his atheism, Hazlitt for his immorality, Keats
for an imagination 'better adapted to the stews'. It was impossible that
any publisher should completely ignore such attacks, or the inflexible
moral attitudes which lay behind them. And if Radstock and Mrs
Emmerson voiced disapproval of indelicacy and seeming political
subversion, Taylor could not but pay some attention to their views –
for in the end, it was people such as they who bought or ignored
Clare's poetry.

The placing of Taylor's editing of *The Shepherd's Calendar* within
this broader context is not an attempt to excuse him for those passages
in the manuscripts which he did censor, and for which he is justly
criticised. But it is an attempt to examine the wider reasons and attitudes which lay behind his suppression of parts of the book. Whatever
comprehensiveness of argument is gained from this perspective is,
indeed, particularly valuable in considering his association with Clare;
for often, as has been suggested, attacks upon his treatment of Clare's
work have simplified the evidence too readily. One fact reveals this
simplification better than most: that although much has been made of
his 'slashings' to *The Shepherd's Calendar*, there has been as yet no

attempt to examine in detail the substantial improvements he made to parts of the title poem.

In Clare's original manuscript of 'February', there are three stanzas the position of which Taylor altered considerably for publication. In the poet's version, they read:[56]

> The gossips saunter in the sun
> As at the spring from door to door
> Of matters in the village done
> And secret newsings mutterd oer
> Young girls when they each other meet
> Will stand their tales of love to tell
> While going on errands down the street
> Or fetching water from the well
>
> A calm of pleasure listens round
> And almost whispers winter bye
> While fancy dreams of summer sounds
> And quiet rapture fills the eye
> The sun beams on the hedges lye
> The south wind murmurs summer soft
> And maids hang out white cloaths to dry
> Around the elder skirted croft
>
> Each barns green thatch reeks in the sun
> Its mate the happy sparrow calls
> And as nest building spring begun
> Peeps in the holes about the walls
> The wren a sunny side the stack
> Wi short tail ever on the strunt
> Cockd gadding up above his back
> Again for dancing gnats will hunt

There is in these stanzas an obvious strength of direct observation; but as sometimes happens in Clare's poetry, beneath the surface is the suggestion of a weakness in poetic realisation. The jump made without warning between the details of village life in stanza one and the quieter, more reflective tone of the second verse is rather abrupt. The fluidity and calm which the words express is not altogether reflected in the structure of the lines which tends to be episodic. Indeed, the structure of 'February' as a whole is uncertain. Clare's viewpoint changes without preparation from detailed descriptions of the countryside (verses 1-10), to a mood of reflection (verse 11), to the countryside again (verses

The concluding verses of 'February'

Clare's MS.	Published version
And oft dame stops her burring wheel To hear the robins note once more That tutles while he pecks his meal From sweet briar hips beside the door	And oft Dame stops her buzzing wheel To hear the robin's note once more, Who tootles while he pecks his meal From sweet-briar hips beside the door.
The hedgehog from its hollow root Sees the wood moss clear of snow And hunts each hedge for fallen fruit Crab and hip and winter bitten sloe And oft when checkd by sudden fears As shepherd boy his haunt espies He rolls up in a ball of spears And all his barking rage defies	The sunbeams on the hedges lie, The south wind murmurs summer soft; The maids hang out white clothes to dry Around the elder-skirted croft; A calm of pleasure listens round, And almost whispers Winter by; While Fancy dreams of Summer's sound, And quiet rapture fills the eye.
Thus nature of the spring will dream While south winds thaw but soon again Frost breaths upon the stiffening stream And numbs it into ice – the plain Soon wears its merry garb of white And icicles that fret at noon Will eke their icy tails at night Beneath the chilly stars and moon	Thus Nature of the Spring will dream While south winds thaw; but soon again Frost breathes upon the stiff'ning stream, And numbs it into ice; the plain Soon wears its mourning garb of white: And icicles, that fret at noon, Will eke their icy tails at night Beneath the chilly stars and moon.
Nature soon sickens of her joys And all is sad and dumb again Save merry shouts of sliding boys About the frozen furrowd plain The foddering boy forgets his song And silent goes wi folded arms And croodling shepherds bend along Crouching to the whizzing storms	Nature soon sickens of her joys, And all is sad and dumb again, Save merry shouts of sliding boys About the frozen furrow'd plain. The foddering-boy forgets his song, And silent goes with folded arms; And croodling shepherds bend along, Crouching to the whizzing storms.
(*The Shepherd's Calendar*, ed. Eric Robinson & Geoffrey Summerfield, pp. 27-8)	(*The Shepherd's Calendar*, 1827 ed., pp. 25-6)

12–18), thence to a more deeply meditative tone (verse 19 and part of 20), and the section concludes finally with the brilliant fantasy of 'croodling shepherds . . ./Crouching to the whizzing storms'.

To compare the manuscript of the final verses of 'February' with the published version is to realise how greatly Taylor improved the structure of Clare's draft, and with what assuredness he gave it a sense of direction and poetic movement leading to a climax (see p. 114). Not only did he remove the reflective stanza 'A calm of pleasure . . .' from its rather incongruous context and place it where it more truly belonged among the concluding verses, but he produced a firmer transition between the descriptive and more meditative lines by reversing the order of the two quatrains in the stanza. Clare's original draft, as can be seen, jerks too abruptly from the description of the hedgehog to nature's dreaming of spring time – the sudden dislocation of tone is without reason, and the poet's use of the word 'thus' merely an attempted disguise for the absence of any poetic logic. But Taylor's reorganisation not only does away with this abruptness but also gives the final stanzas a positive sense of movement towards the climax. Each successive line both echoes and expands upon previous lines. The south wind murmuring 'summer soft' prepares the way for 'a calm of pleasure'. The 'dreams of summer's sound' lead forward to nature dreaming of the spring. Imperceptibly, the large transition between the purely descriptive verse of the dame's spinning wheel and the fantasy of the shepherds 'crouching to the whizzing storms' is made. The concluding verses are infused with a sense of imaginative logic and evolving structure which the original version had only imperfectly realised.

The conclusion of 'February' is not the only example of the improvements Taylor made to Clare's drafts. The ending of the whole poem in 'December' was also substantially improved by a reorganisation of stanzas similar to the change in 'February'.[57] Yet however much Taylor altered the order of verses, it was obvious that he could not correct the uncertainty of realisation which lay beneath more extensive sections of the poem. In one sense, the absence of any firm structure in the conclusion to 'February' points to the chief weakness of *The Shepherd's Calendar* as a whole, and indeed, of Clare's purely descriptive poetry in general. Often, the strength of his union with the natural world pressed so forcibly that he was not always able to enforce upon his direct observation that sense of form which would relate his thumbnail sketches to a larger poetic unity. In many of his shorter poems, clearly, this lack of form is not so vital. But in a long poem such as *The Shepherd's Calendar*, the absence of any underlying pressure or synthesising force results at times in an impression of structural hap-hazardness. There are too many stanzas which may be shifted from their context to another without any loss of meaning or effect. At times, the poem lacks that sense of a firm imaginative centre which controls the accumulation of vignette upon vignette.

Yet this is not always so, and Taylor clearly realised as much. For if he did improve parts of the poem by infusing a sense of structure where that structure was previously lacking, he saw too precisely those places where a new force had come into play, where Clare's direct observation of the natural world had not been transferred immediately to the page, but had been distilled and tightened by a deeper imaginative synthesis.

At the beginning of 1826, when dissension between Clare and himself had again arisen, he criticised the original draft of 'July' in exaggerated terms, calling it 'a descriptive catalogue in *rhyming prose* of all the occupations of the Village People, scarcely one feature of which has not been better pictured by you'. Ill and tired of his task of editing, he wrote of this section, which extended for over 500 lines: 'Instead of cutting out of the Poem on July what is bad, I am obliged to look earnestly to find anything that is good.' But immediately in his letter, he added:

> Pray look it over yourself, & tell me whether there are in this long Piece any Lines worth preserving but these which I am happy to say are very beautiful

> 'Noon gathers wi its blistering breath
> Around and day dyes still as death
> The breeze is stopt the lazy bough
> Hath not a leaf that dances now
> The totter grass upon the hill
> And spiders threads is hanging still
> The feathers dropt from moorhens wing
> Upon the waters surface clings
> As steadfast and as heavy seem
> As stones beneath them in the stream
> Hawkweed and groundsels fairy downs
> Unruffld keep their seeding crowns
> And in the oven heated air
> Not one light thing is floating there
> Save that to the earnest eye
> The restless heat swims twittering bye'

This is in my opinion the only *Poetry* in this long Poem.[58]

In the letter, Taylor did not, unfortunately, go on to elaborate upon the distinctive qualities he so much admired in these lines. But six years previously, in his introduction to *Poems Descriptive*, he had pointed out, and warmly praised, a particular aspect of Clare's use of language, which is clearly to be seen in the sixteen lines from 'July':[59]

> CLARE, as well as many other poets, does not regard language in the same way that a logician does. He considers it collectively rather than in detail, and paints up to his mind's original by mingling words, as a painter mixes his colours. And without this method, it would be impossible to convey to the understanding of the reader an adequate notion of some things, and especially of the effects of nature, seen under certain influences of time, circumstance, and colour.

By 1826, Taylor would not perhaps have asserted so firmly that the collected impression rather than the detail of language was always the stronger force in Clare's poetry. Yet he exempted from his criticism those very lines in 'July' where Clare had begun to exploit the potential reverberations of language, where words did not simply describe a detail of the countryside but gave that detail a greater imaginative resonance and fluidity. The difference in both tone and language between the lines Taylor found 'very beautiful' and the mere 'catalogue of rhyming prose' is immediately apparent. For some thirty lines preceding 'Noon gathers . . .', Clare had written a detailed description of the antics of a shepherd's dog 'licking his skin and catching flyes' (see p. 118). As ever in his descriptive poetry, the accuracy of observation is finely conveyed, and the details of the dog's movements and reactions minutely recorded. But again, the lines are too episodic, and the movement of the verse progresses only through an accumulation of small sketches, none of which is imaginatively predominant. Each vignette (the dog playing, catching sticks, resting, licking his skin, picking at a bone, and so on) plays an equal part in the overall description, with the result that there is no imaginative centre to the sequence as a whole. But immediately following these lines, without warning, the very fabric of the poetry is suddenly drawn taut. The unstructured freedom of natural description is tightened and refined into a greater

From 'July'

To his old haunts he hallows bye
Wi dog that loiters by his side
Or trotts before wi nimble stride
That waits till bid to bark and run
And panteth from the dreaded sun
And oft amid the sunny day
Will join a partner in his play
And in his antic tricks and glee
Will prove as fond of sport as he
And by the flag pool summer warm
He'll watch the motions of his arm
That holds a stick or stone to throw
In the sun gilded flood below
And head oer ears he danses in
Nor fears to wet his curly skin
The boys field cudgel to restore
And brings it in his mouth ashore
And eager as for crust or bone
He'll run to catch the pelted stone
Till wearied out he shakes his hide
And drops his tail and sneaks aside
Unheeding whistles shouts and calls
To take a rest where thickly falls
The rush clumps shadows there he lyes
Licking his skin and catching flyes
Or picking tween his stretching feet
The bone he had not time to eat
Before when wi the teazing boy
He was so throngd wi plays employ
Noon gathers wi its blistering breath
Around and day dyes still as death
The breeze is stopt the lazy bough
Hath not a leaf that dances now
The totter grass upon the hill
And spiders threads is hanging still
The feathers dropt from morehens wings
Upon the waters surface clings
As stedfast and as heavy seem
As stones beneath them in the stream
Hawkweed and groundsels fairey downs
Unruffled keep their seeding crowns
And in the oven heated air
Not one light thing is floating there
Save that to the earnest eye
The restless heat swims twittering bye
The swine run restless down the street
Anxious some pond or ditch to meet
From days hot swoonings to retire
Wallowing in the weeds and mire
The linnets seek the twiggs that lye
Close to the brook and brig stones drye
At top and sit and dip their bills
Till they have drunk their little fills . . .

poetic density. Clare begins suddenly to exploit the imaginative resonances of his material:

> Noon gathers wi its blistering breath
> Around and day dyes still as death
> The breeze is stopt the lazy bough
> Hath not a leaf that dances now. . . .
>
> And in the oven heated air
> Not one light thing is floating there
> Save that to the earnest eye
> The restless heat swims twittering bye

There is in these lines a firm centre of tone and idea which sustains and synthesises the various descriptive touches. The blistering heat of a noonday in summer is at the centre of Clare's imagination; and all incidental detail derives from it, and relates back to it, as parts to a whole. No longer is there here that direct perception of the external world in which microscopic detail exists, poetically, in its own right. On many previous occasions, the feathers of the moorhen or the down of hawkweed and groundsel would have been of fundamental importance to Clare's purpose of description – accuracy and fullness of observation were vital. But in the lines from 'July', such details are important only in so far as they augment and enrich the portrayal of a noonday heat. They have been distilled through the alembic of his imagination and controlled by the sense of stifling heat and stillness which acts as a synthesising force. The section possesses an imaginative core, the realisation, no less, of the idea of the 'one only String' in Taylor's early sonnet.

This transformation of direct observation, the ability to inform passages of pure description with a deeper imaginative synthesis, was to become increasingly marked in Clare's later poetry. It was, of course, a quality which had never been entirely lacking from his work, even from the very beginning of his association with the house. But throughout these years, as hundreds of purely descriptive poems continued to be sent from Helpstone, Taylor constantly urged him to move beyond this kind of factual poetry. He was not alone in his advice. Before leaving for Italy, Keats too had argued that the 'description' of his first volume prevailed too much over the 'sentiment' or 'prevailing Idea' of the verse. Taylor reported his views to Clare:[60]

I think he wishes to say to you that your Images from Nature

are too much introduced without being called for by a particular
Sentiment. . . . His Remark is only applicable now & then when
he feels as if the Description overlaid and stifled that which ought
to be the prevailing Idea.

Later, De Quincey also voiced the same criticism:[61]

> The description is often true even to a botanical eye; and in that,
> perhaps, lies the chief defect; not properly in the scientific accuracy,
> but that, in searching after this too earnestly, the feeling is
> sometimes too much neglected.

Throughout these years, Taylor reiterated this point. His chief advice
to Clare was that the poet needed now to infuse into his description a
deeper awareness:[62]

> What you ought to do is to elevate your Views, and write with
> the Power that belongs to you under the Influence of true
> Poetic Excitement – never in a low or familiar Manner, unless at
> the Time some strong Sensibility is awakened by the Situation of
> the Writer or those he writes about.

However firmly Taylor's initial admiration for Clare's work may have
been based upon the belief 'Simplicity is Strength', it is clear that that
simplicity was, for him, a quality achieved by contrasting poetry with
ordinary life, not by confounding them. As his association with Keats
so frequently revealed, he believed that poets were of a demonstrably
different nature from those who did not write; and similarly, 'true
Poetic Excitement' was an experience radically different from the lives
of most human beings. Of Clare's early poem, 'The Lodge House',
he argued[63] that although as a story it might appear 'capitally told',

> yet . . . it has not the Superiority about it which makes good
> Poetry. Poets do not tell Stories like other people; they draw
> together beautiful & uncommon but very happy Illustrations,
> and adorn their Subject, making as much Difference as there is
> between a common Etching and a fully painted Picture.

The full implications of this theory were finally expressed in their most
defined form in 1826:[64]

> I have often remarked that your Poetry is much the best when
> you are not describing common Things, and if you would raise
> your Views generally, & speak of the Appearances of Nature
> each Month more philosopohically (if I may so say) or with
> more Excitement, you would greatly improve these little poems;

some parts of the November are extremely good – others are too prosaic – they have too much of the language of common everyday Description; – faithful I grant they are, but that is not all – 'What in me is low, Raise & refine' is the way in which you should conceive them as addressing you. . . .

It is precisely for this desire to see 'sentiment', 'elevation' and 'refinement' in Clare's poetry that Taylor has been most fiercely attacked in recent years. Two of his most vigorous critics, quoting a part of this last letter, comment:[65]

With all Taylor's education and refinement, his rich and varied acquaintance with the world of literature, his taste was essentially artificial. Like the reading public for the Victorian annuals, he wanted everything blown up, he wanted significant statement pushed into poetry, and his attitude, despite his radical political sympathies, was a moralising and condescending one.

How a man who recognised, from the mass of contemporary writers, the genius of Keats, Lamb, De Quincey, Hazlitt, Carlyle, Landor, Cary, Hood, and Clare, may be said to have an 'essentially artificial' taste is perhaps scarcely worth discovering. But what is chiefly misleading about this criticism is again the way in which the evidence is simplified. Certainly, it cannot be denied that, in several respects, there is some justification for such a judgment, and Taylor's use of language may well be to blame for this. His quotation from Milton ('"What in me is low, raise and refine" is the way in which you should conceive [these poems] as addressing you') does indeed suggest a somewhat ingenuous, moralising attitude, which cannot be dismissed. Yet to argue that this single example reveals an habitual condescending attitude towards Clare's poetry ignores too much evidence to the contrary. The 'sentiment' and 'elevation' urged by him (and, it should not be forgotten, by Keats and De Quincey too, though in a less sustained way) was not a desire for a contrived moral earnestness so unnatural for a poet of Clare's kind. They were, before all else, poetic qualities which scarcely touched upon the fields of morality and didacticism. What Taylor desired to see in Clare's work was not so much emotion and ideas forced upon poetry, as poetry instinctively created from these qualities. He advocated an emotional and mental attitude behind his writing, a dominant idea or tone, the 'one only String' which refined into a unity the varying strands at work in any single poem. Constantly, he argued that, however delightful his miniatures of the countryside were, they too easily became a mere catalogue of incidents, without a firm imaginative centre. As both Hessey and he recognised, Clare had succeeded brilliantly in describing the natural world in his first collection; but thereafter, both believed that he needed to develop beyond 'the Sheep & Cattle & Poultry & Pigs' towards a deeper synthesis, a more insistent sense of poetic form which would control his direct and unalloyed observation of nature. In the years that followed, Clare did in fact explore increasingly this new ground, in which a dominant tone or idea activated the poetic impulse and provided his poetry with the same kind of disciplined centre as had been achieved in the section from 'July'. And in this exploration, he was to realise, as Taylor had always argued, that poetry, as well as being a statement and a description of experience, was also a refining of it.

The Shepherd's Calendar finally appeared in 1827. It was not a success. The Eclectic Review discerned and warmly praised an 'intrinsic merit' in the new volume;[66] but other criticisms were less generous. The Monthly Review praised Clare for a 'deeper poetical feeling' than Bloomfield, but criticised him for his 'cataloguing' which savoured 'more of matter of fact than poetry'. The number of dialect words in the book too, did not go unnoticed, and the sharpness of the Monthly's attack illustrated how intransigent the opposition to rusticisms could be, and what independence indeed Taylor had shown in retaining many of them. The review[67] objected to

the use of vulgar epithets, or expressions; not provincialisms merely, but absolute specimens of patois, and whose expressive qualities by no means atone for their inelegance . . . they are the progeny of a vicious taste, that cannot be too sparingly indulged in, nor too soon abandoned altogether.

But the poor reception of The Shepherd's Calendar was due to a larger apathy in the reading world. Poetry was in a slump. The public that had so eagerly bought Poems Descriptive only seven years previously had turned from imaginative literature towards the greater immediacy in their daily lives of political and social reform. The audience which Clare had so brilliantly captured in 1820 had barely survived. Taylor wrote to him six months after publication:[68]

The season has been a very bad one for new books, and I am afraid the time has passed away in which poetry will answer.

With that beautiful Frontispiece of De Wints to attract attention, and so much excellent verse inside the Volume, the Shepherd's Calendar has had comparatively no Sale. It will be a long time I doubt not before it repays me my Expenses, but ours is the common lot.

Clare responded quietly:[69]

I feel very dissapointed at the bad sale of the new Poems but I cannot help it if the public will not read ryhmes . . . to tell them what they ought to think of Poetry would be as vain I fear as telling the blind to see   the age of Taste is in dotage & grown old in its youth

By July 1829, two and a half years after its first appearance, *The Shepherd's Calendar* had sold only 425 copies of the edition of 1,000; and even when Clare, on Taylor's advice, began to hawk the remaindered books around Helpstone in the hope of arousing some local interest in his poetry, only a few more can have been sold. In 1831, Taylor reported that he was selling 'not above 12 [copies] in the year'.[70] In terms of sales, at least, the book had failed.

To compare the correspondence between Taylor and Clare after 1827 with those earlier letters when the poet had been the darling of the London literary world is to be aware of an eclipse. Talk about poetry and the promise of new volumes was now increasingly obscured by the more urgent, personal necessities which illness and poverty brought in their train. Money, as ever, caused many problems. In the summer of 1829, Taylor finally sent to Helpstone the full statement of accounts between them both, which had been promised and delayed for many years. Justifiably, Clare had anticipated that, even if there were not a large sum owing him, there should at least be a reasonable balance between credit and debit. In fact, in the account which covered transactions between 30 December 1820 and 30 July 1827, Taylor had estimated that he owed the firm nearly £150. Yet, as Clare justly pointed out, the vagueness of Taylor's unbusinesslike approach, and the length of time elapsed since many of the transactions had been made, had given rise to several mistakes and omissions. The £100 which had been entered in Radstock's Subscription List in 1820 as a gift from the firm was included on the debit side of the account, as was Hilton's portrait of him, which had been painted at Taylor's desire, not his. No account had been taken of his contributions to the *London Magazine*, a matter of some £36; and his half share of the profit on the sales of *Poems Descriptive* was not mentioned at all in the statement. Yet there can be no doubt that Taylor had not made a profit from publishing Clare's work. The omissions in the accounts seem likely now to have made the difference between credit and debit almost negligible, and even to have given Clare a small profit; but Taylor still had on his hands the unsold copies of *The Village Minstrel* and *The Shepherd's Calendar*, which had by 1829 realised only a part of the capital invested in publication. *The Village Minstrel* had sold only 1,250 of the two editions of 1,000 copies each, and there was nearly £300 worth of unsold volumes remaining. And *The Shepherd's Calendar* had failed to pay for money invested by nearly £60, which did not include the £105 that was the unrealised return at that time on the 575 unsold copies.

Discussions over the intricacies of the account were prolonged for months,[71] and there were further financial difficulties too when Clare tried unsuccessfully to realise part of the principal of his Trust Fund in order to meet his needs. Yet throughout these years, Taylor continued to encourage the poet in his work. He contributed to a scheme of establishing him in a small-holding with some livestock. In July 1831, he was sending him a collection of verse with the suggestion that he should compose an anthology;[72] and four years later, he helped in the editing of his manuscripts for *The Rural Muse*, which appeared in 1835 under the imprint of How & Whittaker. It was clear that neither his faith in Clare's genius nor his affection for him personally had in the end been diminished by the repercussions over the account. And Clare needed such faith and affection now more than ever. In 1831, he wrote to Taylor with a personal intimation which was soon to be proved tragically accurate: 'my future prospects seem to be no sleep – a general debility – a stupid & stunning apathy or lingering madness & death. . . .'[73] At night, he had begun to feel a pain in his stomach, a 'prickly feel' about his face, and 'a sobbing & beating' whenever he laid his head down on the pillow. He began to imagine too that 'the Italian liberators' were kicking his head about like a football. In 1835, he complained to George Darling, the doctor who had attended Keats, about sleeplessness and 'sounds' and 'a sort of nightmare awake'.[74] And to Taylor, he wrote helplessly:[75]

> I am in such a state that I cannot help feeling some alarm that I may be as I have been. You must excuse my writing; but I feel if I do not write now I shall not be able. . . . I cannot describe my feelings; perhaps in a day or two I shall not be able to do anything, or get anywhere.

In December 1836, Taylor, returning from a visit to Retford, visited him in the cottage at Northborough to which he had unwillingly moved four years previously. He was accompanied by 'a medical gentleman of Stamford, who was to give . . . his opinion respecting poor Clare's health'. The two men found the poet sitting in a chimney corner, 'looking much as usual'. 'He was not amiss while I was there', Taylor wrote to James,[76]

> but his Wife said that he was under Restraint from seeing me, and that he would afterwards become violent. He knew me, and seemed much pleased at my mentioning former occurrences and Friends to him –

> He talked properly to me in reply to all my questions, knew all the people of whom I spoke, and smiled at my reminding him of the events of past days. But his mind is sadly enfeebled. He is constantly speaking to himself and when I listened I heard such words as these, pronounced a great many times over and with great rapidity – 'God bless them all', 'Keep them from evil', 'Doctors'. But who it was of whom he spoke I could not tell – whether his children, or doctors, or everybody. But I think the latter.[77]

The doctor who accompanied Taylor advised that Clare should be sent to an asylum, and Taylor, however much he may have tried to dismiss such a solution from his mind previously, must now have seen that it was the only way. Within months, arrangements had been made for Clare to enter High Beech Asylum on the edge of Epping Forest, under the humane care of Dr Matthew Allen.

Finally, on 5 May 1837, Clare wrote his last brief letter to Taylor:[78]

> I am scarcely able to write. I have got the drawing done here. You and Mrs Emmerson are the best friends I have and just as you was. . . . I should like to see Hilton and Cary. . . . God bless you. Yours ever, John Clare.

By June, the final details of the arrangements had been completed. Taylor sent to Northborough a last letter:[79]

> I am happy to send you by the Bearer *Seven Pounds* as usual to pay the Half yearly Dividend & it is my sincere Hope that the

Medical Care which is provided for you near this place will be effectual to your recovery. The Bearer will bring you up to Town and take all care of you on the Road

    I am
          Ever your sincere Friend
          John Taylor

Whatever his emotions were, they were scarcely disclosed. But perhaps enough had been done and said in the past seventeen years to render any dramatic statement of faith superfluous. Many years previously, in what must have seemed in 1837 another world, long dead, Clare had written of Taylor: 'he is a kind of screne between me and the world – a sort of hiding place for me in the hour of danger.'[80] It was the most vicious of ironies that, when the chief danger finally came, that screen, by force of circumstance, was sufficient only to a certain point. Beyond it, in the different kind of reality which Clare was now to experience, he had to work out his own salvation, without Taylor's companionship.

At the beginning of this chapter, it was suggested that, of all the relationships between Taylor and the writers he published, his association with Clare was the one in which he most deeply influenced the development of a poet. The reorganisation of stanzas in *The Shepherd's Calendar*, the several perceptive analyses of dialect, the many attempts to infuse a deeper poetic discipline into purely descriptive poetry – these events among many others clearly reveal Taylor as a literary midwife for much of Clare's poetry. And yet, such a relationship as this chapter has tried to trace could scarcely have been sustained for over seventeen years upon a common love of literature alone. From advice and talk and encouragement about poetry, a literary sympathy was undoubtedly created between them, which both felt keenly. But the true grounding of their friendship seems finally to have rested upon qualities both more mundane and more profound than intellectual kinship. Those moments at which their relationship appears suddenly in a steady clarity are not particularly moments of any great importance for the cause of literature. But in an unostentatious way, these spots of time often focus more finely the many aspects of their association. In 1834, as part of his ordinary routine, Taylor sent Clare a small gift of £5, to help him buy some pigs for his small-holding. Years previously, troubled with his illness and intimations of madness, he had written to him more profoundly:[81]

I will faithfully discharge all those Duties you require of me, my dear Clare, if unhappily the Necessity of the Case calls for it. But still I cling to Hope & cannot believe that we have met for the last Time. Nor can I ever think that your Mind, my Friend John, is dead, whatever the Body may be. The Mind says itself in all its actions and expressions 'I am immortal'. It never limits itself to the Duration of the Body, but looks beyond the Grave. Addison says somewhere in the Spectator, that he feels conscious already of Immortality. When I begin to live, he says, I begin to live for ever; for I will never believe that the momentary change which Death makes has any power to interrupt that Course which I then began to run & shall continue to pursue thro' all Eternity. Death is a change of Scene, the pulling off an old Coat, & putting on a new one, and I never do such an act of Treason against the native Sovereignty of the Soul as to believe that it is possible for her to be destroyed by an accidental connection with the Body. . . .

Earnestly wishing you a speedy Recovery and at all Costs eternal Happiness if the other be denied. . . .

Neither of these two acts – money or letter – is of especial significance as far as Clare's poetry is concerned. Yet perhaps Taylor's gift of £5 and particularly his attempt to convince the poet that his mind was not dead demonstrate his sympathy more surely than anything else could. It was not the least of his achievements throughout his career that he recognised the need to encourage his writers in their ordinary living, as well as in the uniqueness of their creativity.

What Clare would finally have achieved without him is impossible to know, though inevitably the question remains a fascinating speculation. On several occasions, as has been seen, serious quarrels on both personal and literary grounds arose between them; and there can be no doubt that Taylor was often at fault for the delays and censorship which temporarily alienated Clare's sympathy. And yet it is more than likely that, without his encouragement and sheer doggedness in deciphering and arranging manuscripts, Clare would never have seen his poetry published in his lifetime, still less recognised. John Murray, whom the poet met during his visit to London in 1822, might praise his work; but could he, or Constable or Blackwood or any of the more renowned publishers, ever have devoted the amount of time and patience that Taylor had? Could any of them have looked beyond the hours of laborious transcribing and maintained the clear and steady belief in Clare's genius that Taylor invariably had? The question is worth emphasising. For, even during the periods of most acute dissension between them, one searches in vain for any hint on Taylor's part that he had lost faith in Clare's talent or that his regard for him personally had diminished.[82] Even as late as 1835, when his whole life was far from the romance of Fleet Street and Waterloo Place, he could still talk to him about 'the Imaginative Faculty in Poetry, in which your Genius excels'.[83] In spite of the dissensions, indeed, the words of his introduction to *The Village Minstrel* crystallised a sympathy which endured:[84]

> [Clare] deserves our favour, as one who tries to please us – our thanks, for having so richly increased the stores of our most innocent enjoyments – our sympathy, and something more substantial than mere pity, because he is placed in circumstances, grievous enough to vulgar minds, but to a man of his sensibility more than commonly distressing; – and our regard and admiration, that, sustaining so many checks and obstructions, his constant mind should have at length shone out with the splendour which animates it in these productions.

The *London Magazine*: 1821-5

Throughout this study of Taylor's association with Keats, Hazlitt, Cary, and Clare, there has been a substantial emphasis so far upon the interaction which existed between individual writers and the firm, both in the actual making of literature and in the fostering of personal friendships. Yet, clearly, to emphasise too greatly this context of individual relationship is not without its dangers. It is possible that the very nature of this perspective, firmly focused as it is upon personal success or disappointment, may enlarge disproportionately that sense of isolation and of an ungovernable breach between writer and reading public, which so many of the firm's authors felt. The apprehension, shared by Keats, Clare, and Hazlitt, that few imaginative writers could ever speak directly and permanently to their society, may well have been a feeling intensified and even exaggerated by the personal wretchedness so deeply woven into their lives. Keats's consumption, Clare's fight against 'lingering madness' in Helpstone, the undeserved acrimony of the public attacks levelled against Hazlitt – these were forces in their lives too persistent not to turn them in upon themselves, not to deprive them of the sustained energy needed to counter a lack of public acclaim.

But although Taylor and Hessey continued to foster close relationships with individual authors throughout the house's greatest years, in April 1821 they bought from Robert Baldwin the proprietorship of the *London Magazine*, and with this accession, the nature of their association with writers acquired suddenly a far larger perspective. No longer did their work involve simply the encouraging of individual genius. They were dealing now with a collective talent, whose very brilliance often derived from the community of spirit and intellect that an intimate society produced. In an imaginative sense, the context of much of their work shifted from Clare's isolated cottage in Helpstone to the monthly dinner parties in Fleet Street and Waterloo Place, where Hazlitt and Lamb, Cary, Wainewright, and Reynolds, sat down to dine, pun, and talk themselves half-way to the stars. Their responsibility now lay not only in sustaining the creativity of individual writers, but also in moulding many talents into a communal spirit, without at the same time destroying the variety of attitudes and thoughts which individuals gave it. More important even than this was the task of interpreting the imaginative energy of such a society to the reading public at large. Individually, few of the firm's serious authors had been recognised by the public. Neither Keats nor Clare nor Hazlitt could ever have been reckoned among the more profitable glories of Scott or Byron. To the public mind, indeed, it might have been that they had spoken in too muted and isolated a voice to capture attention. Yet under a common flag of literary excellence, with the power of a regularly appearing magazine at hand, it might have seemed possible to Taylor and Hessey that a collective talent would succeed where individual writers had failed.

The desire to include a literary magazine under the firm's imprint had been in Taylor's mind for some time. As early as 1817, nearly four years before the house took over the *London*, he had written to his father:[1]

> We have long entertained the Wish of establishing a 'Quarterly Magazine' of genuine original Writers – Do you think 1000 could be sold without Doubt? – If so, we could make it pay, [   ][2]
> if we gave 5/5/- p Sheet 8vo for the Authorship

The emphasis upon 'genuine original Writers' again recalls one of Taylor's foremost policies as a publisher; but for a year, during the financial crisis of 1817–18 and the threat of a dissolution of partnership, the plan to establish such a periodical remained no more than an idea. Yet talk of magazines continued to be in the air. In December 1818, Taylor met the publisher of Walter Scott and the *Edinburgh Review*, Archibald Constable; and a remarkable proposal came out of their meeting, as Taylor reported home. Constable, in London in search of an editor for the *Edinburgh*, was trying to persuade him to visit Scotland for a few weeks:[3]

> [Hessey] fancies that Mr C. has certain Ends in View, by getting me into the North, the Result of which he suspects to be an offer of some Connection with me. . . . C. said yesterday that if I were unconnected with Trade here, & would reside in Edinburgh, & edit his Edinburgh Magazine, he would give me 500 £ a year.

Having survived the worst of the financial crisis of the preceding months, though, Taylor had no real desire to leave the firm, and he decided finally not to accompany Constable back to Edinburgh. But the idea of a magazine remained in his mind, and from various letters to and from Fleet Street, it became increasingly clear that he had one purpose above all in wishing to establish such a work – the desire to rid criticism of those ghosts who had wielded for too long an unchallenged judgment upon the merits of new literature. At the beginning of 1819, Cary wrote to his brother-in-law and explained the chief policy of the magazine the firm proposed to create:[4]

> Their wish is that the task [of criticism] should be performed
> with a better temper than has been usually shown on such
> occasions, and that more pains should be taken to search out for
> the beauties than the faults of the books that are to be reviewed.

The house's desire was for a Review conducted 'on principles of fairness, without any bias from party spirit';[5] and Cary himself was invited to edit it. But this was not the happiest of proposals, and the poet realised as much. The magazine, as Taylor envisaged it, was to be on a scale large enough to require a polymath as well as an exceptional organiser as its editor, for it was to include not only literary topics, which Cary might have competently supervised, but also articles upon the whole range of science and politics, as well as criticism of the fine arts. Cary was realistic enough to allow that it would be 'unpardonable folly' to make himself responsible for what he would not be 'competent even to understand';[6] and he declined the post. For a second time, plans were quietly shelved.

Over two years later, though, an opportunity was presented to the firm which they might have wished to have gained in a happier way. On the night of 16 February 1821, a duel occurred at Chalk Farm which precipitated a tragedy scarcely conceivable even against the background of intransigent bitterness which the most notorious Reviews revelled in. John Scott, who had edited Baldwin's *London Magazine* since its establishment fourteen months previously, was seriously wounded in a duel by one of *Blackwood*'s men, John Christie – the result of an antagonism which had for six months clouded the pages of *Maga* and the *London*. For some days, although he lay in a critical state, there were good hopes that he would recover. The editorial for the March issue of the *London*, dated 26 February, reported to its readers that 'the danger which was at first apprehended is considerably diminished'. But it was a false optimism. A day later, he was dead.

The occasion of the duel between Scott and Christie, acting as Lockhart's second, has become part of the darker side of literary history, and is too well known to need repeating here. It is enough to say that with Scott's death, there died an editor who had succeeded in little over a year in establishing the *London Magazine* as the most brilliant of contemporary periodicals. His personal magnetism and liberalism, together with a remarkable critical perception, had not only attracted the support of such writers as Hazlitt and Lamb, but had also evoked a spirit in which their genius was revealed at its most abundant. Both Hazlitt's *Table Talk* and the immortal character of Elia had been created under his editorship.

But with him now gone, the fate of the magazine immediately began to appear uncertain. Deprived of his rare talent for edging contributors into a community of spirit which heightened rather than dulled their individual brilliance, the *London* was adrift, without clear directives. Between them, Baldwin, Hazlitt, and Reynolds seem to have edited the April and May issues, but the need for a new editor to take undivided responsibility for each number was obvious. Throughout April, there were involved negotiations for the post. Hazlitt was an applicant, as indeed was Cary, who had evidently undergone a change of heart regarding magazine editing. But by the end of the month, it became clear that for some days, discussions had been centring upon a more radical change than the appointment of a new editor. On 28 April, Taylor wrote to James with startling news:[7]

> You will be surprised, but perhaps not sorry to hear that I am likely to be forced into more active Life – We have bought the goodwill of Baldwin's London Magazine, to commence with the July number. . . . The Bargain is not to be publicly known for a fortnight to come, that Baldwin may have Time to take the necessary precautions to secure Contributors &c.

The agreement had been signed two days previously, on the twenty-sixth. Baldwin and his partners had at first wanted Taylor & Hessey to take the remaining back stock at 2*s.* a copy; but the outlay of £1,500 that this would have involved was too high a price for the firm. Negotiations had concluded finally with the house's offer of £500 for the goodwill of the magazine, which was accepted.[8]

The reason why Baldwin resolved to sell the *London* upon Scott's death, rather than appoint a new editor only, remains something of a mystery – the more so because Taylor's letter to James of 28 April clearly shows that the initiative in the discussions had come from Baldwin himself, and not from the firm. It is possible that Baldwin was not exaggerating when he spoke of Scott's death as a 'chasm', and that, faced with the rival claims of various men, none of them automatic choices for the editorship, he felt the magazine could not sustain its brilliance without Scott's authority. Yet at the same time, he could scarcely have failed to realise that he held a pearl of some worth in his hands, even without his former editor. Lamb and Hazlitt, Wainewright, Talfourd and Reynolds, were regular contributors, eager to pool their talents in a magazine of liberal policy. No definite reason for his willingness to sell suggests itself, but Taylor's letters clearly hint at a possible explanation. In his letter to James reporting the purchase of the magazine, he wrote that the sale was '1800, out of 2000 printed – this just pays the Expenses'.[9] But only four months later, he reported: 'We sold last Month 1700 Copies. . . . I suspect that the Sale had actually sunk to 1600 when we entered on the Work.'[10] To add to these suspicions, he might well have recalled the question of the back stock which Baldwin had been anxious to sell with the goodwill of the magazine. It required little mathematical ability to calculate that the £1,500 which had been asked for unsold stock at 2s. a copy meant that 15,000 copies remained unsold within the first fourteen months of the *London*'s appearance. Was this a matter of ridiculously inefficient over-printing or of a very poor sale? Again, no clear answer to the question is now to be had, but there remains a strong suspicion that, even with Scott's editorial acumen and the brilliance of his contributors, the magazine had not answered financially during the months of his editorship. He himself had admitted that what he would have most liked to have culled from the *Quarterly* was 'its sale';[11] and *Maga*, quick as ever to expose the weakness of rival publications, reported in October 1820 that the *London*'s circulation was a paltry 1,100 copies.[12]

Serious enough though these figures were in themselves, they might well have been aggravated in Taylor's mind by a further thought. Compared with the 1,700 copies which the *London* was selling during the summer of 1821, the circulation of the *Quarterly* regularly topped 14,000; and *Maga*, if its own figures could be trusted, was selling a little below 17,000.[13] Perhaps, as Cary had noted two years previously, there was a most vicious kind of irony at work as far as magazine sales were concerned. Fair-minded policies, directed towards truth rather than effect, might not be a financial proposition: 'My neighbour, Mr.

Gillman, is of opinion that without a strong spicing of ill-nature, nothing of this kind can be made palatable to the public, and that the attempt [to create a liberal periodical] would therefore probably fail.'[14] It might well be invective, and not liberalism, which sold magazines.

These questions were to occur again more persistently in the later history of the *London*, but for the moment they were forgotten. Looking back at the bargain he had struck with Baldwin, Taylor viewed the recent accession to the firm's imprint with a cautious pleasure. Against the background of an 'extraordinary Stagnation of Trade' since the beginning of the year, and the financial uncertainty produced by the 'Casualties of retail Trade', the magazine was clearly a worthwhile investment. Appearing monthly, it offered 'the Advantages of a public Situation equal to a perpetual Advertisement'.[15] But in a few lines of dispassionate self-analysis,[16] Taylor recognised that, on a personal level, inevitable tensions might arise:

> My Antipathy to be *tied to Time* is as great as ever – my Talents whatever they may be in other Respects, are not of the *impromptu* Kind – and the Subjects which suit me best now are too grave, too dull I should say, for Magazine Readers –

Within two years, these words were to echo again, not unjustifiably, in the mouths of the *London*'s contributors. But aware though he was of the ways in which his mind was moving, aware too of the grave taxing upon his time and energy the magazine would involve, he had by the end of April not only bought the *London*, but resolved to edit it himself. On the last day of May, he wrote to his father with a suitable sense of occasion:[17]

> My editorial Duties begin on my own Responsibility this Day. But I don't feel the Weight of them yet & perhaps I shall not. All our Contributors are so kind & friendly & well wishing to the Success of our Undertaking that everything which can be done I am sure will be, to prevent my finding my new Employment irksome. – We appear to have plenty of Materials, or Makers of Materials, in hand; & that Source of Anxiety which is one of the greatest is therefore removed. –
>
> Everybody speaks so well of the Mag. & everybody is so confident of its Success in our hands that it will not suffer us to feel much Despondence – You will be able to get us a few Subscribers at Retford – We are pretty sure of increasing by our Connection here the Number to 2000, which is 200 more than Baldwin's have.

It was a fair prospect.

Taylor's immediate decisions as editor were wise ones. He had in the list of established contributors to the magazine a wealth of talent. Lamb and Hazlitt were regular writers. Allan Cunningham, an author whom Taylor believed to be 'a jewel of the finest water',[18] was in the middle of an interesting series on 'Traditional Literature'. John Hamilton Reynolds, the irreverent iconoclast of Wordsworth, was a regular contributor on the eccentricities of the world; and Thomas Griffiths Wainewright, the 'genius' of the magazine for Lamb, veiled himself monthly under the guises of Janus Weathercock and Egomet Bonmot, and addressed himself as 'critic, fiddler, poet and buffoon'.[19] The talent of the circle, though, was becoming increasingly evident, not only to Taylor, but to rival publications as well. Henry Colburn, proprietor of the *New Monthly Magazine*, had already begun to make strenuous efforts to attract the best writers away from the *London*. Taylor immediately countered by increasing the rate of payment for articles to a guinea a page, or sixteen guineas a sheet; and Lamb, as the chief star of the magazine, was paid even higher than this. The best poetry too was paid for at the same rate, and it was with justifiable pride that Taylor offered Clare in August a guinea a page, 'the highest price we have ever paid for Poetry'.[20] The increases had the desired effect. Cary found the new rate that the firm offered 'good pay',[21] and De Quincey felt that 'the terms they held out to contributors were ultramunificent – more so than had yet been heard of in any quarter whatsoever'.[22] Having ensured that the continuity in the list of established contributors would not be broken by questions of payment, Taylor turned to introduce even more talent into the magazine.

In August of the previous year, he had invited to dine with him Thomas Hood, the son of the master under whom he had gained invaluable experience during his first years in London; and a proposal was made at the time that Hood should help to carry some of the burden involved in the firm. Taylor himself was greatly impressed with his ability both as poet and prose-writer,[23] and he felt much inclined to engage him; but for some reason, the suggestion was not followed up immediately. Nine months later, however, faced with the additional work involved in the magazine, he realised that he could not manage without some assistance, and on 9 June,[24] he offered Hood a job as 'a sort of sub-Editor':[25]

> I . . . have proposed to him to allow him 5 Guineas a No for the Assistance he can give me in correcting Proofs &c for the Mag,

and in looking over some of the immense Load of Communications which are poured down before me – He can render me some Assistance in this Respect, and I am happy to think that I can return to him by this way some of the kindnesses I received from his good father.

Hood's reaction to his new appointment was one of unqualified delight. As he wrote later, 'to judge by my zeal and delight in my new pursuit, the bowl had at last found its natural bias.'[26] He immersed himself as a labour of love in writing and dreaming up article upon article; he corrected proofs with an eagerness which can scarcely have been equalled before or since; he jumped '*à la Grimaldi*, head foremost' into what John Scott had once described as 'the turbulence, presumption, heats and regrets that form the atmosphere of an Editor's workroom'.[27] He was twenty-two, and he revelled in the kind of minor anarchy that reigned in Fleet Street.

Taylor could have made no happier choice in his sub-editor, for Hood's spontaneous energy corresponded exactly with the tempo and corporate vitality of the Londoners as a whole. He caught the mood of the circle at once:[28]

> my top-gallant glory was in 'our Contributors!' How I used to look forward to Elia! and backward for Hazlitt, and all around for Edward Herbert [the pen-name of Reynolds], and how I used to *look up* to Allan Cunningham! for at that time the *London* had a goodly list of writers – a rare company.

He himself took over 'The Lion's Head', the editorial column which introduced each number and commented upon articles offered to the magazine, and infused into it a verbal virtuosity which not even the most outrageous of puns could dim:

> T. says his tale is out of his head. Is he a tadpole?
> We suspect H.B.s 'Sonnet to the Rising Sun' was written for a lark.
> The 'Essay on Agricultural Distress' would only increase it.
> 'Lines to Boreas' go rather 'too near the wind'.
> 'The Echo', we fear, will not answer.
> The following are (to use a tender word) rejected . . .
> W's Tears of Sensibility had better be dropped.

The very energy and outrageous delight in this kind of verbal juggling reflected the spirit of the *London* as a whole; and from the very beginning, indeed, Taylor was well enough aware of the distinctive tone of the magazine, the imaginative back-chat which contributors revelled in, not to attempt a sudden change of policy. As Lamb pointed out to him, the chief delight he found in writing for it was the friendship and cordiality which existed between contributors: 'The *Lond. Mag.* is chiefly pleasant to me, because some of my friends write in it.'[29]

Taylor took the hint. Clearly realising the importance of sustaining the corporate spirit of the magazine, he continued to introduce new talent that was similar enough to endorse rather than disrupt the coherence of tone that the *London* had attained. In July, Hessey and he agreed to give Cary sixteen guineas a sheet for his 'Continuation of Johnson's Lives of the Poets', and by the end of the year, the poet had begun his explorations into early French literature, in a series of pioneer essays which opened up a whole new field of writing to the English reading public. Clare too, as has been seen, was encouraged to submit his poetry to the magazine, and Hood began to pun his way through 'The Lion's Head' and other pieces of prose and verse. As the first number of the *London* under the firm's imprint appeared in July 1821, the circle must have seemed to Taylor rich enough in inspiration to realise the hopes he had long entertained for a magazine of 'genuine, original Writers'. But the list of contributors did not yet contain one name which was to reveal the most strikingly original of the new talent that Taylor introduced. In October, 'The Lion's Head' commented upon the second part of a 'deep, eloquent and masterly paper' which had been placed at the head of the contents for that number. Its title was 'Confessions of an English Opium-Eater'.

Taylor and Hessey had been introduced to De Quincey by Thomas Noon Talfourd, the lawyer friend of Lamb, who was acting as sporadic drama critic for the magazine during these months. The precise date of their first meeting is unknown, but almost certainly it must have been during the summer of 1821, for at the end of August, Taylor was writing to his father:[30]

> One Gentleman has begun a long Article and we have included
> it in our present No. and his Copy comes in so very slow that
> I cannot complete anything more for want of it. That
> Article will be found a very curious one – it is on Opium-
> Eating. What singular Men the literary World abounds with!
> I sometimes doubt whether my Opium Friend be in his Senses.

But by the time De Quincey's article appeared in the September and October numbers, Taylor's doubts had clearly been dispelled. The originality of the 'Confessions' was immediately apparent. They revealed a mind acutely sensitised to areas of experience where the patterns and structures of ordinary living no longer applied. Ordinary apprehensions of time and space were blurred, and expanded or contracted. The rhythms of dream and sleep and music obliterated the rhythms of day-to-day life. A fierce imaginative logic confused the boundaries of dream and intellect to create an ultimate seriousness of vision that no other writer in the magazine was ever to explore so deeply. Despite their passages of rhetoric, the 'Confessions' were an examination of a fearful ambiguity and tension deep in the mind, an exploration finally of imaginative chaos.

How deeply Taylor was attracted by the range and wealth of De Quincey's experience is very evident, for by December, they were visiting each other frequently, and talking long into the night. In one of his Commonplace Books,[31] Taylor noted one line of argument which formed a frequent topic of discussion:

> From a Conversation last Evening with Mr. De Quincey I learn that the old Disputers about the Existence of God are likely to have a third Claimant of the Honour of Philosophy in this Department, in the Person of a German, who asserts that God neither *is* nor *was* . . . but is *about to be*.

And a little later, a discussion with De Quincey whether philosophy could comprehend the primary nature of the mind, or only the secondary operations of it, reminded Taylor of an image which had especially struck him in the 'Confessions':

> De Quincey has a Figure to express what must take place before the Mind can so act on itself as to conceive itself, in one of his Opium Dreams, where he conceives the Brain so to have protruded itself as to be to itself an Object of conscious Observation: as if the Eye could be so projected from itself as to be able to see itself – And to a Dreamer only can such a State of Things appear for a Moment possible –

Never before or since, perhaps, can philosophic discussion so nearly have attained the spirit of Bosch – yet such conversations helped to foster an intellectual sympathy which could not have been encouraged in any other way. The range and fluency of their talk, as Richard Woodhouse noted, was remarkable. Taylor would lead De Quincey into political economy, the origin and analogies of language, Roman roads, the pronunciation of Greek and Latin, old castles, the works of Shakespeare, the poetry of Spenser – upon all these, De Quincey was informed 'to considerable minuteness'.[32] That Taylor was intrigued by his powers and delighted in his company, there can be no doubt; and on one occasion at least, his ability to sustain armchair conversation provoked a wry comment:[33]

> Mr. De Quincey has this Instant gone off & Hessey & Woodhouse have accompanied him to the Post Office. Like the Thief & the Gallows [?] 'he seemed loth to depart' – and if Hessey had not almost pushed him off he would not have got to the Place in Time. – I never saw an Instance in which so much Reflection so completely deprived a Man of active Energy as in De Quincey – He is wonderfully learned & wise but as remarkably unable to do anything for himself that requires bodily Effort –

Yet, pleasurable though both Taylor and De Quincey evidently found their bouts of mental gymnastics, their friendship seems finally to have rested upon something more substantial than philosophic agility. At the beginning of 1821, after dining in Fleet Street at one of the first *London Magazine* dinners, De Quincey was seized with severe cramp, and Taylor accompanied him home. In the course of their walk, the essayist spoke of fears which were greatly troubling him:[34]

> he had a sort of feeling, or omen of anticipation, that possibly there was some being in the world who was fated to do him at some time a great and irreparable injury – and this thought often weighed upon him. He was not superstitious, but he could not get rid of this impression. Many circumstances seemed to make it not improbable that Wilson might be that man.

The confession reveals something of the closeness which existed between publisher and essayist; and by the end of the year, indeed, the personal concern which both Taylor and Hessey felt towards him was shown in the way that he perhaps needed most. During the summer, one of the chief reasons for his offering the 'Confessions' to them had been their high rate of payment for articles. But despite the great interest and acclaim that his papers had aroused, they had not dispelled the poverty he had endured throughout the year. In the hope of relieving some of his financial worries, he proposed that the firm should publish a novel, as yet unwritten. Taylor and Hessey accepted the suggestion, and gave him £157.10s. for the book in advance. It was only because of this gift that he was able to return to Fox Ghyll at the end of the year to see his wife and children.[35] The novel itself was never written.

This act, like so many others in the firm's career, is of no startling significance in the course of literary history; yet it demonstrates the help and understanding which Taylor and Hessey so often gave to writers on the most mundane of levels. As has been suggested, it was not the least of their achievements that they recognised the need to encourage their authors in the ordinary context of daily life, as well as in the uniqueness of their creativity. And such need was there in De Quincey's case. The following year, 1822, lacked almost any literary activity as far as he was concerned. But it was marked by the kind of personal wretchedness in which the firm often became involved with their writers. On 24 June, he resolved to drastically reduce the amount of laudanum he was taking. For days, with that scientific precision which is so frequently an anodyne for personal crisis, he attempted to reduce the number of drops from 180 to 130, to 80, to 60, and finally to nothing at all. He abstained for ninety hours, then took a little, then abstained again. The physical symptoms of withdrawal were hard enough to bear, but by September, he was writing to Hessey that these were trifles compared with the 'gloom of mind from some unknown bodily cause' which overcame him.[36] By the end of the year, he was again back in London, hoping to rid himself of his creditors by writing an essay a week. Haunted by debt and opium, he asked for, and almost always received, advances from the firm for articles which might or might not be written. His letters to Hessey in particular invariably began 'My dear friend', and indeed, the friendship between the firm and him was tenacious enough to survive the many requests for loans which were scattered throughout his letters of these months. George Darling, the physician who had attended both Keats and Clare, visited and advised him. Hessey offered him board and lodging for several days after his arrival in London when he was very unwell. Taylor lent him shirts and sovereigns.[37] These, again, were acts of no startling literary significance; no bold change in the nature of literary history occurred because of them. But like the £5 which Taylor sent to Helpstone so that Clare might buy some stock for his small-holding, they perhaps helped to sustain an identifiable pattern in De Quincey's life, helped at least to make the sheer persistence of day-to-day living a little more tolerable. As both Taylor and Hessey recognised, the prose as well as the passion of his life needed sustenance.

One of the most important literary results of the association between De Quincey and the firm was an article about the nature of contemporary periodicals, which was drafted by him towards the end of 1821. Never published in its entirety, the essay is of value not simply as a perceptive analysis of the power and influence of periodical literature in Regency England, but also as a clear exposition of the imaginative editorial policy that Taylor intended to pursue in the *London*. Obviously written under his guidance as an advertisement for future numbers, the latter part of the draft promised readers of the magazine many specific improvements. It would explore fully the period between the close of Johnson's *Lives* and the present, a period which, De Quincey argued, was 'but obscurely known amongst ourselves'; and it would present detailed biographies of lesser known as well as major authors from this time. It was intended also to examine early French literature and, in particular, the vast and unaccountably neglected region of German writing. Articles would appear on the *Niebelungenlied*, and there would be translations and detailed critiques of the most eminent of contemporary German authors, the aim being to compile a comprehensive 'Chrestomatheia or Anthology'. There would also be 'a larger infusion of articles connected with the *classical* remains of antiquity'. The proprietors intended to buy translations of Greek drama and of both Greek and Latin lyric poetry. They hoped too to make 'a more steady provision for the wishes of those who seek for papers of *direct instruction*', and De Quincey gave two examples of future titles – his own 'Letters to a young man of talents whose education had been neglected' and 'Letters on the Transcendental Philosophy'. But chief amongst Taylor & Hessey's proposals was 'a greater *variety* of articles' of the Elia-*Table Talk* kind. As for Lamb and Hazlitt themselves, De Quincey concluded, 'to name them is to utter a eulogy'. It would be enough to say that, as far as they were concerned, there would be no improvement. They would simply continue as before.

Even this brief list of specific improvements is enough to demonstrate the imaginative energy with which Taylor was approaching his new position. Few contemporary magazines, indeed, could have laid claim to such a variety of articles, or to such a determination to explore fields of foreign literature hitherto unknown to the English reading public. Yet valuable though this draft is as an exposition of Taylor's specific aims in future editions of the *London*, it is even more important in its clear indication of the more general policy that was to inform the magazine. One of De Quincey's chief points in his examination of contemporary periodicals was the distinction that should always be recognised between Reviews and Magazines. Taking as his evidence the particular political affiliations of both the *Edinburgh* and the *Quarterly*, he argued persuasively that the origin and subsequent development of these reviews along political lines, finally 'reduced the concerns of Literature . . . to the rank of subordinate interests'. The fact that the *Edinburgh* often manifested 'a Parliamentary origin in the class of information communicated', and that the *Quarterly* frequently appeared almost as a 'substitute for Committees of the House of Commons', illustrated their fundamentally political, rather than literary, nature. As he argued not unjustly, such periodicals were in the end 'scarcely parts of the literature, nor in any other sense literary than in virtue of their objects'. The very nature of Magazines, on the other hand, was 'to unite with these offices of criticism those of original production, and contribute to the joint stock of the literature by examples in *every* department of composition'.

Although the fact is not explicitly stated, it is clear that this emphasis upon 'original production' was intended to be one of the *London*'s chief policies in future numbers. Certainly, such a policy clearly echoes Taylor's earlier desire to establish a magazine of 'genuine original Writers', and his constant belief in the superiority of creative writing overcritical. But the final aim of the *London* was to involve more than the encouraging of creative work. The policy was to allow 'original' writers complete freedom of theme and expression. The firm's intentions, De Quincey pointed out,[38] were to avoid

> any one presiding mind studiously impinging its' own stamp upon the whole body of the articles. Such an overruling predominance of any individual mind cannot but be an injury with relation to literature, by cramping and distorting the natural movements of energetic thinkers.

There would not be found in the *London* that consistency of attitude which many Reviews had been obliged to express in their political and literary opinions. Writers to the magazine would not be forced to endorse any specific motif or viewpoint.

There can be little doubt that, for the first eighteen months of Taylor's editorship at least, this policy of 'original production' and artistic freedom was largely followed. No literary or political credo cramped the free expression of ideas by contributors. There existed no developed literary programme in the magazine around which writers gathered, and indeed, throughout its career, the *London* was never to produce a literary document comparable to Hugo's preface to *Hernani*. Nor was there to emerge from its pages a persistent social or political programme to which writers gave their allegiance. Taylor's policy was fluid and elastic. He had endorsed in fact the immensely generalised statement of policy which had heralded the first number of the magazine in January 1820: 'The *spirit* of things generally, and, above all, of the present time, it will be our business, or at least our endeavour, to catch, condense and delineate.'[39]

Despite this lack of a clear political or literary focus to the *London*, one of the magazine's most remarkable achievements was the creation of a community of spirit and endeavour amongst contributors that was unique in contemporary periodicals – and one event reveals more clearly than any other the way in which this corporate spirit was fostered, the *London* dinners. The idea of holding dinners where contributors to magazines met and talked was, of course, not new. The writers for both the *Quarterly* and the *Edinburgh* frequently dined together, and John Scott himself had held several meetings during his brief editorship. But Taylor seems to have recognised that, if such gatherings were to sustain the fellowship of the magazine, they must become a regular institution, a firm point of reference around which contributors might gather. By the end of 1821, a dinner at the firm's expense for writers to the *London* had become a monthly event, which continued for nearly three years.

One fact demonstrates better than any other how important these gatherings were for the success of the magazine. When, in later years, several Londoners came to compose their reminiscences of this period in their lives, they recalled not so much the literature of genius which had appeared with its pages, but the brilliance of personality and conversation that had been displayed during the magazine dinners. And from their accounts of these meetings, indeed, it is not difficult to understand why literature itself was temporarily eclipsed by puns and wine and talk.

Chief amongst the writers who invariably attended the evenings was Charles Lamb. He sat on Taylor's right hand, dressed nearly always in black, his face full 'of wiry lines' and 'physiognomical quips and cranks' which for the young Tom Hood gave it great character and fascination.[40] For all the Londoners without exception, he was the most cherished of their company. Hood was not alone in discerning in him a generosity of spirit, a 'charity' and 'moderation of judgment'[41] which made him beloved even of those who were very different from him in temperament. His punning and conversation constantly delighted the circle. As Clare remembered him during these gatherings, he would dip a plentiful finger into a large snuff box, throw himself back in his chair, and stammer out a pun, his tongue rolling over the joke like 'a packman's strop turning it over and over till at last it comes out as keen as a razor'.[42] It was invariably the best remark of the evening.

Another frequent guest was Tom Hood, who often vied with Lamb as the most outrageous punster of the evening. He would sit silent amidst the talk and then suddenly shoot out 'some irresistible pun' which completely shattered the gravity of the previous conversation.[43] And even Cary, most gentle and amiable of men, with his 'studious brow, deep-set eyes and bald crown',[44] quietly harboured a wit which was the more delightful because so unexpected. On one occasion, a quotation from an English dramatist had provoked a round of puns on the names of various herbs. The last two mentioned had been mint and anise, when Lamb turned to Cary, 'Now, Cary, it's your turn.' 'It's coming' (cummin) was the immediate rejoinder.[45] Lamb stammered an exit.

Reynolds too was another guest whose wit the company revelled in. For the poet Bryan Waller Procter, 'his good temper and vivacity were like condiments at the feast'.[46] Hood remembered him, caught in a moment of time – 'a gamecock-looking head' with his hair combed smooth and one finger hooked round a glass of champagne.[47] For Clare, he was the soul of these evenings, his plump, round face 'the three-in-one of fun, wit and punning personified'. His wit was instinctive, the flash of a moment, so much so that he would seem almost startled by the laughter a remark of his had produced, and appeared to be deep in thought for a moment 'as if he turned the joke over agen in his mind to find the "merry thought" which made the laughter'.[48]

Even those contributors less fluent in wit and argument were remembered by the chief comedians with a unique sense of enchantment. Hood recalled John Clare, seated beside Lamb, in his bright, grass-coloured coat and yellow waistcoat, 'shining verdantly out from the grave-coloured suits of the literati' and looking 'a very cowslip'.[49] Often Lamb would 'cotton . . . very kindly to the Northamptonshire poet, and still more to his ale, pledging him again and again as "Clarissimus", and "Princely Clare", and sometimes so lustily as to make the latter cast an anxious glance into his tankard'.[50]

Allan Cunningham also was a frequent attender, ready to talk 'two ways at once' when the conversation turned to poetry, but quietly musing over his glass when the irrepressible punning started.[51] For Hood, there was something of the 'true moody, poetical weather observable in the barometer of his face'. At times, he would look earnest and gloomy, but then the weather would clear and he would roar out 'a hearty laugh that lifts him an inch or two from his chair', and rub his palms in enjoyment.[52]

Not all contributors, of course, were remembered with equal delight. Hazlitt attended one or two of the first dinners, but he was rather silent; and for Clare at least, he cut a mysterious figure, which did not wholly endear him to the poet. His eyes were always upon the ground, except when he looked up with a sneer which cut 'a bad pun and a young author's maiden talk to atoms'.[53] De Quincey too did not escape the strictures of B. W. Procter. He probably attended only one of the magazine dinners, on 6 December 1821, when Procter found him 'self-involved', and unable to 'add to the cheerfulness of the meeting'.[54] But as Procter later confessed, he did not like De Quincey, and his prejudice was great enough to blind him to an understanding of the essayist's ill-health and poverty at the end of 1821.[55] Yet these two examples of some coolness amongst the members of the dinners stand out alone from the general sympathy which prevailed; and the firmest impression which remains is, not of dissension, but of a society closely bound in a communal vitality and understanding. One final image may perhaps be added, since, in its irreverent spirit, it evokes much of that sense of enchantment and gentle anarchy from which the *London* drew its inspiration and brilliance. After one dinner, which had gone on well into the early hours, a group of men were to be seen in the streets of London. They walked with that deliberation of step that characterises a somewhat blurred vision:[56]

Several *noticeable* men with black silk stockings were returning from a high court-plenary of literature and French wines, – one might see at a glance that they were famous in puns, poetry, philosophy and exalted criticism! Briefly, they were the *Wits* of London! One of them, 'soaring aloft in the high regions of his fancies, with his garlands and singing robes about him', chaunted in the ringing emptiness of the streets, '*Diddle, diddle, dimpkins.*'

The singer who so mellifluously filled the empty London air with nursery rhymes was Charles Lamb. And if another later account of a similar excursion was anything to go by, he would on this occasion have finally given up the task of walking, taken a coach to Islington, nearly fallen in a river and then sat down over a pipe and gin and water, talking for an hour with those who had accompanied him home.[57] The following day, there might arrive for Taylor and Hessey a letter somewhat hazily composed:[58]

> Is it to you, or to some other kind unknown, that I owe my safe arrival home on Friday night? I confess I have no knowledge of the manner how, or time when. Between ourselves, I am not much better this morning.

It was, as Hood justly proclaimed, 'a rare company'.

To read the accounts of the *London* dinners is, even now, to relive a romance – a romance of wine and venison and good fellowship which was vital to the success of the magazine. Yet several guests, whilst delighting in recalling the puns and eccentricities which had especially captured their imagination, were aware too of a deeper effect that the festivity of these occasions produced. In December 1821, Taylor himself pointed to an important aspect of the dinner which the firm had just given:[59]

> It was a pleasant Party from the extraordinary good nature which prevailed, & the no less remarkable Wit of some of the Company, particularly Reynolds & Lamb & Rice. – It was a well timed Dinner, following so closely the Heels of our puffing Advertisement, for it gave one common Impulse to all –

At their best, the dinners sustained the loyalty and endeavour of contributors, becoming a clear focus around which writers of varying talent and temperament gathered. But as important as this community of spirit was the way in which the gatherings fostered also a community of intellect, an exchanging of ideas and attitudes which at the time provided the very material from which articles in the *London* came to be written. In his reminiscences of Lamb, B. W. Procter pointed to the interaction and expansion of intellect that the meetings encouraged:[60]

> the hearts of the contributors were opened, and with the expansion of heart the intellect widened also. If there had been any shades of

jealousy amongst them, they faded away before the light of the friendly carousal; if there was any envy, it died. All the fences and restraints of authorship were cast off, and the natural human being was disclosed.

'With the expansion of heart the intellect widened also'; Procter's words were echoed by Hood and Hazlitt, Bernard Barton, Wainewright and Reynolds. In his reminiscences of Lamb, Hood pointed out the kind of imaginative impulse which even the less significant of his remarks created:[61]

[His puns] had the brevity without the levity of wit – some of his puns contained the germs of whole essays. Moreover, like Falstaff, he seemed not only witty himself but the occasion of it by example in others.

Hood himself never gave, unfortunately, an illustration of the way in which a single round of punning could develop into the inspiration for a whole essay; but his argument of Lamb's influence upon other contributors was accurate enough. Bernard Barton, who wrote much third-rate, fashionable poetry in the magazine during these years, apostrophised Lamb in a way which was often repeated by other members:[62]

> . . . at times, to earnest thought
> Glimpses of truth most simple and sublime
> By thy imagination have been brought
> Over my spirit.

And Hazlitt was not alone in perceiving the interaction which existed between contributors in general: 'We flatter ourselves, that we not only say good things ourselves, but are the cause of them in others.'[63]

Yet this kind of influence was not simply confined to a general level. Horace Smith was directly inspired in the writing of his 'Death-Posthumous Memorials-Children' by Lamb's essay 'New Year's Eve'. And the essay 'The Praise of Chimney Sweepers' by Lamb himself was firmly derived from B. W. Procter's 'On May Day', which had in turn arisen from an idea first suggested by Taylor. T. G. Wainewright also directly influenced several contributors with his prolific suggestions for new articles. He proposed to Charles Elton, who wrote several pieces on classical literature in the magazine, translations of Aeschylus and Euripides, and a rendering of Horace's Odes. To Cary, he suggested translations of Pindar, Petrarch, and Ariosto, amongst many others; and to Lamb he wrote in July 1821 of an exhibition he had visited at the Royal Academy:[64]

> 'Poor Relations', by Stephanoff, evinces very great and deep observation of nature. . . . I have not time to point out all the variety of intelligence which is combined in this little picture; but I think that our *Elia* would manage it beautifully – let me suggest it to him.

Almost two years later, Lamb's essay 'Poor Relations' appeared in the magazine.

This free exchanging of ideas and themes for essays and poems was a direct result of the community of spirit which the *London* dinners had fostered;[65] and the ways in which ideas were developed and bandied forth amongst writers illustrates clearly the constant mutual inspiration that the circle generated. Through the pages of the magazine, the Londoners addressed each other, offered advice, praised and criticised each other's work, and suggested themes for new articles. This kind of intellectual and imaginative reciprocity was the development in literary terms of the personal friendships which the dinners had helped to encourage. Indeed, it is possibly in this aspect of the magazine that Taylor and Hessey made their greatest contribution to the *London*'s success. By encouraging the prose of talk and wine in the dinners, they had helped also to foster an intellectual kinship between writers, which often provided the very material from which articles came to be composed.

For the remainder of 1821 and throughout the following year, the *London* thrived. Early in 1822 Cunningham wrote to Hessey: 'I must congratulate you on the excellence of the Magazine; it is by far the best of them all, and this is not my own opinion alone, but what I have heard pretty freely confessed in company.'[66] By the autumn, Taylor was engaged in extensive plans to make the magazine even 'more *literary*' and 'more *entertaining*'. He proposed to omit altogether the trading and agricultural reports 'which every Magazine can do as well or better than ourselves', and convert the final sheets into a review of new books, together with important extracts from foreign journals about literature and science.[67] By the end of the year, he was clearly delighted by the success the *London* had attained. He commented to his father on the 'extraordinary Inclination just now manifested by a Number of the best Writers to gain a Place in our Pages',[68] and thought that such a desire must spring from

a *general* Impression that the Work is of such a high Character
for Talent that to be engaged in it confers Honour on the
Individual Contributors, – & this Impression will I trust
be the Forerunner of an Increase in the Number of its Readers.

But the magazine was not without its troubles, and Taylor's reference
to the number of subscribers reflected one of the chief problems.
Circulation had not increased as much as might have been reasonably
expected. In August 1821, a little over 2,000 copies had been sold, a
substantial increase of 300 upon the previous month's sales;[69] but by
the end of the year, comparing the *London*'s number of readers with
the circulation of 4,000 that Colburn's *New Monthly* had reached,
Taylor admitted that there was 'Room to improve in this Respect'.[70]
A month later, it was evident that sales had been disappointing: 'I
wonder the Mag does not sell better at the beginning of the New
Year – it is so very superior to all the others. The Flam of Blackwood
& the Namby pamby of Colburn are more suited it seems to the Taste
of the Age.'
Increasingly too, other difficulties were beginning to arise. In the
spring of 1822, Lamb wrote to Hessey with some searching questions:[71]

What is gone of the Opium Eater, where is Barry Cornwall,
& above all what is become of Janus Weathercock – or by his
worse name of Vink – something? He is much wanted. He was
a genius of the Lond. Mag. The rest of us are single Essayists.
    You must recruit. You will get too serious else. Janus was
characteristic. He talked about it & about it. The Lond.
Mag. wants the personal note too much. Blackw^d owes everything to it.

Lamb's criticism had point. 'Barry Cornwall' (the pen-name of
Procter) had been absent from the *London* for several months; and
nothing from De Quincey had appeared in the magazine since his
'Confessions'. Hazlitt, another name that might have been in Lamb's
mind at the time, had also begun to write increasingly for rival publications such as Colburn's *New Monthly*. Yet as Lamb perceptively
argued, even these writers, excellent though they were as single
essayists, did not foster the special corporate spirit of the magazine
as extensively as others. T. G. Wainewright, under his guise of 'Janus
Weathercock', was such a writer. By gathering much of his material
from the London circle itself, by addressing it in his articles, he acted
as a synthesising force for the magazine as a whole. Similarly with

Tom Hood. 'The Lion's Head' was the Speaker's Corner of the *London*, an open platform where the views of contributors on any subject could be aired more informally than within the confines of a single essay or poem. But by the middle of 1823, barely a year after Elia's letter, both these contributors had written their last pieces. Hood's final article appeared in June of that year,[72] and Janus had disappeared six months earlier, with an article which apostrophised Lamb ('thou hadst the gaiety of a boy, with the knowledge of a man') and offered high-flown yet perceptive and generous advice to John Clare. Lamb wrote to Bernard Barton: 'I cannot but think the *London* drags heavily. I miss Janus. And O how it misses Hazlitt –'[73] Four months later, his sense of foreboding was even more persistent:[74]

> The London I fear falls off. – I linger among its creaking rafters, like the last rat. It will topple down, if they don't get some Buttresses. They have pull'd down three, W. Hazlitt, Proctor, and their best stay, kind light hearted Wainewright – their Janus.

By the autumn of 1823, it was clear that the *London*'s glory was fading. Some indication of the reasons for the falling-off of the magazine was given by Lamb himself:[75]

> Proctor too is affronted (as Janus has been) with their abominable curtailment of his things – some meddling Editor or other – or phantom of one – for neither he nor Janus know their busy friend. But they always find the best part cut out.

This idea of a phantom editor had been first presented by Wainewright himself in his final article for the magazine. He was 'without form', a '*nominis umbra*' who cut away pages and obliterated the climaxes of Janus's work. Procter too was another contributor who seemed undecided as to who in fact was editing the *London*, and in a long letter to Taylor & Hessey, he argued that this ambiguity was proving increasingly detrimental to the magazine:[76]

> Last month half (certainly the best half) of the Miscellany was struck out, as I understand it at Mr Reynolds's suggestion. This month my paper is approved on the Saturday – & on Tuesday this decree is revoked. What am I to think, except that there is some one to whom even the editors' opinion is subservient –...
> Not only I, but, I may say, four of your *principal* contributors feel that this system is not the best. If there be any thing

contrary to morals or good feeling strike it out – if a man
make his papers too long tell him so in plain terms.
He will, if he has any sense, fashion his labours accordingly.

Procter's letter to the firm was eminently fair. He hoped it would be
received as it had been written, 'in a sincere & friendly spirit', for he
admired the 'general good nature' of Taylor and Hessey, and trusted
that by stating his criticisms openly instead of brooding upon them,
he would be able to restore the good relations between the house and
its contributors. Yet although the letter probably had some short-term
effect upon the firm's attitude, neither Taylor nor Hessey seems to
have appreciated the potential gravity of the situation. Even after the
letters of Lamb and Procter, several important writers were still unsure
of a crucial question: who was the editor? Taylor, Hessey, Hood,
Reynolds, or even Woodhouse?

Had this criticism been the only one to trouble contributors, the
ambiguity of editorship and the delegation of editorial rights to
others might not have seemed particularly important. But it was not.
Several leading writers became disheartened by the possibility of
alterations to and even rejection of their work. Even as early as
October 1821, Hessey had reported to Taylor that Hazlitt was concerned about the fate of his *Table Talk*: 'he wished to continue but
said that he felt so annoyed and cramped in his mind by the fear of
alteration or perhaps rejection altogether that he could not write freely
as he was accustomed to do.'[77] Procter too spoke of another source of
discontent that was becoming increasingly frequent. He had sent an
article, 'The Gallery of Portraits', which had at first been thought
'very good' by the firm. Three months later, it had been returned as
rejected. Was it that Taylor really disliked the article, or was it simply
'a civil method of dismissing' him?[78]

In addition to these complaints, the vexed question of the copyright
of those pieces appearing in the magazine was also becoming a reason
for growing contention. Hessey put the firm's case succinctly in a
letter to Cary: 'we object to giving up the whole of the Copyright,
because we do not like the appearance, even, of losing an Author for
whom we have published, or a Work which we have first brought
out.'[79] In many ways, this was clearly a fair argument. It was a rough
justice for the firm to encourage writers, often against a background
of critical attack and poor sales, only to find them turning to other
publishers in palmier days. But, as both Cary and Procter argued in
their different discussions with the house, to claim the whole copyright

of articles was equally unjust to those who had written them. During Baldwin's proprietorship of the *London*, according to Procter, his 'title to copyright' had been fully admitted, as he suspected had that of Lamb and Hazlitt. But now, all that had been changed.

At first, these criticisms of the handling of the magazine were made, as Procter constantly emphasised, 'without anger'. But within months, feelings of frustration and resentment became more persistent, and he warned that 'if to these [reasons for complaint] you add another which touches the feelings more – you will I suspect receive some very distinct tokens of disapprobation'.[80] It could not be that the magazine itself should long escape the growing discontent of several important contributors; and when Hazlitt, Wainewright, and Hood had gone, the community of spirit sustained for over two years began to break up. In the spring of 1821, Taylor himself had spoken of his interests as 'too grave, too dull I should say, for Magazine Readers'.[81] Now, nearly three years later, these words were echoing again, not unjustifiably, in the mouths of several writers. Dullness and gravity were beginning to creep into the *London*.

No clearer illustration of the change in the magazine could be given than a comparison of one of Taylor's remarks in 1822 with the actual contents of the *London* two years later. In 1822, he had urged a writer on phrenology that, to recommend any examination of this topic to the public, 'the Article in question should not exceed 8 pages of the Mag^{ze} & . . . it should be written as *popularly* as possible; for the Readers of Magazines are not much disposed to philosophize'.[82] But two years later, the gradual usurpation of space by learned disquisitions upon political economy, currency, theories of population, as well as phrenology, was destroying the imaginative brilliance of previous numbers. The sense of 'the Colloquial', which Reynolds had urged the firm to foster above all in the magazine, had given way before the sense of the scholarly and the useful. The eight-page limit on phrenology, as well as other Useful Knowledge subjects, had gone. De Quincey's studious and lengthy examinations of 'Malthus', the 'Measure of Value', and 'The Services of Mr. Ricardo to the Science of Political Economy' illustrated the shifting emphasis of the magazine. There could be no greater irony, indeed, than to compare these three articles with one of De Quincey's own remarks in the 1821 draft advertisement for the *London*. Then, he had justly criticised those 'articles of disproportionate length on Political Economy' which had taken over in the *Edinburgh Review*. But now, three years later, his 'Dialogues of Three Templars' ran for two numbers and covered in all over thirty-five pages, nearly a third of the *London*'s total number of pages. Blackwood's *Maga* had good reason to crow, 'Political Economy is not a subject fit for a Magazine';[83] for indeed, it was clear by the autumn of 1824 that the *London* had been caught on the reefs of Useful Knowledge, and that no amount of effort would refloat her.

The magazine dinners, on so many occasions the thermometer of the health of the journal, reflected the change. In 1821 and 1822, they had been held monthly. Now, in 1824, 'the gatherings of the clan to eat, drink, and be merry, were few and far between'.[84] At the December dinner of 1821, Taylor and Hessey had entertained De Quincey, Wainewright, Lamb, Reynolds and Talfourd, Cunningham, Rice, Hood and Woodhouse. It was, in Taylor's words, 'a pleasant party from the extraordinary good nature which prevailed'; it had given 'one common Impulse to all'.[85] In 1824, Thomas Bennion, the faithful factotum to the firm, wrote to Clare:[86]

> The Dinner that was given to the Contributors of the L. Mag this last time was attended by only two of the old contributors that you know, the one was Reynolds and the other Mr. C. Phillips. . . . Your old friend Elia was prevented from being one of the party thro' being ill, . . . there wanted him & you & then there would have been more mirth among them.

On the back of the letter, Bennion scribbled down the names of the guests: 'Mr. Van Dyke, Mr. H. Taylor, Mr. G. Darley, Mr. C. Phillips, Dr. Darling, Rev. Mr. Percival, Mr. Reynolds, & T & H. This was the whole.' A comparison of the guests at these two dinners demonstrates, as clearly as any statement could, the sea change suffered by the magazine. In a metaphorical sense, Bentham was now seated in the throne once occupied by Erato.

But the *London* was an unconscionable time a-dying. 'They keep dragging me on', Lamb bewailed, 'a poor, worn mill-horse, in the eternal round of the damn'd magazine; but 'tis they are blind, not I. Colburn . . . hath the ascendency.'[87] He had written nothing in the magazine for nearly a year, and was to compose his final piece for the number of August 1825. Cary's last contribution too was to appear in the first number for that year. On the editorial side, the ambiguity of editorship, a question which continued to perplex and annoy contributors,[88] was finally resolved at the end of 1824, when Taylor relinquished all responsibility as editor. Henry Southern, editor of the *Retrospective Review* and of the *Westminster Review* with John Bowring, had for some months been acting as an associate editor on the *London*;

and on 2 December, he proposed to the firm that he should take over sole editorial responsibility. Taylor and Hessey accepted. One brief sentence from Taylor's letter to James reporting the change, shows how greatly indeed the emphasis of the magazine had changed: 'They mean to make it answer the better by infusing into it a great deal of temporary Interest.'[89]

To compare this new policy with Taylor's often expressed desire to publish literature that would endure is to recognise the eclipse which the imaginative genius of the magazine had suffered through the more immediate concerns of social and political reform. For a few months, the firm remained proprietors of the *London*. Taylor tried to save some remnants of its past glory by exchanging the closely packed, double-column pages of previous numbers for clearer single-column pages; and he also increased the price by 1s. to 3/6d. But neither a resetting of type nor an increase in price improved the contents. The February number of 1825, Lamb reported, was 'all trash': 'It is whip syllabub, "thin sown with aught of profit or delight." Thin sown! not a germ of fruit or corn.'[90]

Taylor too saw clearly what was happening: 'The Mag. has not sold quite so well, the 2nd No as it did the first – & this perhaps is owing to the more useful Articles which are in the latter – a Hint is thus afforded us which we must not neglect to profit by.'[91] But this realisation had dawned too late, and if anybody did profit by such hints, it was not Taylor & Hessey. Within four months, Hessey was writing to Clare with news that might easily have been anticipated:[92]

We have resolved on disposing of the London Magazine and have I believe found a purchaser for it on pretty fair terms. It may perhaps cause something like a sigh at parting, as even people who have quarrelled with each other all their lives feel sorrow when the hour which is to separate them arrives. The Mag has been to us a source of much interesting incident & has brought us acquainted with much Talent & worth. But the labour it imposed upon us almost wore us out & we were at last compelled to depute the management of it to another Person whose views, in some particulars, do not quite coincide with our own, & whose style of management, though calculated to make the work sell, would entail upon us too many personal enmities & quarrels for us to continue with it comfortably. We therefore took advantage of an Opportunity which offered, & in future another set of People will reap the honours & rewards.

Thus it was finally agreed that Southern should take over the whole concern. Charles Lamb, on so many occasions the inspiration of the *London*'s old contributors, recorded now its passing into the realms of philosophical radicalism: 'It was indeed a dead weight. . . . It had got silly, indecorous, pert, and every thing that is bad.'[93] His final article on 'Imperfect Dramatic Illusion' appeared in August. Now, 'I shall shift myself out of it. It is fallen.'[94]

Why did the *London* fall? Faced with the richness of personalities and events which the magazine fostered, several studies of its history have sought to answer this question, somewhat paradoxically, by presenting a relatively simple argument of cause and effect. The judgments upon Taylor's editorship derived from such an approach may be easily anticipated. Because of his interference with manuscripts, his personal pride, and inability to fully understand the imaginative genius of the magazine, he is at times presented as the man who directly contributed to, and even unwittingly engineered, its decline.

Certainly, this view is not wholly unjust. Taylor was not a second John Scott. There can be no doubt that he cut and rearranged the manuscripts of some contributors, or that he was largely responsible for the ambiguity of editorship which justly annoyed several writers. Neither can it be doubted that there did sometimes appear in his general personality a certain distance and reserve, which might easily have been interpreted as a sign of arrogance or emotional coolness. He was not always able to bridge, by diplomacy and understanding, the differences of opinion which arose between the firm and its authors. As Clare argued during a period of temporary dissension between them both, his conversation, learned and fluent though it was, sometimes appeared as a mere exercise in verbal juggling rather than a means of coming to understand the minds and aspirations of his contributors. His caution and sense of his own rightness also, tended only too easily to dishearten several of his authors, and to alienate their sympathies. And in the latter months of his editorship, his whole mind seemed to be moving in a way which no longer made him as sensitive as he had once been to the imaginative genius of the magazine. Yet these criticisms, just though some of them are, point to only one aspect of the truth; for the reasons for the decline of the *London* were more various than Taylor's partial weaknesses as an editor.

In 1823, an article by Hazlitt in the *Edinburgh Review* exposed one serious deficiency which the *London* possessed throughout the editorships of both Scott and Taylor:[95]

The fault of The London Magazine is, that it wants a sufficient unity of purpose and direction. There is no particular bias or governing spirit, which neutralises the interest. The articles seem thrown into the letterbox, and to come up like blanks and prizes in the lottery – all is in a confused, unconcocted state, like the materials of a rich plum-pudding before it has been well boiled.

For *Maga*, similarly, the *London* appeared as a 'jumbled stew of goodish, badish'.[96] Even allowing for the heightened language understandable from rival publications, these criticisms of a certain nebulousness and lack of direction in the magazine's editorial policy were not unjustified. Late in 1821, De Quincey had stated that the firm's policy was to avoid 'any one presiding mind studiously impinging its' own stamp upon the whole body of the articles'. But worthy though this liberalism was in allowing contributors a relatively free rein in what they wrote, it held very obvious dangers. Too easily the absence of any presiding individual mind involved also the absence of any clear focus to the magazine as a whole. Most obviously was this true of the *London*'s political attitudes, a crucial field for any Regency periodical. Some ten years previously, in his prospectus to the *Reflector*, Leigh Hunt had persuasively argued the need for a firm political framework in both reviews and magazines:[97]

> Politics, in times like these, should naturally take the lead in periodical discussion, because they have an importance and interest almost unexampled in history, and because *they are now, in their turn, exhibiting their re-action upon literature, as literature in the preceding age exhibited its action upon them.*

Yet the examination of such an interaction between literature and politics was scarcely a persistent theme in the *London*'s policy, under either Scott or Taylor. Even as early as 1819, indeed, Horatio Smith had commented to Scott upon the noticeable lack of any political emphasis in the prospectus to the magazine:[98]

> How little you say in the Prospectus about Politics! What are they like, for it will not do in the times that are coming to be neutral or lukewarm, and I trust the London Magazine will leave to the Quarterly Review a full monopoly of political baseness and personal scandal.

Certainly, it was the *London*'s avowed policy to avoid the 'monopoly of political baseness' at all costs; but the subtleties and sophistication of liberal argument were scarcely appropriate to a reading public versed in the clear-cut dramatic conflicts of *Maga* and the *Quarterly*. No better indication of the general public reaction to such liberalism could be given, indeed, than the words of two critics in 1823. Writing to Clare in October of that year, Thomas Bennion fulsomely admired the 'fine lashing' that *Maga* had recently inflicted upon both the *London* and the *New Monthly Review*.[99] And in a letter to the *New European Magazine* in the same month, a certain Tudor Anwyl pointed out the chief weakness of Taylor & Hessey's magazine:[100]

> I have myself always considered the *London Magazine* as inferior to *Blackwood's*, and infinitely superior to the *New Monthly*; which is calculated to please nobody beyond a delicate dandy, or a nervous lady of fashion. There is a manly strength and vigour in *Blackwood*, which, with one or two exceptions, is never displayed in the *London*, whose *forte* is lightness and ease, with much benevolent pleasantry.

These criticisms were symptomatic of a general reaction. Only too readily in the eyes of the reading public, the political liberalism which the *London* propounded might have been construed as the kind of liberalism which was, more accurately, a passive and uninterested neutrality, without bite or flair. The desire to be fair at all costs could well have been interpreted as a fairness involving no cost at all. An advertisement for the magazine in May 1824[101] might proclaim with justifiable pride:

> Party-spirit, which usurps so large a portion of almost every contemporary periodical, is excluded from this work, as foreign to its nature, and tendency. Every article offered for insertion is judged of by its internal merits, and needs no other recommendation than what it may justly derive from these.

Even a cursory comparison of these remarks with the rigorous political framework of many of the contemporary Reviews reveals the innovations in policy which the *London* followed under Scott and Taylor. New literature was to be judged by its own rules and not by the artificial code of its political allegiance. Yet laudable though this policy was, it is clear why the magazine never attracted readers with as strong a magnetism as the political beacons of *Maga* and the *Quarterly*. To be just in critical judgment is one of the most praiseworthy of attitudes, but in a time of political unrest, it is also one of the most uninteresting.

This lack of a sustained focus in the magazine's policy was not confined to its political attitude. It was extended also into the field of literature itself. During its greatest years, as has been suggested, the *London* was essentially a magazine of personalities, not of literary credos. If any firm framework was to be seen in its pages by contemporary readers, it was a framework created by a communal spirit of personality, not by a defined literary programme around which contributors gathered. And if this variety of utterance, the gentle imaginative anarchy of its spirit, are the very qualities for which it is now most justly prized, they could not but seem to the Regency public a muddle of private jokes and unknown eccentricities. The original policy of the magazine had been to portray 'the *spirit* of things generally'. Yet, at its most brilliant, the *London* concentrated not upon the breadth of human activity implied by these words, but upon the reciprocity of a close circle of friends. It became as specialised in its wit as in its disquisitions upon political economy. And here, almost certainly, lay one of the reasons for its comparative failure in terms of circulation and contemporary influence. The literature which appeared in it was essentially private, not public. Contributors addressed themselves finally to the close society which had inspired them. Only in sporadic and isolated bursts did the magazine firmly focus upon the world beyond Fleet Street and Waterloo Place. And when those bursts appeared, they were invariably made in the language of the specialist, not of the common reader – in the language of Bentham rather than Cobbett.

The inability of the magazine to act as an interpreter of its contributors to the reading public, and not merely as a reflector of their intimate circle, was clearly indicated by its sales. At the time that Taylor & Hessey took it over, its circulation was about 1,700 copies a month. By November 1822, it had dropped to 1,600; and at no time during the three years of its most sustained brilliance did sales rise above 2,250. Two of Taylor's unpublished letters reveal, indeed, just how little the magazine answered in terms of sales and profit. In 1824, he informed James that a steady circulation of 2,000 copies would 'make it pay on the whole £500 a year'.[102] Six months later, after the sale to Southern, he wrote again and reported that during the four years of the firm's proprietorship, the *London* had suffered a loss of about £2,000.[103]

These figures show clearly how much the absence of a defined political or social emphasis affected the circulation of the magazine amongst the reading public. And it seems probable too that this lack of any firm framework finally affected the work of contributors more substantially than has been previously recognised. Without a clear banner of literary belief around which writers might gather, may it not have been almost inevitable that the magazine should gradually decline, and that contributors should have been unable to sustain such a high level of writing month after month without repeating themselves or descending into banality?[104] It seems possible, indeed, that the *London* could have attained such brilliance at no other period than the three or four years during which it did. It is possible that it was the product of special conditions: in the assembly of writers not only sympathetic to each other, but also at the height of their powers. Without a clear social or political focus, could such a magazine have existed at all five or ten years after it did? Could even John Scott have sustained for many years after 1824 the same creative reciprocity and the same level of inspired writing, as contributors began to tire and the whole interest of society became increasingly engaged with Reform Bills and works of Useful Knowledge?

Questions such as these do not seek to excuse Taylor's considerable failings during the final eighteen months or so of his editorship, but they perhaps point to the dangers of simplifying the reasons for the *London*'s decline. Perhaps too, in spite of his weaknesses as an editor, he also did enough for the magazine not to need an extensive apologia. He was directly responsible for introducing into it the work of Hood and De Quincey, Clare and Cary, Landor and Carlyle, as well as several writers of lesser brilliance. Under his editorship, the *London* explored the fields of German, French, Italian, and Greek literature, as well as English. The essays of De Quincey and Lamb, together with Hazlitt in the beginning, opened up the immense resources of English prose, and demonstrated that it possessed qualities of structure, music, and rhythm no less abundantly than poetry. Such things could scarcely have appeared had not Taylor been in broad, imaginative sympathy with the ideas of his contributors. And throughout his editorship, he managed also to resolve many mundane problems, which only too easily might have exhausted the energy and enthusiasm of a less dedicated man. There were difficulties, of no great moment in the history of literature, but requiring nevertheless some measure of tact and understanding. Procter might voice the justifiable complaint of writers who did not wish their work to be altered. Yet, on the other hand, there were always those such as De Quincey who wrote: 'Do not scruple out of any tenderness for my trouble, to cut away – without limit: – whatever best suits the interests of the Mag. is what I am [   ] bound to like best – and *do* like best.'[105] To adjudicate for the best between these opposing attitudes towards editorial rights, and between many similar arguments, to understand the reasons for delays in the submission of promised articles, to encourage and sympathise with men of various temperaments and beliefs, *hic labor est*. For some two years, there can be little doubt that Taylor very largely succeeded.

There remains a final image to which the mind returns, because in its irreverent spirit, it especially captures the beneficial influence which Taylor had during the first two years of his editorship. The *London* dinners, which Hessey and he instituted as a regular monthly meeting for contributors, came to be remembered as the focus of personal friendships in a way that the actual articles in the magazine never did. Over haunches of venison and French wine, the evenings blurred, and talk flowed gloriously.

Several years later, Tom Hood, remembering these things, wrote the *London*'s finest obituary:[106]

> It is with mingled feelings of pride, pleasure, and pain, that I revert to those old times, when the writers I had long known and admired in spirit were present to me in the flesh – when I had the delight of listening to their wit and wisdom from their own lips, of gazing on their faces, and grasping their right hands. . . .
>
> . . . perhaps no ex-periodical might so appropriately be apostrophised with the Irish funereal question – 'Arrah, honey, why did you die?' Had you not an editor, and elegant prose writers, and beautiful poets, and broths of boys for criticism and classics, and wits and humourists. . . . Hadn't you an Opium Eater, and a Dwarf, and a Giant, and a Learned Lamb, and a Green Man? . . . Arrah, why did you die?

{ 6 }

The years 1821-5:
Lamb, De Quincey, Carlyle,
Landor, and Coleridge

The editorship of the *London Magazine* was, in itself, a task large enough to demand all of Taylor's time and attention. To direct the magazine's broad policy, to introduce and encourage new writers, to read and judge hundreds of manuscripts, and to deal with the countless mundane matters in the publication of such a work – these were the demands made upon him almost daily for four years. Yet the magazine always remained an addition to the firm's publishing activities, not a substitute for them; and throughout the period of his editorship, Taylor continued to supervise the whole of the house's other publications, employing no reader and with only Hessey and occasionally Woodhouse to assist in management. The care and thoroughness he brought to this aspect of the firm's business has already been partly seen in his association with John Clare. The poet's work was read, criticised, and organised, not simply in general ways but often in minutest detail. Yet Clare was only one of many writers with whom the house was concerned during the years of the *London*. By 1826, in addition to publishing in book form the work of regular contributors to the magazine – Lamb, Cary, and De Quincey, Allan Cunningham and John Bowring – Taylor & Hessey had brought out new volumes by Carlyle and Coleridge, George Borrow and Landor, Darley and Richard Ayton. Far from diminishing their activity in the publishing line, indeed, the *London* increased it. As Taylor had hoped in the spring of 1821, the magazine had given the firm 'the Advantages of a public Situation equal to a perpetual Advertisement'.[1]

There can be no doubt that the monthly publication of the magazine placed the house more firmly in the public eye; and throughout these years, there were several signs that the partnership was attaining some sort of recognition and security. On 1 January 1823, the publishing department, together with the magazine, moved to new and more opulent premises at 13 Waterloo Place, thus leaving the shop in Fleet Street free for the retail trade. Taylor viewed the change with a characteristic uncertainty of emotion: 'I do not feel as if I were too anxious, or too sanguine – it seems a reasonable Experiment, & in that lies much of my Comfort.'[2] The new premises, though, situated as they were in a new and fashionable area of the city just south of Nash's Regent Street, undoubtedly aroused public curiosity and increased confidence in the progress of the firm, for a fortnight later, he was able to write to James:[3]

> the Magazine rises in Sale, having increased about 200 since the Year began – It is certainly making more Noise in the World than it did – & perhaps this apparent Prosperity may be partly owing to the secret Recommendation of this more public Demonstration in its Favour, the taking a New House for publishing it.

But in spite of the gradual expansion, neither new premises nor the public advertisement afforded by the *London* were able to dispel entirely the old problems of publishing which continued to plague the firm. A new location alone could not provide the panacea to combat poor or only moderate sales, and the apparent lack of public interest in the new books of imaginative literature the house brought out. Certainly, the firm was well enough acquainted with such difficulties from past experience; but experience, needless to say, did not make them any the less acute. Indeed, the problems of publishing fine literature might well have seemed in the years after Keats's death even more perplexing than before. On several previous occasions, the house had experienced a natural and perhaps inevitable difficulty in recommending unknown writers to the public. But this problem persisted even with those authors who had gained a considerable celebrity through the pages of the *London*.

With the firm's desire to bring out works of literature that would survive a constant influence upon their choice of books for publication, it must have been clear to both Taylor and Hessey that many of the articles in the magazine deserved a more enduring and spacious setting than the closely packed, double-columned pages in which they had first appeared. Yet as both must certainly have realised also, there were obvious problems in transferring such articles from magazine to book form. Not only was there the danger that the repetition of material would hinder sales, but also that the reading public would judge such books upon their intrinsic merit, as the work of a single author. They would not automatically place them within that wider context of imaginative and colloquial back-chat upon which the *London* depended so greatly for its brilliance. In book form, the articles would be seen in an unintended isolation, not as part of that communal spirit in which Clare had spoken to Elia, Elia to Hazlitt, and Wainewright to all three. Extracted from the context for which they had been written, would such articles appear even more brilliant to the ordinary reader, or more pedestrian?

The work of two contributors in particular might have seemed distinctive enough to transcend the medium for which it had been originally composed. Although Lamb's 'Elia' essays clearly owed something to the corporate spirit of the magazine, in the humane, comprehensive wisdom of their themes, in that attitude of tolerant sanity which always endeared Lamb to his contemporaries, they revealed a complete individuality. Even more was this true of De Quincey's 'Confessions'. The tone of his articles was deeply private, deriving nothing from the atmosphere of public gossip which the most fervent Londoners revelled in. Taylor, certainly, seems to have been confident that the originality of these two works was striking enough to allow them to stand by themselves, for in August 1822, the first edition of the *Confessions* appeared, to be followed at the end of the year by Lamb's *Elia: Essays which have appeared under that Signature in the London Magazine.*

There could be few better examples of the vagaries of public taste than the fate of these two volumes in the reading market. The *Confessions* sold immediately. The first edition, which was almost certainly of 1,000 copies, was quickly bought up, and within four months, a second edition of a further 1,000 had been seen through the press and half of it subscribed for. On 18 December, Taylor reported to his father that the house had already delivered 500 copies to bookshops, and as he justly commented, this was 'a good Subscription so near the End of the year'.[4] By June 1823, only nine months after publication, a third edition had been brought out and was in the shops. Within a year, the book cannot have sold less than 2,500 copies.

At first, it seemed that Lamb's *Elia* volume too would meet with a similar success. Shortly after its publication in December, Taylor was hopeful of its progress: 'we have . . . subscribed nearly 200 out of 1000, which we reckon is a good beginning.'[5] Even apart from its intrinsic merit as literature, the volume had much to recommend it. Both Taylor and Thomas Davison, the printer, had clearly seen the book through the press with more than usual care. Gone was the tightly crushed and claustrophobic setting of the *London*'s pages. There were generous margins and spacings between each line. The type was clean and firm, and the volume as a whole possessed a fine clarity of design and execution which did Lamb's words full justice. Yet in spite of these recommendations, the book did not sell. A year after its appearance, Lamb wrote to Bernard Barton: 'I judge I shall put forth no second volume. More praise than buy, and T. and H. are not particularly disposed for Martyrs.'[6] Even these words, though, distressing enough in themselves, did not tell the whole story. Not only was no new volume published by Taylor & Hessey, but no second edition of the first was ever called for by the public. Despite the considerable renown of Elia as the star of the *London*, six years later in 1828, Taylor was still advertising the first edition of his essays.[7]

If he ever tried to, Taylor might have been justifiably perplexed to define the reasons for De Quincey's success and Lamb's failure in terms of sales. The timing of publication, clearly, could have made little difference, for the *Confessions* and *Elia* had appeared within four months of each other at most, and during this period, there had been no public scandal of the kind that had so quickly buried Keats's *Lamia*. Critically too, both books enjoyed a favourable response, for despite the unnecessary criticism of Robert Southey in a *Quarterly* article that *Elia* wanted 'only a sounder religious feeling, to be as delightful as it is original', which occasioned a minor storm in a teacup, both works were generally well received by the Reviews. Perhaps after all, Lamb had been too close to the community spirit of the *London*; and, extracted from the context for which they had been written, his essays seemed to the public less strikingly original than De Quincey's. Perhaps too, Southey's remark, a passing reference in an article upon a totally different subject, was enough of a hint to morally minded readers to reduce sales considerably.[8] But however obscure the reasons, the result was clear enough. De Quincey's volume went through nearly three editions within a year. Six years after publication, Lamb's book had still not exhausted its first edition of 1,000 copies.

When the theorising was over, this was the plain, economic reality to which Taylor and Hessey had to return, and, as so persistent a problem, it could scarcely avoid affecting their association with writers. Faced with the growing financial difficulties arising from such uncertainty in sales, their policy of gradual expansion became increasingly coloured during these years by a greater caution – a caution, not in publishing works of imaginative literature at all, but in paying so highly for the copyright. In 1819, they had offered Cary £109 for the thousand remaining copies of his Dante, and £125 for a new edition of 750 copies. It was a generous agreement. But four years later, in the autumn of 1823, the proposal to publish another of his works, a translation of Aristophanes' *The Birds*, illustrated how greatly the impact of uncertain sales was beginning to affect their policy. On 9 October, Hessey wrote to Cary and tried to insure the firm against loss should the book not answer. He offered £50 immediate payment for the translation, but a further £50 only when the first edition of 1,000 copies was exhausted. In his reply, Cary stuck firmly to his original demand for 100 guineas before allowing the book to go to press. Hessey responded with a catalogue of the facts in the case. The firm's offer was 'in fact very liberal'; for if he were to receive his 100 guineas, and if the whole edition were exhausted, the firm would still be left with a profit of under £50 on an outlay of £50 – and they had, of course, always to run the risk that the volume would not sell. Cary was not impressed. If the house was unwilling to accept his terms, he would call for the manuscript. Finally, however, at the end of October, a compromise was reached. The poet was to receive fifty guineas immediately, and fifty more as soon as half the edition had been sold.[9] The translation, which Hessey thought 'very spirited & . . . very faithful', appeared the following year, 1824. Four years later, this first edition was still being advertised in Taylor's list of publications.

Increasingly, the financial risks involved in this type of publication were forcing Taylor to recognise the influence of public response upon the firm's work. Beneath the surface of letters which speak with growing frequency of economic difficulties, it is possible to discern, indeed, his deepening awareness that the very nature of his profession was forcing him into a kind of no-man's-land between writer and reading public, between artistic values and economic realities. On the one hand, he could scarcely ignore the fact, so often mentioned in this study, that the promulgation of literature was now a trade, subject to the same laws of supply and demand as any other. No longer was it possible to argue that literature was a product protected in some special way from the pervasive influence of economics and a free market, for that tradition had died with the passing of private patronage. Yet Taylor was not so dull of soul as to believe that what answered public demand was thereby necessarily the best literature; and throughout his work after 1821, indeed, there remained despite the caution about copyright the same unwillingness to compromise more than was necessary with the reading market, which had so strongly characterised his association with Keats and Hazlitt. In attempting to wrest from the public some part of its power of patronage, he was attempting also to foster the foremost tradition of the firm – the belief, quite simply, that literature could be judged by its own rules, without constant reference to its economic potential or to public response.

A policy such as this, which sought to weaken the influence both of finance and of the reading public upon the publishing of new literature, could hardly have been sustained for long without Taylor's own strong spirit of independence. Indeed, it was precisely this spirit, the autonomy of his judgment, that had been very largely responsible for the house's continued encouragement of Keats and Hazlitt after the attacks of the Reviews. Such self-reliance was not, of course, without its dangers; and on several occasions, as has been seen, it caused a good deal of friction between Taylor and his authors. He appropriated too many of their own functions to himself; he cut and altered and censored too readily. Yet if this kind of independence sometimes offended, it was just as frequently the very quality which encouraged him to take risks, to experiment with new works, and to have faith in new authors. And for yet another writer who made his way to the firm during these years, the price of such a spirit was not too high; for, as with Clare and Hood, it was through Taylor that he gained his introduction to the literary world. The writer was Thomas Carlyle.

Carlyle's work was first brought to Taylor's attention by Edward Irving, the Scots divine who visited London in the early months of 1823 on an extensive evangelical crusade. Taylor, evidently, had attended several of the meetings organised and had been much taken with the eloquence of Irving's oratory, for in July he gave Clare a lengthy account of the imaginative brilliance and power of his sermons:[10]

> He looks like what you could imagine John the Baptist to have
> been – and he talks to the Congregation, especially the rich and
> the intellectual, in a Style more like John's Address to the Jews
> than anything else – . . . . We have not had such a Writer since
> the Days of Milton, nor such an Orator at any Time, for he
> combines the Imagination and Eloquence of Jeremy Taylor with
> the Zeal of Knox.

With such admiration on his part, it was almost inevitable that when Irving spoke warmly to him of Carlyle's project for a 'picture-gallery of literary great men', he should willingly accept the proposal to publish it. Carlyle was asked to inaugurate the series with a biography of the German playwright, Schiller.

The form in which Taylor intended this first essay to appear is a little uncertain, but it is very possible that he hoped it would initiate a new venture of the firm – 'a Biographical Work, to appear Quarterly'.[11] Certainly, as his letters from this period reveal, some such idea of entering upon another substantial publication was in his mind at the time, and the new periodical may well have been intended as a companion to the *London Magazine*. But by the autumn of 1823, the idea had been abandoned. The difficulties, he thought finally, were too great: 'on maturer Consideration this project required such unity of purpose and equality of talent in the writers, Qualifications which are not easily found, that I gave it up.'[12] Instead, he inserted the first part of the essay on Schiller in the October number of the *London*, and wrote a letter[13] which, as Carlyle acknowledged, was 'full of that "essential oil", flattery':[14]

I think most highly of the Execution of this part. It surpassed what I had allowed myself to expect from Mr. Irving's Description, though you thought his Estimate demanded a considerable Reduction. I am certain it will be thought in general a very able & interesting paper.

The appearance of this essay in the *London* was Carlyle's baptism in print, the first piece of writing by him ever to be published. Yet the firm's encouragement did not end there, for by the summer of the following year, they had offered to publish the complete biography in book form. Carlyle was to receive £50, in return for which the house would be allowed to print 1,000 copies. After the sale of the first edition, the copyright would remain entirely in his hands.[15]

The Life of Frederick Schiller was finally published on 1 March 1825, a fine octavo volume of some 300 pages, and both biographer and publisher evidently anticipated that the book would succeed. Eight months even before its appearance, Carlyle felt that the edition of 1,000 copies should sell 'with tolerable rapidity'.[16] And the firm's faith in him was clearly demonstrated when, three weeks before publication, Hessey wrote expressing their willingness to bring out another work – a life of Voltaire, for which they offered improved terms, £100 for the first and for each subsequent edition.[17] But in the end, no biography of Voltaire was ever destined to appear under Taylor & Hessey's imprint, and one of the reasons for this became clear nearly three years later. In December 1827, Carlyle wrote to Taylor enquiring of the progress *The Life of Schiller* had made since its appearance:[18]

There is some talk here of publishing my *Life of Schiller* a second
time, and in a more cheap and popular form. As an indispensable
preliminary it becomes necessary to inquire whether *your* interest
in the little Book had expired; whether the first Edition is all off
your hands; and if so, whether a second would be of any value
to *you*. . . .

. . . I begin to have some touch of sympathy for that unhappy
first-born of my brain, which certainly I left in a most ostrich-
like fashion; never having heard one syllable good bad or
indifferent respecting it, except once or twice that *here* it was out
of print.

But Carlyle had certainly been misinformed. The book was not out
of print – far from it. Taylor replied: 'I have had the number of
Schiller on hand ascertained and I am sorry to say it differs widely
from your expectation. There are 650 copies in my warehouse.'[19] In
nearly three years, only 350 copies of the volume had been sold. As a
last resort, Taylor offered to sell the remaining stock to Carlyle at
1/6d. a copy, suggesting that the book might then be remaindered
at 2/6d.:

I need not tell you how great a Loser I must be by such terms,
but I see not otherwise how the book can ever be got rid of;
and yet it *ought* to sell. But here we have no medium; if a work
is not a mere novel, it must be absolutely useful & even
necessary, or it will not be cared for.

'We have no medium' – this single phrase crystallised the continuing problem. Twenty years after its beginnings in publishing,
and despite the regular monthly appearance of the *London*, the house
had still failed to discover a constant medium by which works of
literary excellence could be advertised and firmly impressed upon the
minds of the reading public. Their problem, difficult enough though
it was to resolve, could be stated in relatively simple terms. For those
works of imaginative and critical literature they published – books
such as Carlyle's *Schiller* or Lamb's *Elia* or Keats's *Lamia* – no clear
process seemed to exist by which the enduring value of such volumes
could be interpreted to the public at large.

This difficulty of reconciling popular taste and demand with an understanding of true literary worth was, needless to say, nothing new in

the firm's activities. Yet in the years following Keats's death, the very persistence of this problem in Taylor's work only served to highlight a further difficulty. Looking as he did both towards the reading public and towards the writers of the house, he was compelled increasingly to come to some clearer definition of his responsibility as a publisher. Earlier in 1816, as has been seen, he believed that the firm's chief effort should be simply to encourage, and even to originate by direct proposal, those works of literature which might survive their own age. Yet, laudable and momentous though this policy was, it scarcely took into account those questions of editorial control which began to arise more and more frequently in the house's later career. The several pertinent questions posed by contributors to the *London* were, indeed, symptomatic of a more general unease amongst writers of the house as a whole. Over what areas in the diffusion of literature, it was queried, was it justifiable for any publisher to exercise direct control, and over what areas did he hold only an indirect responsibility? Was he merely to publish books, following the manuscripts of his authors word for word, comma for comma, or to advise them, attempt to interpret their work, and even to alter their manuscripts where necessary as an essential part of his work?

None of the great publishers in literary history have, of course, recognised any clear line of demarcation between their province and the province of critics or authors. Indeed, the greatest of the associations between publishers and writers have invariably been those in which these boundaries have been most confused and ill-defined. The role of the publisher has not been static and circumscribed, but fluid and dynamic. He has not been the passive servant of his writers, merely transforming manuscripts into the printed book, but has often played a vital part in the making of literature, not only in suggesting and influencing the themes of new works, but on several occasions even in controlling directly the kind of statements which authors have made.

There can be little doubt that this question of control, of a publisher's right to alter or censor material, was by far the most controversial problem Taylor faced in his career. It occurred, as has been seen, in the debate over the conclusion to *The Eve of St Agnes*. It occurred with Clare in the arguments over radicalism and supposed indelicacies in *Poems Descriptive* and *The Shepherd's Calendar*. It occurred yet again with several articles submitted by contributors to the *London Magazine*. On occasions, it is clear that Taylor was uneasy of his responsibility in this matter. The questions he put to Clare about several passages in the poet's first two volumes – 'Are these to be omitted also?', 'Have I altered them for the better?' and so forth – reveal an uncertainty of mind which in these cases was undoubtedly genuine. And yet, as various parts of this study have shown also, his alteration of several writers' work was often seen, and sometimes justifiably, as an unwarrantable intrusion into the province of the writer, which could not be tolerated. In 1823, this particular dissension arose again with yet another of the firm's authors, but on this occasion, Taylor's blue pencil provoked an argument which reverberated more fiercely than ever before. A publisher's responsibility, it was claimed, was little more than the practical business of translating manuscript into book. By trying to control the themes and contents of new books, particularly in the application of moral sanctions upon works of creative literature, he was meddling unjustifiably. The writer around whom these discussions raged was Walter Savage Landor.

Taylor was introduced to Landor's work in early 1823 by Julius Hare, a classical tutor at Trinity College, Cambridge, and a regular contributor at that time to the *London Magazine*. With Landor away in Italy, Hare had been entrusted by him with the task of finding a publisher for his *Imaginary Conversations*; but from the very beginning, there had been difficulties. Hare had tried three publishers and had failed to get the manuscript accepted before finally turning to Taylor as 'one to whom our literature has been so much indebted'[20] and as 'the most honourable man in the trade'.[21] For a short while, he seemed to have made a happy choice. Taylor replied immediately to his request:[22]

I shall be glad to see Mr. Landor's MS. and to publish it on the Terms you propose, if it answers the Expectation I am led to form of it, both from your Description & from the acknowledged Ability of the Author. I have often heard my Friend Mr. De Quincey speak of him in such Terms for his extraordinary Powers of Mind, as surpass the Estimation in which he is generally held; & I cannot but hope therefore that this Work will extort from the Public that Praise to which he is justly entitled. –

But even at this early stage, there was a warning light:

If I . . . endeavour to judge for myself of the Work . . . you must not think it unreasonable, for unless I exercised some Discretion I could feel no Right to appropriate to myself the Compliment you pay the Publishers of Elia, &c.

By the middle of April, he had read the Conversations and had become very uneasy about several passages which he felt he could not accept. If they were not omitted, he argued, the sale of the book would be 'materially affected', and this would be particularly regrettable with a work 'so capable of interesting & instructing'.[23] In reply, Hare reported that Landor himself was willing to bear any loss the book might make. Taylor's chief concern, though, was not a financial one:[24]

> If I looked only as a Man of Business on the Speculation of publishing Mr Landor's Work, I could not hesitate after his liberal Proposal to bear the Loss; but that has not been in my Thoughts. . . . My Objection lies deeper; I am averse to become instrumental to the appearance of such of these Conversations, or such Parts of them, as I cannot honestly approve. . . . I have no Right however to require more – I must therefore decline the Publication, & regret that I cannot feel justified in undertaking it –

Hare, though, had had enough of trailing around publishers. He discussed the matter with Taylor at great length and finally, in his own words, almost 'forced' him to undertake the work.[25]

But few things are more uneasy than an uneasy publisher, and Taylor's objections were not quietened. For weeks, letters full of involved argument and negotiation passed between him and Hare. 'As a Reader merely', he found little in Landor's work offensive; indeed, he admired a great deal even in those passages to which he was most opposed. But as a publisher, he argued, his responsibility lay deeper than personal reaction. On political grounds, several passages, he contended, were unsuitable for publication because of prejudice. The account Landor had given of Edmund Burke's change of party was untrue, and he had unjustly branded him 'with the most barefaced Dishonesty'. Even more disturbing were the attacks against contemporary politicians, for here the laws of libel became a vital consideration. The charges Landor had made against Sir William Bentinck and the whole tenor of the dialogue between Pitt and Canning might well be considered libellous, and with a good deal of justice, Taylor argued, 'as the Law at present stands I have no desire to incur the Penalties of such a Verdict'. In several other instances too, the pervading freedom of Landor's writing worried him. In a poem read by Cecil to Queen Elizabeth, he admitted that the line 'Too late the goddess hid what hand may hide' made for 'an excellent Picture', but he considered it 'done with a Freedom almost beyond the Era of

Elizabeth'. Oliver Cromwell's exclamation to Walter Noble, 'I must piss upon these firebrands, before I can make them tractable', also disturbed him for the licence of its expression. The critic William Gifford had been no friend to him, but he could not accept the way in which Landor had attacked him:[26]

> Gifford is spoken of . . . too much in his own Style, & . . . the Contempt is over-acted. I sho^d like to see him punished, but with Justice & Dignity, – so that even his own Party wo^d not be able to find in it an Excuse for taking his Part. –

These objections, though, all expressed in a letter to Hare of 26 April 1823, were only minor sources of dissension compared with the chief object of Taylor's concern – the Middleton-Magliabecchi dialogue. In this conversation, Conyers Middleton, the eighteenth-century divine who had sought to divorce the true nature of Christian doctrine from the elaborate trappings of ecclesiastical ritual, had attacked the Bible and firmly rejected the efficacy of prayer. This dialogue in particular clearly touched a sensitive area of Taylor's beliefs, for radical though he was in many aspects of his Christian morality, prayer remained for him throughout his life a corner-stone of faith. Yet he argued to Hare that his chief objection to publishing the conversation was not that Landor had attacked views he personally held:[27]

> I know what Mr Landor means, & I should find little Difficulty myself in agreeing with him in his Views; but I cannot consent to loosen Mankind from one set of Obligations before they are fitted for the Reception of another equally or more operative on their Consciences – . . . because a Man is wise & able to do without a Schoolmaster, that is no Reason why Boys, by whom I mean the less wise & the uneducated, should be left as much without a Go[al?][28] as without Discretion. – We begin at the wrong End when we [atte]mpt to remove Superstition before Ignorance –

How far this argument was in fact a rationalisation on Taylor's part for his own dislike of the attack upon prayer is debatable. To contend that, as a publisher, he was morally obliged to censor the offending passages for fear that less educated readers would misunderstand them, was scarcely a convincing response. Debatable too is the question of whether the good he believed he would do by suppressing the dialogue was not greatly outweighed by the harm of censoring freedom of speech and opinion. As Hare hinted to him not unjustly, there was more than a suspicion of exaggeration and false rhetoric in the position he was maintaining.[29] But it is likely that the debate did in fact produce some tension in his mind. On so many occasions previously, he had persistently advocated the need for a disinterested judgment of literary merit, for a judgment which consciously divorced the value of litera-ture from a writer's political or religious affiliation. Yet now, he was himself attempting to judge in just the way he had condemned. Finally, however, he agreed to let the matter be taken out of his hands. Hare suggested appealing to Wordsworth and Southey to mediate in the disputed passages, and he responded: 'Let them see the Proofs, & if they approve of what I condemn, I will consent to forego the Right of private Judgment, & be bound by their Decision.'[30]

The summer passed. Taylor, still uneasy, continued to try and relieve the firm of the book. He offered to have the work printed whilst Hare sought another publisher, and suggested that Longman's might be interested. Yet, despite the various disagreements, he remained con-vinced of the book's exceptional quality: 'We have not had so much Wisdom put into a Book since the Days of Lord Bacon – I have ordered 750 Copies but am willing to make it 1000 if you wish it.'[31] Finally, in March 1824, still under the house's imprint though only just, the first two volumes of *Imaginary Conversations of Literary Men and Statesmen* appeared.

The book was generally well received by both critics and public. Both the *Examiner* and the *Edinburgh Review* praised it, and Hare himself generously advanced its cause by advertising its genius in the *London*. By July indeed, only four months after publication, Taylor was able to report that 'the *Trade* are beginning to send for more Copies of the Work, which shews that it is moving. On Saturday the 5 principal Houses in the Row had fresh Numbers.'[32]

Although at first the book did not 'spread like wild-fire',[33] by the end of the year it was clear that it was answering. The first edition had sold out, and Taylor had already begun preparing a second, as well as arranging material for the third volume.[34] But good sales and reviews did not succeed in dispelling old arguments, and in Novem-ber, preparations for the second edition caused the dispute about the Middleton dialogue on prayer to break out again. Taylor expressed his views now with fiercer conviction:[35]

I believe this to be wrong, & if it is so, it cannot be a Trifle which I am asked to grant, in publishing it. You think me over scrupulous I know, but I am bound, by what I conceive to be

right, to act in the Way I do. . . . You may be as sincerely convinced that you are benefiting Men as I am, on the other hand,
that you are injuring them – & I believe not only that you
are equally sincere, but that your Judgment is as good an
Authority for your Action, as mine is for my Refusal to act. . . .

I refused Lord Byron's Vision of Judgment long before it was
offered to John Hunt – yet I did not think *that* a Production so
likely to prove pernicious as the Article in Question.

To add fuel to the fire, there also arose a misunderstanding about
payment which gave the *coup de grâce* to the association between
Landor and the firm. The house's business arrangements with its
authors had never been a model of clarity or organisation, and in
Landor's case, it proved disastrous. Almost a year after the appearance
of the book, Taylor wrote to him apologising for the delay in sending
the money due to him, but pointing out rather tactlessly that the cost
of bringing out the second edition might initially absorb the profit
made on the first. Not without justice, Landor erupted. He wrote to
Hare with a fury reminiscent of Hazlitt's reply to Gifford. Even if he
had agreed to a second edition, which he had not, he failed to see
what that had to do with what had already been published:[36]

> Greatly do I regret that I have had anything to do with so
> insincere a man, with such an impudent coxcomb . . . this honest
> man says I may be indebted to him *at some future time*, and
> gives that as a reason why I shall not receive a farthing now!
> Does he consider himself as a man of business, or (as these
> people in our days are apt to do) as a gentleman? . . .
> To delay the payment of what is due, on the plea that I may
> hereafter be indebted to one for *something* not ordered, nor
> contemplated by me, is the conduct of a scoundrel.

He ordered Taylor to stop the printing of the second edition, and
began legal proceedings against him through his cousin, Walter
Landor. Hare immediately wrote to him, protesting that he had been
responsible for the commissioning of the second edition, not Taylor,
and that the publisher's delay in making payment was not as repre-
hensible as it seemed. But the damage had been done. Taylor wrote
to Hare about Landor's remarks:[37]

> He says on the authority of Hazlitt that those Booksellers who
> take half the Profit never take half the Risk. This is true of us in
> one Sense: we have never taken half because we have always

taken the whole Risk when the Profits were to be divided,
(& our Loss has often been very heavy from it). . . . Equally
absurd is the Notion he has taken up that I had any sinister End
or selfish View in the reprinting of the Work . . . so far from
Profit being an Allurement I have repeatedly offered to give up
the Work on Principle at various Stages of its Progress. . . . He
need be under no Apprehension of my taking Advantage of
him. . . . I renounce him and all his Works with the greatest
Willingness –

Hare replied immediately on receiving the letter. The only fault he
found in Taylor's actions was a delay in replying to one of Landor's
letters requesting payment. But this furnished 'no justification for any
part of the language' Landor had used. Hare was convinced that
Taylor's conduct had, from the very beginning, been that of a
'thoroughly upright, liberal, and conscientious man'.[38] He suspected
that Hazlitt, who was at that time in Italy with Landor, had had a
finger in the pie. Taylor, for his part, acknowledged that he had been
at fault for the delay in payment,[39] and quickly advanced some £90
to Landor's bankers. But the house had lost heavily. Some £175 had
already been spent in preparing the 1,000 copies of the second edition
and the 1,500 of volume three before Landor's edict forbidding further
publication had arrived,[40] and there was no hope of recouping the
deficit. From the works of Keats, Lamb, Carlyle, and Cary, the one
book of substantial talent which had seemed likely to answer with the
public had been smothered, not by poor sales or critical attack, but by
carelessness and too ready a temper.

The outcome of the association, though, was not altogether clouded
in bitterness. Taylor found great comfort at least in Hare's fair-
mindedness when the argument with Landor was at its height, and
he wrote to thank him for his support. Their relationship, he felt, had
produced 'the pleasantest Correspondence my Publishing Avocations
ever introduced me to'.[41] In fact, 'this Service of yours [is] the first,
I might almost say, & certainly the greatest, I ever received from any
Friend.'[42] And his good feelings towards Landor also were not
altogether broken by their dispute. Both had been at fault. The anger
died. A fortnight after receiving the letter forbidding publication, he
wrote again to Hare[43] observing that in one of the conversations,
Landor had depicted a man, Lord Manvers, whom he had known as a
boy: 'I . . . fancy I hear him speak in the Words which are attributed
to him – The dramatic Faculty by which this Impression is conveyed

is sometimes very perfect in Landor.' Freed from a book that he had been uneasy about from the very beginning, he was now able to estimate its worth dispassionately and generously: 'Now that I have nothing to do with the Work or the Author, I shall be able to enjoy the Reading of it more than ever.'

Throughout these years, the firm continued in different ways to build upon its tradition of fine publications, bringing out works which, although understandably eclipsed now by the greater glories of Lamb, Clare, and De Quincey, were still worthwhile additions to their list. In spite of the fate of *Elia*, the *London Magazine* continued to provide both writers and materials for new books. In 1822, two volumes of poetry and prose by Allan Cunningham appeared; and two years later, Hazlitt's *Sketches of the Principal Picture-Galleries in England* was published, a sign that the old association created in the days of *Maga*'s scourge had not been entirely forgotten. In 1825 the house also brought out the work of another *London* contributor, perhaps deserving of a wider recognition – Richard Ayton's *Essays and Sketches of Character*. Two substantial productions of this time in particular, demonstrate the breadth of interest which continued to inform their editorial policy. In 1820, they published Henry Brooke's *A Guide to the Stars*, a beautifully printed volume of astronomical maps and diagrams, presented with a fine clarity of design and execution. Three years later, they were bringing out *The Italian School of Design*, a magnificently produced art book, edited by William Young Ottley, which contained drawings and etchings by Michelangelo, Raphael, Leonardo da Vinci, and Andrea del Sarto. The price of this volume too was equally magnificent – some seven and a half guineas for subscribers and anything up to thirty guineas for special bindings and sizes. But one book, much cheaper in price, was destined to capture the public imagination more completely than any of these works; and its publication reintroduced a poet and critic who had remained on the friendliest terms with Taylor and Hessey for many years.

During the late summer of 1823, Samuel Taylor Coleridge approached the firm with a somewhat random collection of material which he wanted published. The book was to be called *Aids to Reflection*, and consisted of a compendium of extracts from the writings of Archbishop Leighton, to which Coleridge hoped to add a biography, notes, and a detailed critique of Leighton's thought. Taylor in particular must have been greatly attracted by the proposal. His admiration for Leighton's work was great ('Next to the Bible I sho[d] deem it the wisest Book in our Language,' he once wrote to James)[44] and arrangements for publication were soon completed. By October, Hessey was able to report: 'Mr. Coleridge has been with me again to-day with his Title and Preface, and on Saturday the whole will be in my hands. It will be a delightful Book and will be sure to sell well.'[45] The material was arranged and the book put to press. But a work of Coleridge's was really safe from alteration only when out in the bookshops, for the poet possessed the distressing habit of having second thoughts. As soon as he saw the proofs for the new volume, he began to be worried:[46]

> I was struck with the Apprehension of the disorderly and heterogeneous appearance which the Selections intermixed with my own comments &c would have – I had not calculated aright on the relative quantity of the one and the other – and the more I reflected, the more desirable it appeared to me to carry on the promise of the Title Page (*Aids* to Reflection) systematically throughout the work – – But little did I anticipate the time and trouble, that this *rifacciamento* would cost me –

Nor, it might be added, did Taylor and Hessey. The vagaries of Coleridge's proposals evoked throughout the following year an impression of mild anarchy, for in addition to *Aids to Reflection*, he also suggested the firm should publish three further, related works. The first, a book on the 'Elements of Discourse and Criterion of True and False Reasoning'; the second, a volume to be entitled 'The Wanderings of Cain'; and finally, a series of six disquisitions on faith, the eucharist, prayer, the church, Hebrew scripture, and the 'right and superstitious use . . . of the Scriptures'.[47] The aim, Coleridge explained, was to produce 'a compleat System of the Philosophy of Religion'. But he was rather unsure of the title 'Six Disquisitions'. What did Hessey think of '"Conversations on Stainmoor" (n.b. the dreariest and longest Waste-land in England)'; or perhaps, if this would not do, 'The Young Chaplain and the Grey-headed Passenger: or Conversations on Shipboard during a Voyage to the Mediterranean'? He was happier composing poetry, clearly, than book titles.

Aids to Reflection finally emerged in July 1825, and gained a quiet and reasonable success.[48] But in contrast to the administrative chaos surrounding its preparation for the press, its publication marked also an event of far greater moment for the firm itself. Coleridge had made his proposals just in time, for *Aids to Reflection* was one of the last books ever to be published by the house. On 30 June 1825, an event so often threatened in past years could no longer be avoided. Taylor and Hessey dissolved their partnership.

The decision to end their association, which had lasted for almost twenty years, had probably been reached during April or May of that year. At the end of May, Taylor wrote to Clare, forewarning him of the event:[49]

> When Midsummer comes, my old Friend Hessey & I shall have dissolved Partnership. He retains the retail trade of the House in Fleet Street – & I shall keep the publishing Business and manage it here myself. The two Businesses are perfectly distinct, & may be separated with Advantage to both Concerns, & I am sure of the Benefit to Hessey's health, who having had all the Care of both has had more Fatigue and Closeness of Attention than he could well endure.

Hessey too wrote to Helpstone, hoping to reassure Clare that the dissolution would make no difference 'in our ancient friendship nor in any of our Connections I trust'.[50] To Philip Bliss, an old friend living in Oxford, Taylor explained that dissolution seemed the logical outcome for the firm as it was then organised:[51]

> As there were two separate Businesses and two Houses adapted for the Management of them . . . each of us took the Business which he felt best qualified for. . . . I am happy to say that the Friendship which existed between us before we went into Business is not likely to be injured by the Dissolution of Partnership.

But reassured though friends of the house might have been that no personal ties would be broken, some might have sensed also during these weeks that an era was now drawing to a close. A world had begun to pass. The new societies in which Taylor and Hessey would soon find themselves would not be the society of the Londoners or of Keats's circle. For almost ten years, they had pursued a policy of considerable glory in encouraging writers in whom they believed; but many of those authors had not answered in terms of sales, and the financial risks involved in such publishing were finally too great a burden. The house had lost on Carlyle, on Landor, and Lamb, and probably on Hazlitt also. The *London Magazine* had left them with a deficit of £500 a year. With perhaps the single exception of the books of Ann and Jane Taylor, they had failed to discover a best-selling author, another Byron or Scott, whose work was assured of high sales on its first appearance and a steady circulation thereafter. In the end, the partnership could not survive on the basis of constant loans from friends in Bakewell and London. On 7 June 1825, Taylor reported to James that Mr Bonsor, a London financier who had often come to their rescue in times past, had seen a full statement of their accounts. He regarded them, quite simply, as the forerunner of 'complete insolvency'.[52]

It was not until 1829 that all the complications of dissolution were eventually settled, but there was something of an irrevocable finality during these few weeks of 1825. The firm had wavered once before, during the financial crisis of 1817, but now it seemed that the only solution was to decide permanently one way or the other. Once the decision had been taken, Taylor was able to stand back and view the state of their affairs dispassionately. He wrote to his sister Jenny in July:[53]

> The Sum of the whole Matter is this: I would rather part with all I have than be under Obligations which I cannot answer. But if I am not compelled to make such a Sacrifice I should be very glad, – & if any clear Sum should be left me, after all Debts due from T & H are paid, sufficient to buy any of the Copyrights, & to afford me a Chance of conducting Business again without Injury to others, I shall have great Pleasure in availing myself of it.
>
> Adding Hessey's Portion of the Stock &c to what would have been mine makes a Total of . . . 11653 £ To this must be put 6085 £ accounts owing us (6085) and the Copyright and Stock of the London Magazine —— 1400 – These Sums on the one Side amounting to —— 19138 comes to a little more than our outstanding Debts which including Bonds & all other Obligations amount to 18260 £ –

This letter, never previously published, reveals for the first time precisely how close the firm had come to complete insolvency. After nearly twenty years of partnership, the final profit made by them amounted to £878 – an annual profit, on the average, of just £46.

At the beginning of 1816, Taylor had first written in explicit terms of his desire to create a publishing list of 'genuine, original Authors'. Now, a mere nine years later, the success of his policy was indisputable. Within these few years, Hessey and he had published the work of Keats and Hazlitt, Lamb, Cary, and Carlyle, Hood, De Quincey, and

Landor, Clare and Coleridge; and through the pages of the *London*, they had brought out also the work of lesser talents, Reynolds and Procter, Cunningham, Ayton, and Wainewright. To encourage, understand, and publish the writing of such an illustrious company was truly the work of a lifetime. Yet for Taylor, it had been concentrated within a mere nine years of his life. During this period, he had had only Hessey, and occasionally Woodhouse, Hood, or Reynolds, to assist in the many tasks of the house. He employed no reader. He acted as adviser, letter-writer, business manager, transcriber, editor, and publisher, as well as the host and friend of many writers. The final toll of such constant activity was almost inevitable. It was impossible that the sustained application demanded of him during these years could finally be borne without seriously injuring his health. In the end, indeed, it wore him out.

During the first years of the firm's expansion, he seemed able to withstand the many demands made on his time and energy. But his health was never good, and with the added burden of the *London Magazine* in 1821, his letters begin to speak with increasing frequency of tiredness and depression. At the end of May of that year, he had written to his father with bright hopes for the future of the firm and the magazine. But a week later, he wrote again: 'I am well nigh tired already of the Cares & Fatigues of my new Avocation, which has come upon me when I am too full of other Work to be able to take it with any degree of Comfort.'[54] And to James, a few days later,[55] and at the end of June:[56]

I have not Time to say much, my letter-writing has so much increased that my pen is seldom out of my hand till midnight – Joined with the Accession of reading & writing which the Mag brings is an Influx of MSS. for Opinion – . . . I suspect in time it will fill up more of my Time than is consistent with a due regard to Health –

I never felt so much oppressed with Care and never felt my Hands so full of Work as since you left London. . . . I only fear that my Health will not stand all this.

By the end of the year, the magazine was 'haunting' his mind,[57] and a single phrase in a letter to Clare defined the whole trouble: 'we have no *Repose* in London.'[58] By the autumn of 1822, George Darling, the firm's doctor, told Hessey that if Taylor did not give up 'the present Application & Confinement', he would seriously damage his health.[59]

Plans were mooted that he should either retire completely from the firm, or take on an assistant, and even that the *London* should be sold.[60] Hessey was convinced that he could not 'bear up under eighteen more such months of Anxiety'; but he did, for there was no change in the management of the house or the magazine. The toll was inevitable. He was 'very seriously unwell' in July 1822, and away from London for six weeks during the autumn. A year later, the same pattern of overwork and enforced recuperation was repeated. At the beginning of 1824, he was writing to Clare: 'I have been very ill since I last wrote. . . . This is the first Day that I have taken up my Pen since. . . . I feel tired with even this little Writing.'[61] In the autumn of the year, he was again away from London, ill. Finally, in 1825, with the many problems arising from the sale of the *London* and the dissolution of partnership on his mind, he collapsed. About 10 August, he suffered an attack of 'brain-fever', and for some days, Hessey wrote to Clare, there was scarcely any hope that he would live.

'For ten days', Hessey reported, 'he was in a high state of delirium. . . . A bilious attack with inflammation in the bowels was the first form of his disease, but when the bowels were better his head was affected.'[62] His mind began to wander. He became suspicious of those about him and felt a 'pressure & tightness upon his brain', which reminded him of the symptoms that Clare had experienced during his illnesses. George Darling attended him throughout the fever, and administered 'very severe medicines' as well as bleeding him profusely.[63] But even with the constant help and vigilance of Darling and Hessey, the fever remained. On 21 August, Hessey wrote to James: 'Yesterday we were all very much alarmed & so was the Doctor – the long continuance of the fever, and the unyielding obstinacy of the delirium, made him feel very doubtful of the issue –'[64] As Taylor continued to fight his illness, several friends read to him. He still remained 'under some false impressions', but was not altogether unable to form 'a tolerably correct judgment of what was going on'. He delighted most in hearing the Acts of the Apostles, Shakespeare's sonnets, and the poetry of Keats and Clare – before all others, these books seem to have been the points of reference from his past life upon which his mind now rested. Most especially, his thoughts turned at the height of the fever towards those deepest beliefs which had informed his own life:[65]

> I had . . . the same convictions (I am happy to add) of the indestructible Nature of my own Soul. It seemed to glow like a spark of Fire beneath a pile of Mountains, & nothing would

extinguish or injure it – had the whole World been heaped together over it I felt as if it was impossible to be crushed.

Slowly he began to gain strength, and after 20 August, each day brought a better hope of his recovery. On the twenty-first, Hessey was able to write to James that his pulse was lower, and his mind calmer. Darling could not yet declare him out of danger, 'yet if he continues to go on in his present state there is every reason for a good hope of his recovery – that of course will be a work of time, but we shall be very thankful for any Conditions –'[66] A fortnight later, although he was still 'very weak from the vigorous measures that men of necessity pursued with him', he had begun to gain some strength, and there was no longer a fear for his life. But it was to be many weeks before he was able to return to work. As Hessey realised, 'he never had so severe an illness before';[67] 'he has had a very serious shock and I fear he will not get over it for some time.'[68]

The reasons for Taylor's illness are clear enough. The concentrated energy and application that he had devoted to the firm and its business during the previous nine years had finally exhausted him too completely. He was now no longer able to draw upon reserves of strength to tide him over the most exacting periods of mental fatigue. He had done too much in too short a time with too little assistance. And the price of such application had now been exacted. He had finally worn himself out.

Few eras in publishing history can have ended so precisely in time. At the end of June, the firm dissolved partnership; in July, the *London Magazine* was sold; in August, Taylor was seriously ill. Each of these events of the summer of 1825 was, in itself, momentous enough. In combination, they marked clearly the turning point of Taylor's life. He was now forty-four, and his illness seems to have marked not only a physical but also a mental climacteric. It had emphasised without ambiguity what Darling had been warning him for years – that he could not continue the work he had been doing without permanently injuring his health. If he had once been able to turn a blind eye upon such advice, it was now impossible. From this summer onwards, his mind began increasingly to turn away from publishing imaginative literature towards the demands of a new generation – a generation which was reading, not Keats and Clare, but works of education and Useful Knowledge; not poetry, but the new sciences. The romance of Fleet Street and Waterloo Place was all but over.

'No publisher of poetry now':
the years 1826-64

As the summer of 1825 passed, an era came to a close. A few vestiges of the firm's old interests did in fact survive until the following year, but these few publications, the odd letter or conversation about literature, began to appear increasingly out of place in an alien world. Having slowly recuperated from his illness during the autumn, Taylor spent part of the new year organising material for Clare's *Shepherd's Calendar*, and during these months too, he was involved in publishing a book by the 'gypsy gentleman', George Borrow. A collection of Borrow's verse entitled *The Romantic Ballads* had been published in Norwich on 10 May 1826; but seemingly the poet was convinced that local demand would far from exhaust the edition of 500 copies, for immediately after publication he enquired of Allan Cunningham whether Taylor would be willing to accept the book under his imprint. A London connection might invigorate sales: 'They are well printed, as you see, and in his hands, with a little reviewing and advertising, would most likely go off.'[1] Taylor was evidently eager to publish the work, for Cunningham replied only three days later to say that he had accepted the offer. Later that year, the book duly appeared under his imprint, but it did not answer. The poetry was uninspired. The Reviews ignored it. Not unjustly, it appeared and disappeared in silence.[2]

In much wider contexts also, it could be sensed during 1826 that the literary world which Taylor and Hessey had known was fast passing away. The dissolution of partnership seemed indeed to reflect the critical state of imaginative literature in general, which appeared to be almost on the verge of crumbling completely. In the early months of the year, the country was caught in an economic crisis which hit severely many sections of the trading community. The whole of London, Taylor wrote to James, was suffering from 'money fever',[3] and the lack of public confidence exacted an especially heavy toll of booksellers and publishers. As Charles Knight later recalled, 'half the

Row was shaky',[4] and many houses, unable to meet the sudden run upon them for payment, crashed into bankruptcy. On 16 January, Taylor wrote to Bakewell that the whole of the publishing trade was in 'a terrible State':[5]

> Hurst Robinson stopt on Saturday for near 500,000 £ – & it is not doubted that T. Hurst (late Longman's) is ruined by the Assistance he has pledged himself to obtain for them. . . . I am sorry to add that so far as Constable is alluded to I fear the Suspicion is too well founded. . . . Several smaller Houses in the Trade have failed. . . . Bonsor . . . feels sure he says that not more than *2* or *3* Houses in Paternoster Row can stand – I never saw him so alarmed.

The collapse of many firms in London – among them one of the giants, Constable's – must again have brought home to Taylor in a particularly immediate way the impossibility of divorcing the cause of serious literature from the firm financial structure of the publishing house. But, as he saw clearly, the bankruptcies of 1826 revealed more than the financial instability of many firms. They augured a slump in literature, particularly in poetry. As a writer in Blackwood's *Maga* accurately remarked: 'Few write poetry . . . and nobody at all reads it. Our poets . . . have over-dosed us.'[6] The public had been satiated. No longer was it conceivable that 10,000 copies of a poem would sell on the very day of publication, as had happened in 1814 with Byron's *The Corsair*. Taylor wrote to Clare:[7]

> The season has been a very bad one for new books, and I am afraid the time has passed away in which poetry will answer.

> All the old poetry buyers seem to be dead, and the new race have no taste for it. The fact is, Men's circumstances are not so good as they formerly were, and fancy book buying is a luxury which they can't afford to indulge in as they once could.

In Helpstone, Clare quietly mourned that 'the age of Taste' was 'in dotage & grown old in its youth',[8] and for others of the old *London* circle too, the years of glory had almost vanished. In 1824, during the last months of the magazine's existence under Taylor's editorship, a contributor had commented upon the 'sensuality, effeminacy, fluency, eloquence, and lack of intellectual content' in contemporary poetry.[9] Now, in the years immediately preceding the Reform Bill, these words rang out even more persistently. Charles Lamb complained of 'the vague, dreamy, wordy, *matterless* poetry of this empty age',[10] and lamented the decline of authorship as a profession: "tis useless to write poetry with no purchasers. 'Tis cold work Authorship without something to puff one into fashion.'[11] 'The best thing', he thought, 'is never to hear of such a thing as a bookseller again or to think there are publishers; second hand Stationers and Old Book Stalls for me. Authorship should be an idea of the Past.'[12]

For many, of course, authorship remained very much a thing of the present, and there could be no greater mistake than to suggest that the slump in poetry and imaginative literature reflected a general decline in the number of books published each year, or the public interest they aroused. On the contrary, despite the economic crisis of 1826 and the subsequent bankruptcy of many houses, the number of books brought out in England between 1826 and 1832 shows a small but steady increase.[13] Even more indicative of the relative health of much of the trade is the fact that vast sums for copyright and high sales were still common. In 1827, *The Keepsake*, an example of those 'combinations of show and emptiness, yclept Annuals' that were detested by Lamb,[14] sold an estimated 15,000 copies.[15] As another illustration, the cheap fashionable novels with which Henry Colburn flooded the reading market from 1826 onwards were reputed on a conservative estimate to earn him an annual profit of over £20,000.[16] In 1829, to take a further example, Harriette Wilson's *Memoirs* went through thirty editions within twelve months;[17] and a year later, 4,000 copies of Samuel Rogers's *Italy* were sold within a fortnight.[18] There remained an energy in the trade and a ready public for these kinds of books. But the sense of buoyancy suggested by these figures was little more than a buoyancy created by the invincible sentimentalism of the reading public, its unquenchable thirst for scandal and intrigue, and the desire of middle-class readers to peep through the curtains of the aristocrat's drawing-room, thereby gaining a gentility by proxy. The books revealed a tinsel world. They were the superficial ornaments of an entrenched philistinism. Literature which sought to express an enduring seriousness of vision became lost, for a few brief years, in a no-man's-land, with few writers and few readers.

The whole mind of society was beginning to move elsewhere. As Bulwer Lytton perceptively remarked: 'Every time has its genius; the genius of this time is wholly anti-poetic.'[19] The *Westminster Review*, the mouthpiece of Bentham's philosophical radicalism, clearly voiced the concerns of a new generation:[20]

we have risen to the station which we occupy, not by literature, not by the knowledge of extinct languages, but by the science of politics, of law, of public economy, of commerce, of mathematics; by astronomy, by mechanics, by natural history. It is by these that we are destined to rise yet higher. These constitute the business of society, and in these we ought to seek for the objects of education. . . .

. . . Literature is a seducer; we had almost said a harlot. She may do to trifle with; but woe be to the state whose statesmen write verses, and whose lawyers read more in Tom Moore than in Bracton.

However perverse the philistinism of this viewpoint, however much it ignored the complex ways in which literature can and does affect the whole fabric of a society, it epitomised the tone of an age in which poetry had been eclipsed by mechanics, literature by politics. There was no dearth of books, but they were little more than fashionable and anaesthetisingly genteel. Literature had become a decoration. Education and above all politics began to touch the lives of ordinary readers more deeply than poetry ever could. 'Society is become a sort of battlefield', Fanny Kemble wrote in 1831, 'for every man (and every woman too) is nothing if not political.'[21] And T. F. Dibdin, who some twenty years previously had written *The Bibliomania or Book-Madness*, now composed a melancholy sequel entitled *Bibliophobia. Remarks on the Present Languid and Depressed State of Literature and the Book Trade.* 'The wished for *Reform in Parliament*', he commented, 'like Aaron's serpent, has swallowed up every other interest and pursuit.'[22]

Taylor himself saw too how greatly the growing political concerns of the public were eclipsing the cause of imaginative literature. In July 1831, he spoke with Longman's, who argued to him that the substantial decline in the sales of their *Cabinet Cyclopaedia* was due to 'the unsettled State of the Country on the Reform Q[uestion]'.[23] He heard throughout the year persistent complaints of a dearth of trade in London, and realised clearly that 'unless a Change takes place soon . . . many will be ruined'.[24] His prognosis was not wrong, for by the autumn, to take a single example, over six hundred London printers were out of work.[25] *The Athenaeum* commented: 'all in literature continues dull as a great thaw', and briefly diagnosed the chief cause:[26]

in truth, till the great question of reform is settled, we need look for no commanding works in either literature or art . . . the great market of literature will not open its gates full and wide, till the public mind is settled – and perhaps not then.

If so much of Taylor's genius as a publisher had previously derived from his unwillingness to blindly endorse the fashions of public taste, his activities now began to reflect more and more the concerns of his age. For many months after dissolving partnership with Hessey, he was undecided whether to continue as a publisher or to retire altogether from the trade. 'If I had a Partner with Money,' he wrote to James, 'I should still be most willing to continue. My Dread is that I may involve my Friends & this paralyses me.'[27] Finally, in the summer of 1827, he applied for the post of publisher and bookseller to the newly created University of London. He had distinguished support. Henry Brougham, Sir James Mackintosh, and Dr Birkbeck promised to argue his case, and on 8 December, a meeting of the University Council appointed him to the post.[28] Two brief sentences from his letters to Clare[29] about this time reveal how greatly indeed the emphasis of his work had shifted:

I think in future I shall confine my Speculations to Works of Utility. . . .

. . . I am now surrounded by so unpoetical a lot of men that our old subjects are seldom on the carpet.

His new list of publications reflected as clearly as anything could the change undergone. They were, as he fully recognised, 'of the slow & useful Kind rather than the obviously desirable.'[30] His interest had been caught by the growing public demand for textbooks and studious educational works, for volumes introducing science and mechanics and economic theory to an age awakening to new forms of knowledge. In 1827, he began a series of Interlinear Translations, volumes in which the classics of ancient literature were rendered line by line into English. Parts of Homer, Virgil, and Caesar appeared, as well as a Latin Grammar; and within nine months of publication, almost the whole of the first edition of each book had been sold.[31] George Darley, a former contributor to the *London*, was one of his writers who also discovered in science a readier public than he had ever done in literature. His *System of Popular Geometry*, published in 1826, was followed a year later by a book on *Popular Algebra*. He continued to build up his 'Scientific Library' with another work on geometry, one on *Popular Trigonometry*, another on *Familiar Astronomy*, all of which were published by Taylor before 1830. Hessey was convinced that Darley's works were 'the best Speculations' Taylor had ever embarked upon;[32] and indeed, it was only too clear that the 'Scientific Library', together with the Interlinears and the books of Dionysius Lardner on *The Steam Engine* and *Euclid*, provided a steadier sale than Keats, Clare, or Lamb had ever achieved:[33]

> I have the Pleasure to inform you that my Interlinears for some Reason or other sell very well, & so do Darleys Scientific Library – The Second Editions are published of the Homer, Virgil, & Geometry – & those of the Latin Grammar & Algebra are in the press. – Lardner's Steam Engine is also just published 2nd Edit – it bids fair to sell well – But the Euclid which will appear in March is the Book which in all Likelihood will benefit most by the Connection its Author & I have formed with the London Univ[y]. – It is greatly enquired for –

To compare the hopefulness of this letter with those many complaints in previous years of poor sales and lack of public recognition is to realise the ways in which Taylor was now gaining some measure of financial reward for his efforts. Far from trying to enlarge and create new directions in the taste of the reading public, he was now content to follow and endorse its demands. Yet even with the steady sales of textbooks to the University, his security still seemed likely to crumble at any moment. At the end of 1829, he suddenly wrote to James about a sum of money owed to a certain 'G.H.' He had not been able to pay the loan on the date due, for 'the only Way in which I could have given it to G.H. was by letting myself come to a State of Bankruptcy'.[34]

If Taylor just escaped this fate, though, Hessey did not. On 19 May 1829, the name of this man whom Clare had always thought so 'cautious' and 'monied' appeared in the register of bankrupts.[35] His business as bookseller had finally collapsed. Possibly with the financial assistance of Taylor and his other friends, he managed to survive until the following year, when he set up as a book and picture auctioneer in Regent Street. But it was a short-lived business. Early the following year, 1831, he decided to give up the trials of books altogether. He started a small school in Hampstead and began drilling the children of the Victorian age in the world of Lardner's steam engine and Darley's 'systems'.

Taylor too was moving further and further away from his earlier life. Not only his work but also some large part of his personality had clearly begun to change. As early as 1823, in the midst of his activity as editor of the *London*, he had spoken of a certain stillness that he had now begun to feel, a less frantic devotion to the cares of the world:[36]

> another Cause of my Quietness is perhaps to be found in the Trailing off from the World which I have felt growing upon me of late. I have less Ambition than I had, & except as a Measure of Duty I regard all Attempts to get forward in Life as beyond my Views of Happiness, or rather below them –

Now, six years later, the old energy which had sustained him on many occasions when the future seemed bleak had almost run dry:[37]

> To some these Things ['the Cares of Business'] would prove light & easy to be borne – Perhaps they would have appeared so to me once, but I have had a long Period of solitary Anxiety, & the Spring which was once elastic by constant Pressure loses its Activity. – This must be my Apology to those Friends who expect a greater Energy from me. . . . From 1825 (I might go further back) a Succession of Events of a trying Character has filled me with so much Concern, that I cannot recollect any Period (except when I was recovering from Illness) during all that Time when I could take up a Book and give proper Attention to it . . . nor have I looked into any but what in some Degree I was compelled to do – it ought not to seem strange therefore that at last I feel overfatigued & unfit to continue the Strife much longer.
>
> . . . I have so seldom an Opportunity of speaking of what oppresses me, that even to give it silent Utterance thus, acts as a Relief –

The spring had wound down. He had become quieter, less ambitious, and perhaps also more solitary. For the slowing down had been bought at a price. Not only was he now a world away from the books of imaginative literature he had once published, but his old circle of friends also had largely dispersed. From the *London* society, only Clare, Hessey, and Darley remained as friends who were still in touch. The tone of several of his letters to Clare revealed something of the isolation he felt:[38]

> Darley was with me last Night. . . . I am glad you liked him so much. [He] is the only Good that ever came from the London

Magazine – He is a staunch Friend, & one of the gentlest & kindest of Human Beings. It is very odd that I have never seen Reynolds for nearly two years. . . .

And again:[39]

> I am no publisher of poetry now. The rest of our formerly gay party are dispersed, and they seldom think of the quondam [spirit?] of the Magazine which bound us in common bond of brotherhood together.

In 1830 Hessey too spoke the same story in a letter to Clare. Charles Lamb was still 'the same kind-hearted creature as ever', but he had not seen Hood or Reynolds for many months, nor Allan Cunningham 'except by mere chance' – 'they are scattered abroad in various directions and have new pursuits and new friends.' Richard Woodhouse had left for Madeira with 'strong and alarming Symptoms of Consumption', and Hessey feared he was in much danger. Darley too had now left for the Continent. Most grievous of all, Hazlitt was very ill, near dying. With Taylor again in the countryside recuperating from ill-health, Hessey forgot old disputes and visited the essayist whilst there was still time: 'I saw him twice on Monday, but yesterday he was too ill to see me. I fear his mind is quite as ill at ease as his body.'[40] Three days later, Hazlitt was dead. Together with Lamb and Hazlitt's son, Hessey was with him when he died.[41]

In other ways too, old associations were gradually disappearing. Both Taylor and Hessey had gained new societies, but they could not forget earlier days; and at times, the memory of the help they had given many writers whom they now never saw provoked in Taylor particularly a feeling that they had been deserted.[42] Perhaps, in his most depressed state, it seemed to him that the firm's authors had taken what they had offered in palmier days and had now left to follow other pursuits and other friends. In some respects, he may have been justified; but one result at least of such a feeling was deplorable. In 1833, he heard that Charles Lamb was intending to bring out, under Edward Moxon's imprint, a volume to be entitled *The Last Essays of Elia*. Well over half the material for the book was to consist of essays previously published in the *London*, and the copyright of this material Taylor believed was his. At the beginning of March, he wrote to Moxon threatening to apply for an injunction against publication unless he received some compensation. Lamb's eruption is well known.[43] Taylor claimed that he had bought the copyright of the essays from Baldwin, but Lamb had a far different interpretation: 'No *writing*, and no *word*, ever passed between Taylor, or Hessey, and me respecting copy right. This I can swear.' And, in a more imaginative flight of damnation:

> to lay his desecrating hands upon Elia! Has the irreverent ark-toucher been struck blind I wonder –? The more I think of him, the less I think of him. His meanness is invisible with aid of solar microscope, my moral eye smarts at him. The less flea that bites little fleas! The great Beast! the beggarly nit!

He applied to his lawyer friend, Thomas Noon Talfourd, for advice about this 'son of a bitch in a manger' who would neither 'print, himself, nor *let* print'.[44] But Talfourd's reply seems to have been at best enigmatic, for by the end of the year, Lamb had both written to Procter asking him to give Taylor some £30 as a settlement, and had seen Taylor and Moxon at law in a case which Moxon ultimately won.[45]

The argument was not without its moments of comedy, and in earlier days perhaps, there might have been a time for such words. But now, the dispute seemed unfitting, and unworthy of both men's generosity of spirit. Within two years, Taylor was writing to Clare to report that Lamb too had died: 'Poor Charles Lamb is dead – perhaps you had not heard of it before – He fell down and cut his Face against the Gravel on the Turnpike Road, which brought on the Erisypelas, & in a few Days carried him off –'[46] The letter also contained news of the death of another friend in whose company both Taylor and Hessey had delighted on many occasions – the red-haired, philological lawyer, Richard Woodhouse. Like Keats, he had followed the sun in the hope that a warmer climate would cure his consumption; but finally, on 3 September 1834, the disease had killed him. In his will, he gave to Taylor the half-length portrait of Keats, painted after the poet's death by Hilton; also many other portraits, sketches, and busts of him, together with manuscripts and letters in his hand, and much material relating to him. 'In fact', he wrote of Taylor, 'they belong to him but I have collected and kept them.'[47] Reporting Woodhouse's death to Clare, Taylor mourned the 'good kind hearted Friend' of them both,[48] but as for the collection of Keats's manuscripts,

> I don't know whether it will be possible for me to do anything with them. I should like to print a complete Edition of Keats's Poems, with several of his letters, but the world cares nothing for him – I fear that even 250 copies would not sell.

In his diligent way, Taylor continued to publish the textbooks of a new generation. His house, now removed to 30 Upper Gower Street, close by the University, became a favourite resort of scientists and currency reformers; and he himself began to compose those studious treatises on economic theory which he had once despaired of ever having time enough to write. *An Essay on Money* appeared in 1830, *The Standard and Measure of Value* and . . . *an Analysis of the Subjects of Currency* in 1832, *Currency Fallacies Refuted* in 1833, *A Catechism of the Currency* and *A Catechism of Foreign Exchanges* in 1835. He had indeed plunged into the Victorian age with a vengeance. But he was, in his own words, 'no publisher of poetry now', and the romance of Fleet Street and Waterloo Place had vanished completely. Perhaps his last act which echoed back firmly to the days of Keats and the Londoners was his visit to John Clare in December 1836. The two men talked together and remembered the past. But during the pauses in their conversation, Taylor noticed Clare's mouth moving continually, whispering words without sense. Within six months, the poet had begun upon the years of High Beech and Northampton Asylum.

Taylor was to live for nearly thirty years longer, surviving almost all of his contemporaries from Keats's circle and the *London Magazine*. They were years of useful and honest endeavour, but one searches in vain for the inspiration and imaginative energy which had so characterised his mind in earlier days. His breadth of interest and knowledge was still astonishing, and indeed, it is probably during this period of his life that his comprehensiveness of mind, first nurtured by Trye and Stevenson in Retford, flowered most fully. With remarkable scholarship and fluency, he continued to range over many diverse subjects that might well have proved the downfall of a lesser talent. Within the five years from 1841 to 1845, toiling through volume after volume of figures and elaborate calculations, he wrote no less than eleven books and pamphlets on one aspect or another of the country's economic distress and the necessity for currency reform. In 1844, amidst all this, he also plunged into biblical prophecy and attempted to elucidate the Apocalypse of the Book of Revelation in *Wealth the Name and Number of the Beast, 666*. He continued to read in astronomy, in Greek and Hebrew, in antiquities and archaeology. In the early 1850s, he was at work preparing an edition of the New Testament, in which words were emphasised with a view to reproducing as closely as possible 'the tone in which they were spoken by our Lord and his Apostles'. In the early 1860s, he was researching into weights and measures, both ancient and modern, systems of measurement, and the Great Pyramid of Egypt. The sheer mental dexterity and breadth of knowledge displayed in these and many other books is undeniable; and perhaps there still remains a compulsive fascination in these revelations of the adaptability and quixotry of his mind. But save for isolated passages in his economic treatises, which were genuinely concerned to relieve the often appalling hardship of the working classes, these books touched reality only rarely. More often, they were careful works of scholarship, in which it seems as if he had almost become hypnotised by the fluency of his own learned rhetoric. A few pages from his finest letters to Keats or Clare are worth far more.

His publishing career continued to prosper quietly. In 1836, he entered upon a new partnership with a Mr Walton, and together the new firm remained as booksellers and publishers to the London University. Their list was studious and uninspired, and the demands of the university continued to weigh it down with the necessary textbooks for generations of students. Grammars of English, Latin, Greek, and Hebrew appeared; scientific manuals by Dionysius Lardner; treatises on mechanics and midwifery, economics and chemistry; Augustus de Morgan on mathematics. Education had indeed captured his mind.

Yet throughout these years, events occurred which might have brought back to him, if only for a short while, the more imaginative emphasis of his earlier life. From time to time, old friends called at Upper Gower Street to talk and reminisce. In 1838, George Darley called on him in company with Joseph Severn, and for a brief hour or two memories of Keats must have filled the air. A year earlier, there had been a letter from another member of Keats's circle, John Hamilton Reynolds, who nostalgically recalled the events and personalities of another age:[49]

> We are now strangers, – We, who were 'in the better part of your life, & the happiest part of mine' always together, – never now meet. . . .
> What days – were *the* days of the London! – I 'try back' as the Huntsman says – over the hours of Early-Hood – Earnest-Hessey – bleak Dr Darling – twinkling Clare, – 'tipsy-joy & jollity' Lamb – Drear-Carey, – Long-*taled* Cunningham – and beautiful Mrs Jones! – Where are all? – or most of them? –
> I am always dabbling with my pen – like a grey-headed Duckling – old in myself – but young in my love of the stream. You are always publishing good books – which are quite out of my line.

Hessey remained, as always, the closest of friends, continuing to teach at his school in Hampstead. But in 1840, he moved to Huddersfield, where his son Francis had been appointed Principal of the Collegiate School, and yet another of Taylor's friends was now separated from him. Very probably, Taylor visited his old partner several times in Huddersfield, and there would have been time and opportunity then to sustain their friendship and recall past days. But the continuation of their relationship seems the only thread which firmly connects with the years in Fleet Street and Waterloo Place. The pattern of all other associations between the firm and its old writers was now a matter of chance meetings, the odd letter which revived memories, the transient conversation. Even these were becoming fewer. By 1846, Hood was dead, as were Cunningham and Cary. In November of that year, 'one of the real worthies of the earth', George Darley, died also. Hessey much regretted that he had not known of Darley's illness, 'for I should have been most glad to visit him and afford him such comforts as in a Bachelor's establishment are frequently wanting'.[50] But he had been out of touch with him, and the news had come too late.

Taylor, though, was not entirely forgetful of his earlier life. In 1848, he assisted Monckton Milnes in preparing his *Life and Remains of Keats*, and ten years later, Hessey was writing to him to report that Hood's son and daughter were planning the memorials of their father.[51] Information was needed about the old *London Magazine*:

> would you like your name to be known as Editor or not? I have
> added a Postscript containing this information which I think
> ought to be given, as the credit of managing & editing the *best
> Literary Magazine* that ever appeared certainly belongs to you,
> and it is worthy of no slight praise.

Hessey was not willing for the romance of Fleet Street to go entirely unrecorded, and from time to time he attempted to prod Taylor and turn his mind from economic theory and biblical scholarship to the men of great talent he had once known:[52]

> I always regretted that you did not take Keats's Name & Fame
> in hand. You & Woodhouse knew more of him than any one,
> and you might have made a very interesting Book of his Memoirs.
> Even now, you might, I should think do something with the
> materials Woodhouse left you.
>
> . . . I have always lamented that there was no Memoir of poor
> Hilton – His beautiful, retiring, amiable character, and his

decided genius, would form a nice subject, and it is a thousand
pities that such a man should have no record of him preserved....
You see I am chalking out amusement for you in your leisure.

Nothing came of Hessey's suggestions, but there remained one poet
whom Taylor did not forget. Throughout the years of Clare's asylum,
he continued to do his best for the poet's well-being. With Walton's
assistance, he supervised for nearly thirty years the payment of Clare's
expenses in High Beech and Northampton Asylum, as well as con-
tributing his share. In 1854, he was writing to the Surveyor of Taxes
in Kensington for a return of some tax on the poet's stock;[53] and
during this year too, he tried to achieve a more substantial honour for
Clare's name by publishing a complete edition of his poetry. The
copyright of *The Rural Muse* was purchased from How, and an offer
made to Routledge of all the Clare rights for £200.[54] There was
enthusiasm from many of the poet's friends for the venture, and a
willingness to help in editing, but negotiations with Routledge and
later with the publisher John Whitaker eventually fell through, and
no volume was ever destined to appear. Clare still remembered his
former publishers, and during one visit from his son, he 'inquired after
Taylor particularly'.[55] In company with Hessey, Taylor possibly
visited him in Northampton during September 1857;[56] and four years
later, though he could now scarcely move out of doors without
assistance, he was still managing Clare's dividends. These small acts,
like so many in the past, were of no startling significance in the cause
of literature. Yet, as Taylor perhaps realised, there is a kind of sanctity
in the sheer persistence of ordinary living, which deserves recognition.
Like the five pounds he had given Clare in 1834 to help buy some stock
for his small-holding, these undramatic acts perhaps played some small
part in easing the troubles of the poet and his family.

On 1 March 1853, at the age of 71, Taylor retired from publishing,
and for the last ten years of his life, he lived at 7 Leonard Place,
Kensington. He continued to read and write prolifically, and no less
than ten books and pamphlets on political economy, the Bible, and the
Great Pyramid appeared during this period.[57] Friends such as Charles
Strong recommended heavy volumes of comparative linguistics and
Sanskrit grammar to beguile the days of his retirement,[58] and tried to
persuade him to write his memoirs. But although Taylor recognised
that he had had 'such opportunities of knowing many Men of Genius
as fall to the lot of few', he had kept no record of events or conversations, and his memory was not now exact enough for the task.[59] His

health too was failing. He was troubled with a 'severe internal disease', and his eyesight was becoming worse. By 1861, in his eightieth year, he could not tell whether anyone was in a room he entered unless they were to move about.[60] Hessey too was unwell and unable to move without pain. On 25 May 1862, he wrote Taylor a letter which began 'My dear and oldest Friend', and quietly reported the death of his wife, Kate: 'I cannot let the sad Intelligence reach you from any one but myself – No one will or can feel it more than I am sure you will. . . . I can scarcely realise our loss yet. . . . God bless you my dear old friend – pray for us.'[61] And a year later, Taylor's beloved brother James, who had come to the firm's rescue on so many occasions in the past, died too. The two old men had survived them all.

During the last few months of his life, Taylor's mind was drawn more and more to the Christian beliefs which he had held throughout youth and middle age, and he rested now in the belief that death was no more than a 'falling asleep' and a 'momentary forgetfulness'. He tried also to come to some understanding of his life, of the justice of his actions, and the generosity of his spirit. Over thirty years previously, in what now must have seemed another world, he had written to John Clare: 'If my Life does not justify me in the Eyes of those who know me, I deserve Censure, and if it does I need not fear it.'[62] Now, as he neared his eighty-third birthday, he wrote simply: 'In some things I may have been right, and in a great many things I may have been wrong, but of one thing I am sure – I have always tried to be right.'[63] The words might justly stand as his own epitaph. On 5 July 1864, barely six weeks after the death of Clare in Northampton, he died.

Hessey's son Francis wrote, 'we have lost a truly good and great man':[64]

> I scarcely know how to communicate to my Father the sad
> tidings of his removal. They were indeed like Brothers through
> life: and I fear, from the precarious state of my Father's Health,
> that in death they will not be long divided.
>
> There is one little memorial of him that I should like to
> possess: – and one that will be valueless to any one else. It is *his*
> *spectacles*. My eyes and his were of the same degree of short-
> sightedness. . . .

Taylor's body was brought from Kensington back to Retford and the countryside he had known as a boy. He was buried in the village churchyard of Gamston, a few miles south of Retford, by a life-long friend, the Rev. John Twells; and here the University of London erected a tombstone to his memory. Hessey had a few more years to live, but they were uneventful and colourless. When he died on 7 April 1870, he, like Taylor, was buried in a village churchyard far from Fleet Street – in Manningford Bruce, Wiltshire.

The last thirty years of Taylor's life, full as they were with scholarship, writing, and endeavour in the field of educational publishing, brought him substantial honour and recognition from his contemporaries. Yet there can be no doubt that these years, useful and studious though they undeniably were, seem to lack now a clear focus. The recorded events of this period, indeed, often appear strangely unrelated, and one searches in vain for that immediacy and clarity of vision, that imaginative synthesis which had once so deeply informed his work in the days of Keats and the Londoners. The pattern of his life becomes fragmented, a protracted anticlimax after the romance of Fleet Street and Waterloo Place.

But from time to time during these years, events occurred which might, to his mind, have brought together the many aspects of his career in publishing. One such event, perhaps, was the publication of a book in 1833 entitled *Exposition of the False Medium & Barriers Excluding Men of Genius from the Public*, by R. H. Horne. Protesting against the general run of publishers who placed too much trust in ill-qualified 'readers', and who were themselves unwilling to run risks for the cause of serious literature, Horne specifically exempted from his criticism the old firm of Taylor & Hessey:[65]

> Perhaps no Publisher, within a given length of time, ever introduced half so many excellent works as Messrs. Taylor and Hessey; and they were the only publishers who ever accepted a book upon the sheer account of its merit. Mr. Taylor is himself a literary man and did not employ a Reader. What other publisher would have undertaken Carey's Dante? &c. Ayton's Essays were published as a 'work of love', and a memorial of the man.

But a part of Horne's purpose was more than mere encomium, pleasing though this might have been to the old partnership at the time. He tried also to analyse briefly some of the pervasive factors that had seemed to influence the publishing of literature in his generation, and especially the difficulties which Taylor and Hessey themselves had faced as publishers of new literature. He argued persuasively that the house's lack of financial success had been 'owing to the extra-ordinary force of the political tide at that period'. Several of the firm's books had sold well at first, only to be ignored completely after the politically motivated attacks of the Reviews. In a wider context, endorsing Hazlitt's argument, he saw also a reading public almost hypnotised by the brilliantly perverse rhetoric of the great Reviews. It had not been ignorance of the questions involved which had led the public to accept unquestioningly the tablets of stone handed down by Gifford or Croker, but a particular kind of moral cowardice. They were the acolytes who willingly granted the Reviews the role of critical arbiter, against whose verdict there was no appeal.

From the reading public, Horne turned finally to the publishers themselves, and to some definition of the vital part they played in the diffusion of literature:[66]

> A Publisher holds a most important station in the social
> machine, and on his judgment and integrity depend the
> introduction of intellect to the world, and often the direction in
> which it is wielded. Added to this, he should be able to estimate
> genius and talent, and also to calculate the 'form and pressure' of
> the time, and the *permanent* as well as changeful texture of the
> public mind and feeling.

So often in the course of this book, it has been suggested that Taylor's career is important, not simply for its intrinsic interest, but also for the ways in which it frequently reveals the wider problems of promul-gating literature in society. And it is now time to gather up the sug-gestions and to interpret the whole of his career in the light of Horne's analysis. How far did he truly estimate the genius of the writers he published, and in what ways was he able to direct their ideas upon the reading world? What was the 'form and pressure' of the years during which he built up the firm with Hessey, and how seriously did those pressures affect his work as a publisher? Not least of all, how did he adjudicate between the '*permanent* [and] changeful texture of the public mind' – how, indeed, did he help to foster the cause of literature, not only for his own but also for future generations?

{ 8 }

Literature, the publisher, and the reading public

There could be few better illustrations of the importance that the publishing house had attained in the eyes of Regency commentators than the words of one anonymous writer in 1825:[1]

> A literary man of the present day would as soon think of seeking patronage from the Emperor of Austria, or setting forth the talents and the virtues of the Spanish Ferdinand, as of placing his hopes of a hearing with the public upon the foremost noble-man in the land . . . this change has brought the publishers of books into an attitude of the greatest importance and honour; – it has made them the connecting link between the people of England and that which has made, is making, and shall continue to make the people of England superior to the people of every land where intellect has not the same unbounded scope.

There can be no doubt that, by the 1820s, the publishers of books in England had attained a position of far-reaching influence in the creation and promulgation of literature; that, upon their imagination, perception, and critical judgment, new works depended as never before in the history of English letters for their introduction into the literary world. Some of the reasons for this influence have already been suggested in several parts of this biography. The great Regency publishers no longer merely translated manuscripts into the printed book, but had begun in many various ways to influence the writing of literature, proposing some of its themes, justifying its novelty to critics and reviewers, and helping to promote its reception in the reading world. They frequently fostered a community of spirit amongst their authors by organising regular meetings where writers met and talked, and where an interaction of ideas and personalities was directly encouraged. They looked towards the 'sayees' of literature as well as the 'sayers' and, by attempting to reconcile the writer's ideal audience with the public that actually existed, became the adjudicators and 'connecting link' between the different demands of authors and critics, readers and reviewers. For Taylor & Hessey, as for Murray, Constable, Blackwood, and many others, the publisher had become by 1820 the bustling and sympathetic midwife for new writing. Almost every part of the making of literature, from the moment of its conception to its eventual fate in the reading market, was potentially his concern.

None of this emancipation in the world of publishing, of course, would ever have been possible without a similar and parallel emancipation of the writer himself. Indeed, the growing influence of the publisher in literary history begins with the increasing freedom of the writer from the constrictions often imposed by aristocratic patronage. Yet although the nature of this freedom for both author and publisher becomes most clearly formulated in the early years of the nineteenth century, its beginnings had in fact taken place over a century previously. The Copyright Act of 1709 recognised a writer's work as a property of value which could be sold in a free market, and therefore, as a commodity deserving legal protection. For much of the eighteenth century, certainly, the relationship between the writer and his market did not constitute the only process by which literature was written and disseminated. Aristocratic patronage continued to hold considerable sway, and even as late as 1820, as the dispute between Taylor and Lord Radstock has shown, the influence of class and wealth over literature was still wielded occasionally. But during this century, the commercial potential of literature, as a trade subject to the same economic laws as any other, is increasingly recognised. Writers begin to exploit the interests, not of the aristocrat, but of the market, of the growing reading public. Fielding dedicates his *Historical Register* to the public at large. Johnson declares, 'We have done with Patronage', and points to the development from 'the great' to 'the multitude' as the author's only employer. Goldsmith argues that poets now have 'no other patrons but the public'. By 1816, when Taylor and Hessey expanded the publishing side of their activities, the business of literature was clearly seen, not as an extravagance to decorate the lives of aristocrats, but as a trade and profession demanding dedicated specialists. In De Quincey's words, 'literature must decay unless we have a class *wholly* dedicated to that service, not pursuing it as an amusement only with wearied and pre-occupied minds'.[2]

The institution of the market as that point in the diffusion of literature where writer and reader met, and the growing number of authors depending entirely upon it for their livelihood, was an obvious and welcome liberation from the economic and moral influence of aristocratic patronage. But finally, this very emancipation led to a more subtle and devious kind of slavery. Only too quickly, literature became a commodity whose value was measured in commercial terms, not aesthetic or imaginative. Increasingly, writers became dependent upon the financial value of their work in a market where *laissez faire* doctrines allowed of only one criterion by which new works might be judged – their saleability. As Taylor's career has shown, a publisher could frequently assist authors in whom he believed with loans and even gifts of money to counter a lack of financial success; but he too was ultimately dependent upon the market to regain the expenses of publication. No house, obviously, could survive a succession of remaindered books. The publisher who brought out new works with a blithe disregard for their commercial potential invited certain bankruptcy.

Time and again in his career, as this study has often shown, Taylor was forced to recognise that the promulgation of literature could not be divorced from finance. It was indeed one of the most sustained pressures he faced. Throughout the firm's greatest years, the threats of a dissolution of partnership, the countless requests for loans, the many complaints of poor sales – all reveal the pervasive influence that economic forces exerted upon the house. Yet as both he and many of his writers saw, the development of literature into a trade had involved also a far more complex factor: the emergence of an influential reading public. It was no accident that the two had developed at the same time. The more a free market became the focal point in the diffusion of literature, the more powerful were the demands of the public over what was published. Their sheer size alone gave them the greatest economic control. By the 1830s, indeed, they had become to all intents and purposes the collective patrons of literature.

As early as 1803, during his brief stay at Lackington's, Taylor seems to have realised, if only in part, the nature and power of the new public evolving. No longer was it a relatively clearly defined group towards whom the imaginative writer might consciously direct his thoughts. Increasingly amorphous, its reading habits cut across traditional barriers of class and culture. Its interests had expanded to cover every field of knowledge and opinion. The works of Byron sold as much as rigorously orthodox religious publications. The tinsel word of the Annuals attracted as many readers as the passionate realism of Cobbett or other radical propagandists. Books of spelling sold as well as political pamphlets, works of history as much as the third-rate sentimental novel. For some authors, of course, particularly those with specifically political or religious themes, it was still possible to know their audience. In moral and political debate, the public fragmented into smaller groups with recognisably distinctive ideologies, and the writer consequently addressed a relatively clearly defined group within society. But for the poet and imaginative author whose theme was not overtly political or religious, and who addressed society as a whole, it no longer seemed possible to discern a consistency of taste or attitude in the reading public. Increasingly, he saw the public as a muddle and an abstraction, a constantly shifting shadow of confused feelings and beliefs which it was impossible to speak to directly.

The great increase in the numbers of the reading public was not the only difficulty to face writers of new literature. If the public had expanded, so too had the media by which literature was promulgated. The costly and finely embellished book of the aristocrat had long ceased to be the chief means by which the printed word was transmitted to an author's public. Pamphlets, annuals, cheap series, monthly and quarterly magazines, newspapers, reviews – all these had, by 1830, become firmly established media of very different kinds through which the reading population was addressed. Against such a background of expansion, both in the size of the public and in the channels through which new literature was conveyed to the market, it was inevitable that many imaginative writers should view their potential audience with a suspicion often verging upon hostility. The expansion of literacy had brought too much uncertainty to the dissemination of literature. That relatively clear process by which an author had been commissioned to write a book by his patron had now disappeared for ever, and whatever clarity had once existed became a muddle of insoluble problems and unanswerable questions. What permanent concerns of his society was any writer to reflect in his work? What medium did he choose to reach as wide a public as possible? How, indeed, was he to discern a public at all?

As many parts of this book have shown, several of the writers whose work was published by Taylor & Hessey reacted strongly against the increasing power of the reading public. Lamb attacked them indirectly in his contempt for Annuals, publishers, and 'fancy books'.[3] Coleridge explicitly condemned 'the multitudinous "public", shaped into personal unity by the magic of abstraction, [which] sits nominal despot on the throne of criticism'.[4] Clare believed that 'to tell them what they ought to think of Poetry would be as vain . . . as telling the blind to see'.[5] Above all, Keats was their fiercest critic. He saw them quite unambiguously as an 'Enemy', whom it was impossible to address 'without feelings of Hostility'. He claimed never to have written a single line of poetry 'with the least Shadow of public thought';[6] and in a letter to Haydon, he defined the essential conflict he saw between himself and his potential readers: 'I never expect to get any thing by my Books: and moreover I wish to avoid publishing – I admire Human Nature but I do not like *Men*. – I should like to compose things honourable to Man – but not fingerable over by *Men*.'[7]

The courage and integrity of Keats's many affirmations of creative autonomy cannot be doubted. And yet, as has been suggested, such fierce and inflexible independence held several dangers. Too easily the belief in a total imaginative freedom and an unswerving fidelity to the movements of poetic inspiration became a belief in an inevitable separation between a poet and his readers; and what this separation produced in turn was an ingenuous abstraction of the reading public itself. Unable to come to terms with his audience, Keats tried to translate the reality of it into a philosophic generality such as 'Man' or 'Human Nature' which he might address. Yet such an abstraction was a hypothesis which was unworkable from the very beginning, for it was an attempt to divorce the creation of literature from its promulgation. It did not recognise that, to survive, literature must be read by the fingerers as well as written in honour of mankind.

It would certainly be unjust to single out Keats as a lone commentator upon this tension between the ideal and real audience for literature, for his views were symptomatic of a general antipathy towards the public felt by many authors. Wordsworth, scarcely less forceful in his attack, proposed the same kind of distinction between 'Men' and 'Man:'[8]

> Still more lamentable is his error who can believe that there is anything of divine infallibility in the clamour of that small though loud portion of the community, ever governed by factitious influence, which, under the name of the PUBLIC, passes itself upon the unthinking, for the PEOPLE. Towards the Public, the Writer hopes that he feels as much deference as it is entitled to; but to the People, philosophically characterised, and to the embodied spirit of their knowledge . . . his devout respect, his reverence, is due.

Again, there can be no doubt of the courage and artistic integrity reflected in this distinction between the 'PUBLIC' and the 'PEOPLE'; but as with Keats's 'Men' and Man', it was an attempt by Wordsworth to isolate and consequently to elevate one part of the making of literature from the complete process. By emphasising the glory of the People or of Human Nature, both poets raised their own role above the trials of the market, since it was they who addressed 'the embodied spirit' of mankind's knowledge. This attempt to divide the making of literature into two distinct processes – one the actual creation of new works, the other the dissemination of them amongst the reading public – was not of course without beneficial effects. In practice, it manifestly did produce great art. But it revealed also a paradox which lay at the very heart of the debate between writer and public. In a central passage of the 1800 Preface to *The Lyrical Ballads*, Wordsworth argues that the object of poetry is the expression of truths 'not individual and local, but general and operative'. The poet expresses those passions, thoughts, and feelings which are 'the general passions, thoughts and feelings of men'. He writes under one restriction only, 'namely, the necessity of giving immediate pleasure to a human Being possessed of that information which may be expected from him, not as a lawyer, a physician, a mariner, an astronomer, or a natural philosopher, but as a Man'.[9] Yet, for many Romantic writers, this claim for poetry as an exploration of the shared and mutually understood experience of all men existed alongside the firm emphasis upon the difference between the writer and his public, and the result was that the belief in poetry as the finest expression of common experience became a hypothesis, an intellectualisation which was only rarely translated into the actual reality of the market. At the very point in the diffusion of literature where the desire to communicate a shared understanding was most severely tested, in the market itself, writers retreated into abstractions such as 'Man' or 'the People' and rejected the voice of the public. In the end, the audience they sought to address became, indeed, the product of a private imagination, not of the shared knowledge common to both them and their readers.

One of the most astute commentators of Regency society, Bulwer Lytton, recognised perceptively the result of this attempted divorce between the creation and promulgation of literature. In *England and the English*, the Romantic writer was depicted in the figure of Mr Lofty, a man who had built 'a wall between himself and other men':[10]

with all his genius, not knowing how to address mankind and disdainful of the knowledge, he does not a tithe of the benefit that he might: could he learn to co-operate with others, he might reform a world, but he saith with Milton 'The world that I regard is myself' . . . he is melancholic and despondent: he pines for the Ideal: he feels society is not made for the nobler aims, and

sickens at the littleness of daily life: he has in him all the elements
of greatness, but not of triumph: he will die with his best
qualities unknown.

Lytton's analysis is not without its moments of exaggeration, but in
his statement that many writers of his age had in them 'all the elements
of greatness, but not of triumph', he captured the tragedy of a generation. The complex relationship between social and artistic values in the
life of art had, in the end, become too muddled for a clear exposition
of the ways in which imaginative literature might be integrated into
the ordinary reader's common understanding. The separateness of the
artist's experience finally clouded any direct relationship with his
public into a condition of half-lights and uncertainty, distance and
isolation.

The problems of how the serious writer, conscious that he exists
socially as well as individually, may both reflect and disturb his readers'
experience, of how too he may attract both the ordinary reader and
the intellectual cenacle, lay at the centre of the tension between the
Romantic artist and his public. And yet, clearly, to accept unquestioningly these differences between writer and public as an inevitable state
of affairs is not without its dangers. Faced with the disappointments of
poor sales and the frequent acrimony of critical attack, it is possible
that several writers tended to romanticise and thus exaggerate their
isolation from the common reality in which their readers lived. As a
caveat, the argument of a later writer, Arnold Bennett, is worth
remembering:[11]

> The truth is that an artist who demands appreciation from the
> public on his own terms, and on none but his own terms, is
> either a god or a conceited and impractical fool. And he is
> somewhat more likely to be the latter than the former. He wants
> too much. There are two sides to every bargain, including the
> artistic. . . . The sagacious artist, while respecting himself, will
> respect the idiosyncrasies of the public. To do both is quite
> possible.

As a firm statement of faith in a productive relationship between writer
and reading public, this argument is undoubtedly of value. Yet it
bypasses, rather than resolves, the crucial problem. As Keats, Wordsworth, and Shelley found, a point is seemingly inevitably reached when
the serious author finds himself in conflict with the prevailing reading
taste of his age. Beyond that point, who is to compromise and what

form is the compromise to take? Is the writer to sacrifice some part of
his individuality and integrity for the sake of public demand and
understanding, or the reading public itself to be brought finally to
comprehend the exploration of human experience which new literature
expresses?

It would be miraculous indeed if Taylor's career were to provide a
clear answer to these questions, for the difficulty is still with us today
and seems likely to remain. Yet his work does point to one conclusion,
the mere recognition of which may help in future examinations of
the problem. Time and again in his career, he was brought face to face
with the infinite complexity of the ways in which literature comes to
be created and promulgated in society, with the tenuous, shifting
process by which any writer's vision is eventually communicated to
his readers. No two books published by the firm, indeed, ever followed
even roughly the same line of development from the moment of first
inspiration to the eventual understanding of them by individual
readers. The publication of Keats's *Lamia* was affected by moral and
political pressures which were not present in the introduction of
De Quincey's *Confessions* to the reading world. Clare's 1820 volume
was influenced by the last traces of aristocratic patronage, which never
appeared with the works of Lamb or Coleridge. The publication and
sales of Hazlitt's books were deeply affected by attacks from the
Reviews, whereas Cary's translation of Dante and Landor's *Imaginary
Conversations* received high critical acclaim. Acknowledging these
constantly shifting pressures upon the publication of new literature,
many contemporary commentators argued that there could therefore
be no permanent reconciliation between the serious writer and his
public. Isaac D'Israeli was only one of many who viewed the cause of
literature with quiet pessimism.[12]

> It is to be lamented . . . that even a bookseller may have too
> refined a taste for his trade; it must always be to his interest to
> float on the current of public taste, whatever that may be; should
> he have an ambition to *create* it, he will be anticipating a more
> cultivated curiosity by half a century; thus the business of a
> bookseller rarely accords with the design of advancing our
> literature.

An examination of many Taylor & Hessey publications demonstrates well the way in which the firm had often been compelled
merely to 'float on the current of public taste'. Mingled amongst the
work of Keats, Hazlitt, Clare, and the others, many more books

appeared which clearly endorsed the taste of the Regency reading public, without any attempt to enlarge it imaginatively. The Rev. Francis Hodgson's *Poems on Religious Subjects* follows the works of Hazlitt; De Quincey's *Confessions* are sandwiched between George Downes's *Letters from Mecklenburg and Holstein* and George Darley on *Popular Trigonometry*; Keats's poetry stands out between a series of Interlinear Translations and Elizabeth Kent's *Flora Domestica*. Yet although such books as these made up a considerable proportion of the firm's output, what remains chiefly remarkable about the house is that Taylor and Hessey did not compromise more often with the demands of the public. In this very fact, indeed, there perhaps lies some tentative resolution of the complex debate between writer and reading public, for by bringing out a proportion of books regardless of their market potential, the firm had attempted quite consciously to reduce the economic influence of the public. Two examples of their spirit of independence are especially noticeable. Throughout the house's greatest years, Taylor was clearly aware of the immense public appetite for novels of all kinds. Jane Taylor's tale *Display*, published by the firm in 1815, went through six editions in under two years, and the other novels produced by the Taylors sold on a scale which was never repeated by any of the house's other authors. Again, three years after the dissolution of partnership, as has been seen, Taylor wrote to Carlyle about the success of Colburn's series of fashionable tales and acknowledged that 'if a work is not a mere novel, it must be absolutely useful & even necessary, or it will not be cared for'.[13] Yet apart from the tales of Ann and Jane Taylor, the firm published only two other novels in a list of some 110 books.

Similarly with political publications. As this biography has often shown, one of the most intransigent pressures upon the house's activities had been the influence of politics. The scarcely veiled hysteria of *Maga* and the *Quarterly* had effectively killed the sales both of Keats's *Endymion* and of Hazlitt's works. *Lamia*, likewise, had been buried beneath a mass of pamphlets arguing the pros and cons of the case against Caroline of Brunswick. Much of the reason for the curious no-man's-land in which literature found itself during the years immediately preceding 1832 had been the concern felt by all classes for the outcome of the great Reform Bill. Taylor's generation had been, above all else, a political generation, confusedly steering its way from a state of potential revolution to some form of social stability. Yet in the firm's list of publications, the political turmoil of the age is reflected on only one occasion. In the whole of the fourteen years

between 1814 and 1827, Taylor & Hessey published a single, incon-
spicuous volume concerned with politics, *A Letter . . . on the Subject of
the Poor Laws*, by Richard Blakemore.

The reasons why the firm did not publish social works and fashionable novels assured of capturing the public imagination are not difficult
to discern. Throughout the house's finest years, Taylor constantly
emphasised in letters and conversations the uniqueness of the serious
writer's vision. The creative force of his imagination made 'Action,
Thinking, Argument, Description, something different, & superior
to what it would be in any other Person'.[14] Even the act of criticism
inevitably involved 'an Inferiority of Mind' because it was 'founded
upon what the Poet has done'.[15] Although as a publisher, he was often
compelled to acknowledge the demands of the reading public, his
mind rested finally upon the literature itself and upon those who wrote
it. One of his earliest remarks about publishing may be recalled. In
1816, he rejected Leigh Hunt's *Letters of Harry Brown* because some
parts of them, "tho proper for a newspaper, are not well adapted for
a Volume which we should hope would live longer than such Topics
and such Men are likely to be remembered'.[16] It was the statement of
a man whose eye was as much on the future as on the present. The
political situation which Hunt had described would, in the very nature
of things, inevitably pass, and the passionate debates upon reform or
the Poor Laws no longer capture the mind with as great an immediacy
and intensity. *Sub specie aeternitatis*, literature was more likely to
survive.

After 1825, as has been seen, Taylor turned more and more towards
the reading public in an attempt to answer its demands. Increasingly,
he was content to reflect the interests of the age in his publications,
with few attempts to enlarge or create new directions in public taste.
His role, which had once been so deeply concerned with the creation
of a dynamic relationship between literature and society, now saw
that relationship become increasingly passive and static. There can
be no doubt that his later books generally sold well; yet despite this
answering of public demand (perhaps, indeed, because of it), his was
not a Victorian achievement, recognised and esteemed though he
became. His true achievement as a publisher lay in the eight or nine
years between 1816 and 1825, in the struggles for Keats and Hazlitt
and the encouragement of De Quincey and Clare. During these years,
his importance often lies in the fact that he acts as a focus for those
many pressures which were brought to bear upon the publication of
new literature. Looking towards his writers, towards the Reviews,

towards moral attitudes and public demand, he mirrors indeed the confused evolution of a new literacy. Historically, he stands at the beginning of an era in which the publisher becomes one of the chief mediators between writer and reading public, and his career shows how the deep tension between them could, with patience and under-standing, be transformed into a kind of controlled tug-of-war. Yet his importance lies also on a more personal level. By helping several authors with loans and gifts of money, by continuing to encourage their efforts after critical attack, he had directly tried to wrest from the reading public some of its power of collective patronage. In so doing, he had acted not only as a publisher, but indeed, as a patron himself of new literature.

However greatly both Taylor and Hessey were concerned with the problems of fostering new writing, the mind almost instinctively turns finally to Taylor himself, to his literary opinions and his personal force and influence upon the writers he met daily. In his judgments and analyses of literature, at least, there can be little doubt that he possessed a remarkable perception and innate sensitivity to the poetic revolution of his age. The repeated emphasis in his many writings upon imagina-tion and creativity, the sustained battle waged against scholarly poet-asters who 'by dint of Words and the Repetition of certain Greek and Latin lines' dressed themselves up as 'the Sons of Apollo',[17] the constant belief in the superiority of creative over critical writing[18] – all these beliefs, amongst many others, reveal him as one of the great publishers of his generation in his recognition of the new energy, spirit, and direction of Romantic literature. It struck an instinctive chord in his mind, and his reaction to it was complete, and unalloyed by any hearkening back to the less persistently troubled world of eighteenth-century writing. No poet himself, he knew what poetry was; and despite dissension and difficulty, his support for those who wrote it most brilliantly never wavered.

In any lasting judgment about his personal force upon the house's writers, however, one's final impressions tend to be more confused and ill-defined, for as one looks back over his many actions and opinions, so much in his character seems a paradox of conflicting emotions and interests. He was an antiquarian and a scholar, fascinated even during the firm's greatest years with the subjects of linguistics, science, and economics. Yet this decisive intellect, delighting as his friends pointed out in 'order, precision, exactness and fact',[19] was at the same time acutely receptive to the more diffuse workings of the poetic imagination. Ambition and a strong desire for recognition were part of a personality which, in the quietest and most self-effacing of ways, answered the various needs of writers much more than could have been reasonably expected from any publisher. As several parts of this biography have shown, his caution and moral earnestness often tended to alienate the sympathies of authors, yet he undertook the publication of *Endymion* in the very year that the firm's final profit had been precisely £2, and courageously stood by both Keats and Hazlitt after the attacks from the Reviews against their supposed immorality. He was on several occasions criticised for his distance and aloofness, for standing too much upon his dignity, and yet with Hessey, he instituted the *London Magazine* dinners and contributed greatly to the talk and fellowship of those evenings. He generously lent or gave his writers considerable sums of money, often aware that he might not be repaid for many years, if at all; and yet he instituted niggling, legalistic claims for copyright against Lamb and later De Quincey.[20] There can sometimes be seen in his character a certain sternness of final judgment, a certain fixity of attitude which smacks of self-conscious rectitude; but then often, one notices also the uncertainty and fluidity of his opinions, and his manifest delight in conversation and debate. He formed deep and lasting personal friendships with his brother James, with Hessey, Keats, and Clare, and yet he managed to quarrel, often seriously, with many of the writers of the house. At one time or another, Keats, Hazlitt, Lamb, Hood, De Quincey, Clare, and Landor all found cause for complaint with him, sometimes justifiably. But then again, Hessey, who knew him more closely than any of them, could write of him to Clare:[21]

> I am sure you will rejoice with me at anything which benefits
> that most kind and generous and friendly and disinterested of
> men. I have known John Taylor now nearly thirty years most
> intimately, and the more I know of him the more I esteem and
> love him. He has been indeed a true and tried friend to me when
> friends were scarce.

Where, beneath all these seeming contradictions, was the essential nature of the man?

In the end, it is of course only right that it should be impossible to know, just as it is impossible finally to estimate how greatly financial worries and sheer exhaustion may have affected his relationships with authors. Biography can, at best, only intimate the nature of personal associations and suggest the broad rhythms of feeling and perception in a man's life. It can never recreate in a complex richness the reality through which others have lived. And yet, despite this, there can be no doubt that any biographer of Taylor faces special difficulties of inter-pretation, difficulties which arise not simply from the paradox of his personality, but also from the peculiar kind of objectivity that seems to characterise so many of his recorded thoughts and actions. In Edmund Blunden's words, it is often true that a vast number of his activities are 'difficult to feel in the semblance of urgent life';[22] that, despite the thousands of personal letters he wrote throughout his life, from which one naturally expects a degree of self-revelation, there remains a certain distance, an obstinate gap which prevents the bio-grapher from seeing him in a moment of outstanding vision, in a spot of time at which he is uniquely revealed. To argue that such distance and reserve was consciously imposed by him as a safeguard against emotional crises such as may have occurred with Isabella Jones, may be one explanation. But another and perhaps more convincing one is that Taylor seems to have been the kind of man for whom articulation of deep feeling was often difficult – that, as a bachelor who was never to marry, the impulse for profound revelation was never a sustained pressure in his everyday life, but remained something internal, to be pondered in the quiet of the study, or during the countryside walks around Bakewell or Retford he so much enjoyed. Such, indeed, may be a possible explanation for that absence of personal illumination at the moments when one most expects it – in his last letter to John Clare, or to Keats, or in the letter to Clare reporting the deaths of Woodhouse and Lamb. The ultimate emotion was not exposed and recorded, but remained private, to be worked out by him alone.

Despite this apparent objectivity, though, it would be strange, as Edmund Blunden has written, 'if one could investigate the life of a significant human being without discovering that he, or she, became especially clear to the imagination in certain moments perhaps not originally the most striking, but of a keen individuality';[23] and there is no doubt that such moments of illumination do occur in Taylor's life. One, perhaps, is focused in an early letter from him to his brother James, written at his old writing desk which he was sending James as a gift:[24]

At that old Desk I have sat cogitating the best part of the Night away to produce from sterile Brains, half a dozen lame lines, upon some worthless subject – . . . But on the other Hand I have met at that board all my best and dearest Friends – and have

held sweet Concourse with them with my Pen – And therein
I hope you will find what a Comfort & Blessing it oftentimes
becomes, as well as I have done –

The thousands of letters he wrote throughout his life are a clear testimony to the comfort he found in this kind of relationship. Yet beneath
these words, there is perhaps also a glimpse, not so much of any
loneliness, but of the essential solitariness of his nature. For beside
the image of him as the dispenser of wine and venison and good
fellowship during the *London Magazine* dinners, there remains also
the image of the bachelor alone in his study, writing letters and reading
manuscripts until late into the night. Brilliant though he always was
in conversation, and dependent though he remained upon the society
of his friends, his individuality seems as keenly focused in this scene
as in many others more crowded and colourful. And it is possible that
some part of this solitariness was responsible, in the most undramatic
of ways, for the understanding of his finest actions. Out of many which
might be recalled, one final image of a letter written by him to Clare
remains in the memory – a letter which, in its profound sympathy and
perception, was arguably the finest he ever composed. Troubled with
the poet's intimations of approaching madness, of 'blue devils' and
'cold water creeping all about', he had written to him, quite unosten-
tatiously, of the immortality of the soul, trying to convince him that
his mind would not die: '[I] cannot believe that we have met for the
last Time. Nor can I ever think that your Mind, my Friend John, is
dead, whatever the body may be. The Mind says itself in all its actions
and expressions "I am immortal".'[25]
And in the world of literature too, he had helped to bring about
a kind of immortality. What Keats or Clare or the Londoners would
have achieved without him is almost impossible to say. Yet without
his faith and encouragement, it seems very probable that some of them
would never have seen their work published in their lifetime, and that
others would have had to struggle for recognition a little harder and a
little less hopefully. For Taylor, and Hessey too, ultimately understood their writers in the way that mattered most. If there had been one
single impulse in common to them all, it was the desire that their work
should be published and should survive. Keats and Clare, Hazlitt and
De Quincey, Lamb and Coleridge, and all the others, would have
echoed the aspiration of Milton – that they 'might perhaps leave something so written to after times, as they should not willingly let it die'.
This too had been Taylor's hope.

Notes

Abbreviations

Bauer	Josephine Bauer, 'The London Magazine, 1820–29', *Anglistica*, I, 1953.
Clare Letters	*The Letters of John Clare*, ed. J. W. & A. Tibble, 1950.
Jack	Ian Jack, *English Literature 1815–1832*, 1963.
Jerrold	Walter Jerrold, *Thomas Hood & Charles Lamb: The Story of a Friendship*, 1930.
KC	*The Keats Circle: Letters and Papers, 1816–78*, ed. H. E. Rollins, 2 vols, 1948.
Keats Letters	*The Letters of John Keats*, ed. H. E. Rollins, 2 vols, 1958.
KP	Edmund Blunden, *Keats's Publisher: A Memoir of John Taylor (1781–1864)*, 1936.
King	R. W. King, *The Translator of Dante*, 1925.
Lamb Letters	*The Letters of Charles and Mary Lamb*, ed. E. V. Lucas, 3 vols, 1935.
McFarland	G. F. McFarland, 'The Early Literary Career of Julius Charles Hare', *Bulletin of the John Rylands Library*, XLVI, 1963.
MLPKC	*More Letters and Papers of the Keats Circle*, ed. H. E. Rollins, 1955.
Richardson	Joanna Richardson, *The Everlasting Spell*, 1963.
SC, 1827	John Clare, *The Shepherd's Calendar*, 1827.
SC, 1964	John Clare, *The Shepherd's Calendar*, ed. Eric Robinson & Geoffrey Summerfield, 1964.
Taylor	Olive M. Taylor, 'John Taylor, Author and Publisher', *London Mercury*, XII, June 1925.

Abbreviations of unpublished manuscript sources are to be found in Section D of the bibliography.

Chapter 1   Apprenticeship: 1781–1816

1 Bakewell MSS; one of Taylor's notebooks, 31 December 1810.
2 *ibid.*, to his brother James, 8 November 1862.
3 *ibid.*, 19 February 1802.
4 *ibid.*, 1 July [1803].

5 *ibid.*, to his father and mother, 28 August 1804.

6 See A. S. Collins, *The Profession of Letters*, 1928, p. 29.

7 James Lackington, *Memoirs*, 1827 ed., p. 131.

8 *ibid.*, p. 246.

9 *ibid.*, p. 222.

10 Bakewell MSS; Taylor to his father, 26 March 1804.

11 Wilton MSS; manuscript biography of Rev. J. A. Hessey.

12 Bakewell MSS; to his father, September 1807.

13 *ibid.*, to his father, 28 August 1804, and to one of his sisters, 10 June 1804.

14 *ibid.*, to one of his sisters, 10 June 1804.

15 *ibid.*, 6 March 1805.

16 *ibid.*, to his father and mother, 31 March 1804, 8 May [1804].

17 *ibid.*, to his father, 29 April 1804.

18 *ibid.*, to his father and mother, 8 May [1804], 28 September 1804.

19 *ibid.*, to his father, 29 April 1804.

20 *ibid.*, 8 May [1804].

21 R. D. Altick, *The English Common Reader . . . 1800–1900*, 1957, p. 262.

22 Bakewell MSS; 8 May [1804].

23 *ibid.*, 28 August 1804.

24 The details of their agreement are unfortunately lacking, for there is a break in the Bakewell letters between 1805 and 1807.

25 See, for example, *KC*, II, p. 399.

26 *KP*, pp. 26–7.

27 *KC*, II, pp. 379–80, 381–2.

28 *ibid.*, II, p. 395.

29 *ibid.*, II, pp. 381, 399.

30 Bakewell MSS; 4 March 1811.

31 *ibid.*

32 *ibid.*, n.d., but almost certainly written during 1812.

33 *ibid.*, to James, 4 January 1813.

34 Brooke-Taylor MSS; to Taylor, 31 January 1814.

35 Bakewell MSS; 19 August 1806.

36 *ibid.*, to James, 23 August 1813.

37 Egerton MS. 2245, fol. 202; 14 August 1820.

38 Bakewell MSS; 19 September [1807?].

39 Quoted by Richardson, p. 219.

40 Bakewell MSS; to James, 1 February 1812. The identity of the lady in Claverton is unfortunately unknown.

41 *ibid.*, to James, 11 April 1813.

42 Quoted by Taylor, p. 166.

43 Bakewell MSS; to James, 4 November, 9 May 1815. *Grammar made Easy* seems never to have been finished by Taylor.

44 The earliest record of Taylor's interest I have found is in a letter to George Woodfall of 24 March 1806 (Add. MS. 27781, fol. 7).

45 *The Identity of Junius*, 1816, p. 255.
46 *ibid.*, p. 236.
47 *ibid.*, pp. 248–9.
48 *ibid.*, pp. 246–7.
49 Brooke-Taylor MSS; to Taylor, 10 January 1814.
50 Bakewell MSS; to James, 24 February, 6 September 1814.
51 *ibid.*, to James, 9 May 1815.
52 Altick, *The English Common Reader*, pp. 262, 331.
53 Bakewell MSS; to James, 23 November 1816.
54 *ibid.*, to his mother, 24 January 1816.
55 Quoted by Jack, p. 26.
56 Bakewell MSS; to James, 12 March 1818.
57 *ibid.*, 24 January 1816.
58 *ibid.*, to James, 12 March, 26 March 1818.
59 Brooke-Taylor MSS; 18 January 1814. The new novel was *Patronage*, 4 vols, 1814.
60 Keats House MSS; 15 April 1817.

Chapter 2   'A true poet': Taylor and Keats, 1817–21

1 Charles and Mary Cowden Clarke, *Recollections of Writers*, 1878, p. 140.
2 Quoted by Aileen Ward in *John Keats: The Making of a Poet*, 1963, p. 106.
3 *Champion*, 9 March 1817.
4 *Examiner*, No. 497, 6 July 1817, p. 429.
5 *Eclectic Review*, VIII, September 1817, p. 274.
6 The letter is quoted in full by Walter Jackson Bate in *John Keats*, 1963, pp. 150–1.
7 Keats House MSS; fol. 1.
8 Bakewell MSS; to his mother, 26 January 1816.
9 Egerton MS. 2245, fol. 202; 14 August 1820.
10 Berg Collection MSS; vol. 6 of Taylor's Commonplace Books, pp. 12–14. Notes for ch. 2 of 'An Essay on Poetry'.
   To estimate how greatly these thoughts about the poetic imagination may have influenced Taylor in deciding to publish Keats, the date of their composition is clearly important. Unfortunately, the Commonplace Book gives no indication about when they might have been written. The only clue to a possible date I have been able to discover is contained in a letter from Taylor to Clare of 27 April 1820 (Egerton MS. 2245, fol. 103). Criticising the reception given to Keats's work by the Reviews, Taylor writes, 'it makes me feel still more inclined to write "An Essay on English Poesy" which I have thought much of, & shall proceed with as soon as I can find Time.' Although there is no evidence that he ever got down to writing the essay, the notes quoted in the text are very clearly a preparation for it. But how long before or after April 1820 he first noted down

his thoughts must remain debatable. It is, of course, tempting to argue that they were composed between 1817 and 1820, as a direct result of Keats's own theories upon this subject, expressed during one of their many conversations with each other. Tempting too is the suggestion that, in the formulation of this philosophy, the influence did not only come from the poet – that Taylor himself may have played a more substantial part than has ever been recognised in helping to crystallise Keats's beliefs about imagination, creativity, and poetic identity. Whatever the date and inspiration of the notes, however, what remains chiefly important is the close correspondence between the views of poet and publisher – a theme which I examine more fully on pp. 35–6.

11 *KC*, I, p. 69.
12 *Keats Letters*, I, p. 146.
13 Quoted by Robert Gittings in *Keats: the living year, September 1818– September 1819*, 1954, p. 4.
14 *Keats Letters*, I, pp. 147–8.
15 Quoted by Richardson, p. 234.
16 Keats House MSS, fol. 2; 4 June 1818.
17 *KC*, I, p. 69.
18 Keats House MSS, fol. 2; 4 June 1818.
19 *The Poems of John Keats*, ed. H. W. Garrod, 1958 ed., pp. xciii–iv.
20 *Keats Letters*, I, pp. 266–7.
21 *ibid.*, I, pp. 270–2.
22 Bakewell MSS; to James, 15 April 1818.
23 Keats House MSS, fol. 2; to James, 4 June 1818.
24 *Blackwood's Magazine*, III, August 1818, pp. 522, 524.
25 *KC*, I, pp. 34–5.
26 *ibid.*, I, p. 37.
27 *British Critic*, IX, June 1818, p. 652.
28 *ibid.*, p. 654.
29 Increasingly, it seems as if Taylor too was being drawn into the line of attack. The mention of his 'respectability' ('for Brutus is an honourable man') was unnecessary, but childishly effective. For the reader, ignorant of the position he held regarding Keats's supposed indelicacy, an association of personalities had been suggested.
30 *Quarterly Review*, XIX, April 1818, p. 205.
31 *Keats Letters*, I, pp. 373–4.
32 *KC*, I, pp. 52–3.
33 *ibid.*, I, pp. 68–9.
34 A suggestion made by Dorothy Hewlett in *A Life of Keats*, 1949, p. 186.
35 *Keats Letters*, II, p. 65.
36 *ibid.*, II, pp. 15–16.
37 Robert Gittings, *John Keats: The Living Year*, p. 95.
38 *Keats Letters*, II, p. 65.

39 *KC*, I, p. 215.
40 Dorothy Hewlett, *A Life of Keats*, p. 187. Curiously though, in the end pages of a pamphlet, 'The University of London &c.', published by Taylor in 1828, he himself is still advertising the first edition of *Endymion*.
41 See Mabel A. E. Steele, 'The Authorship of "The Poet" and other Sonnets', *Keats–Shelley Journal*, V, 1956.
42 *Keats Letters*, II, p. 144.
43 *KC*, I, p. 82.
44 A conservative estimate. Over a year later, in September 1820, it was still £135 (*KC*, I, p. 139).
45 *ibid.*, I, p. 92.
46 Ann Taylor, *Practical Hints to young Females . . .*, 1814, p. iii.
47 See above, pp. 67–8.
48 *KC*, I, pp. 96–7.
49 *Keats Letters*, I, p. 415.
50 *ibid.*, II, p. 234.
51 *KC*, I, p. 97. It should be added, in fairness to Taylor, that this was not a criticism of the poem as a whole, but only of a single extract from the Feast which Keats had copied out in a letter to him of 5 September 1819.
52 Writing to Clare on 6 June 1820 (Egerton MS. 2245, fol. 140), Taylor quoted extensively those passages in the book which pleased him most. Over three-quarters of them came from 'Lamia'.
53 Egerton MS. 2245, fols. 155, 153; 30, 27 June 1820.
54 Keats House MSS, fol. 6; 26 June 1820.
55 *KC*, I, p. 118.
56 *Keats Letters*, II, p. 298.
57 Keats House MSS; 29 June 1820.
58 Dorothy Hewlett points this out in her *Life of Keats*, pp. 321–2.
59 II, August 1820, p. 173.
60 XXXIV, August 1820, p. 205.
61 *Keats Letters*, II, p. 315.
62 Egerton MS. 2245, fol. 202; 14 August 1820.
63 Keats House MSS, fol. 9; to his father, 31 August 1820.
64 Rollins (*KC*, I, pp. 133–7) includes the cancelled readings of this letter, but for the sake of clarity and continuity I have omitted these.
65 Keats House MSS, fol. 9; to his father, 31 August 1820.
66 VII, September 1820, p. 665.
67 Arthur Bryant, *The Age of Elegance, 1812–1822*, 1958 Pelican ed., pp. 417–19.
68 *Independent Remarks on the Queen's Case*, 1820, p. 29.
69 Edmund Blunden, *Leigh Hunt*, 1930, p. 156.
70 Keats House MSS, fol. 8; to his father, 23 August 1820.
71 Egerton MS. 2245, fol. 245; 28 November 1820.
72 Bakewell MSS; to Taylor, 15 November 1820.

73 Egerton MS. 2246, fol. 143; 18 March 1822.
74 'The University of London &c.', 1828, n.p. (See n. 40 above.)
75 Bakewell MSS; 21 April, 31 May, 28 August 1820, 7 June 1821.
76 In fact, Taylor and Hessey were not repaid until 1828, when George Keats finally reimbursed them.
77 *KC*, I, p. 139.
78 See *KC*, I, p. 200.
79 *MLPKC*, p. 16.
80 *KC*, I, pp. 182–3.
81 *ibid.*, I, pp. 202–4.
82 *MLPKC*, p. 109.
83 Bakewell MSS.
84 *KC*, I, p. 230.
85 The earliest announcement of Taylor's plan discovered by Blunden was in the *Morning Chronicle* of 4 June 1821 (*KP*, p. 93). But in *KC*, I, p. 236, there is a letter from Bailey to Taylor of 28 April 1821, in which Bailey writes that he has seen the advertisement about Keats's Literary Remains. He omits, though, to name the paper he had seen it in.
86 *KP*, pp. 93–4.
87 Egerton MS. 2245, fol. 304; 26 March 1821.
88 XXIII, May 1820, p. 225.
89 Egerton MS. 2245, fol. 304; 26 March 1821.
90 *ibid.*, fol. 293; 9 March 1821.
91 *KP*, p. 92.
92 Keats House MSS, fol. 6; 26 June 1820.

Chapter 3   The years of expansion, 1817–20: Leigh Hunt, Hazlitt, Cary, and the Reviews

1 All extracts from the letters of Shelley, Hunt, and Taylor & Hessey in this section are quoted by G. D. Stout in 'Leigh Hunt's Money Troubles', *Washington University Studies*, XII, Humanistic Series, no. 2, 1925.
2 Bakewell MSS; 31 August 1816.
3 *ibid.*, to James, 11 September 1816.
4 *ibid.*, 16 June 1817.
5 *ibid.*, Taylor to James, 27 November 1817.
6 *ibid.*, to James, 30 January 1818.
7 *ibid.*, to James, 5 March 1818.
8 *ibid.*, to James, 13 July 1818. From January 1816 to Midsummer 1817, the retail had lost nearly £800, although the actual returns for the period were the third highest in the firm's history. In 1815, the profits from the publishing side, on the other hand, were £251; in 1816, £501.11.0.; in 1817, £399.9.0.; and from January to Midsummer 1818, £690.7.7.
9 *ibid.*, to his father, 20 January 1819.

10 *ibid.*, to James, 30 January 1818.

11 *ibid.*, 31 October 1818.

12 *ibid.*, to his father, 20 January 1819.

13 *ibid.*, 17 December 1819.

14 Berg Collection MSS; vol. 3 of Taylor's Commonplace Books, n.p. The note is dated 19 September 1815.

15 Brooke-Taylor MSS; 14 April 1819.

16 Berg Collection MSS; vol. 3 of Taylor's Commonplace Books, n.p.

17 *KP*, p. 33.

18 Bakewell MSS; to James, 8 May 1826.

19 *ibid.*, to James, 29 June 1831.

20 Keats House MSS; fol. 2.

21 XXXVI, January 1818, p. 466.

22 III, April 1818, p. 75.

23 See *Keats Letters*, I, p. 368.

24 *KC*, I, p. 37.

25 Probably for reasons of expediency, this article was not allowed to appear.

26 Full accounts are given by P. P. Howe in *The Life of William Hazlitt*, rev. ed. 1947, pp. 232–47, by Catherine M. Maclean in *Born Under Saturn . . .*, 1943, pp. 363–6, 382–93, 400–2, and by Herschel Baker in *William Hazlitt*, 1962, pp. 364–81.

27 See a letter by P. P. Howe in the *Times Literary Supplement*, 21 March 1936, p. 244.

28 Bakewell MSS.

29 *ibid.*, to his father, 27 November 1817.

30 *ibid.*, 31 October 1818.

31 Berg Collection MSS; vol. 4 of Taylor's Commonplace Books, p. 110, n.d.

32 *The Complete Works of William Hazlitt*, ed. P. P. Howe, 20 vols, 1930–4; VIII, p. 99. Although Hazlitt may well have exaggerated the poor sales of *Shakespear's Plays*, there is little doubt that in general terms his statement was accurate enough. A third edition of the book was not called for, indeed, until 1838, twenty years after the second.

33 *KP*, pp. 56–7.

34 Elie Halévy, *England in 1815*, 1924 ed., p. 443.

35 VIII, October 1820, p. 81.

36 Baldwin's *London Magazine*, I, April 1820, p. 387.

37 *Works of Hazlitt*, ed. P. P. Howe, VIII, p. 99.

38 Jack, p. 8.

39 *ibid.*, p. 20.

40 *ibid.*, p. 14.

41 *Contemporary Reviews of Romantic Poetry*, ed. John Wain, 1953, p. 17.

42 Bakewell MSS; to his father, 31 December 1818.

43 *Edinburgh Review*, XL, November 1812, p. 280.

44 Quoted by Jack, p. 9.

45 *Edinburgh Review*, XXXV, May 1811, p. 45.

46 *ibid.*, LIX, June 1818, pp. 98-9.

47 *England and the English*, 2 vols., 1833; II, p. 71.

48 See Charles Knight, *Passages of a Working Life*, 3 vols, 1864-5, I, p. 112; Bulwer Lytton, *England and the English*, II, p. 96; *The Prose of John Clare*, ed. J. W. and A. Tibble, 1951, pp. 99-100.

49 Berg Collection MSS; to Julius Hare, 22 April 1825.

50 *ibid.*, 19 April 1825.

51 King, pp. 111-12.

52 *The Collected Letters of Coleridge*, ed. E. L. Griggs, 6 vols, 1956- ; IV, p. 832.

53 *ibid.*, IV, p. 827.

54 Bakewell MSS; to his father, 14 April 1819.

55 King, p. 118.

56 *ibid.*, p. 338 and King's own transcriptions of Taylor's letters.

57 Bakewell MSS; to James, 28 August 1820.

58 Bakewell MSS.

59 Northampton MS. 43, fol. 1; [April 1819].

60 *KP*, p. 67.

Chapter 4   Taylor and Clare: 1819-37

1 University of Texas MSS. The poem is dated March 1818.

2 *John Clare: Selected Poems*, ed. J. W. and A. Tibble, 1965, p. 215. It should be noted that Clare wrote 'The Flight of Birds' at some time between 1824 and 1832, and thus Taylor could not have initially recognised the strength of his dialect from this particular poem. I have chosen it as an illustration simply because many rustic words occur within a few lines. The first manuscripts Taylor received contain as much dialect as this later poem, but the words tend to be less concentrated within a few lines.

3 *Poems Descriptive . . .*, 1820, 1st ed., pp. xiv-xv.

4 *ibid.*, p. xvi.

5 Northampton MS. 43, fol. 4; to Taylor, 3 June 1819.

6 *ibid.*, fol. 11; Drury to Taylor, 2 January 1820.

7 *ibid.*, fol. 12; to Taylor, 17 January 1820.

8 *ibid.*, fols. 13, 14; to Taylor, n.d. and 5 February 1820.

9 King, p. 133.

10 Bakewell MSS; Taylor to his father, 25 May 1820.

11 *Poems Descriptive*, pp. 148, 149.

12 Egerton MS. 2245, fol. 118; 11 May 1820.

13 *Clare Letters*, p. 49.

14 Egerton MS. 2245, fol. 225; Taylor to Clare, 27 September 1820.

15 *ibid.*, fol. 225.

16 *ibid.*, fol. 271; 6 January 1821.

17 *ibid.*, fol. 271. 'I cannot print the 4th Edit. from not thinking it right to omit them.'

18 *ibid.*, fols. 253, 254; 12 December 1820.

19 *ibid.*, fol. 257; 15 December 1820.

20 Northampton MS. 34; [about 20 December 1820].

21 Egerton MS. 2245, fol. 324; 5 June 1821.

22 *ibid.*, fols. 277, 285, 287; 23 January, 10 and 11 February 1821.

23 *ibid.*, fol. 359; 29 August 1821.

24 Northampton MS. 44; 30 November 1819.

25 *ibid.*, 2 August 1820.

26 *ibid.*, Gilchrist to Hessey, 23 April 1820.

27 Egerton MS. 2245, fol. 21; 13 January 1820.

28 *Clare: selected poems and prose*, ed. Eric Robinson and Geoffrey Summerfield, 1966, pp. 114–15.

29 *The Prose of John Clare*, ed. J. W. and A. Tibble, 1950, p. 210.

30 Egerton MS. 2246, fol. 405; 3 November 1824.

31 IV, November 1821, pp. 544–5.

32 Bakewell MSS; 22 June 1807.

33 *The Village Minstrel*, 2 vols., 1821; II, pp. 120, 122. The poem may be found in many modern editions of Clare's poetry.

34 IV, November 1821, pp. 540–1.

35 A suggestion made by Geoffrey Grigson in his *John Clare: Selected Poems*, 1950, p. 10.

36 Northampton MS. 34; n.d.

37 *The Village Minstrel*, II, pp. 124–5.

38 *Clare Letters*, p. 132.

39 Egerton MS. 2246, fol. 228.

40 *Clare Letters*, pp. 136, 151.

41 Peterborough MS. F 1, fol. 102; 2 October 1824.

42 *ibid.*, fol. 103; 15 March 1825.

43 Egerton MS. 2246, fol. 469; 18 March 1825.

44 Egerton MS. 2247, fol. 34; 31 May 1825.

45 In fairness to Taylor, though, part of the delay must also have been due to Van Dyk. The first mention of his offer to Taylor that I have discovered is in a letter from him to Clare of 21 August 1824 (Peterborough MS. F 1, fol. 93). Seven months later, he is still correcting the first section of 'January' (fol. 105; 29 March 1825).

46 Egerton MS. 2247, fol. 132; 28 January 1826.

47 The manuscript is Peterborough MS. A 20.

48 These two examples are quoted by Eric Robinson and Geoffrey Summerfield in 'Taylor's Editing of *The Shepherd's Calendar*', *Review of English Studies*, xiv, 1963, p. 362.

49 Egerton MS. 2250, fol. 329; n.d., but almost certainly written during the summer of 1825.

50 See Robinson and Summerfield *RES* article mentioned above.

51 *Clare: selected poems and prose*, ed. Robinson and Summerfield, p. 23; and the same authors' *RES* article, p. 367.

52 The page references are, of course, to the 1827 edition.

53 *SC*, 1964, p. 69.

54 *ibid.*, p. 135 (*SC*, 1827, pp. 66–7).

55 Egerton MS. 2245, fol. 172; 11 July 1820.

56 *SC*, 1964, p. 25.

57 Slightly out of place in its context is the stanza beginning 'Old customs O I love the sound . . .' (*SC*, 1964, p. 126). These eight lines Taylor transposes to the very end of 'December' (*SC*, 1827, p. 99), and thereby creates a more fitting climax than the rather perfunctory one Clare had originally composed.

58 Egerton MS. 2246, fol. 132; 28 January. A further example of the simplification that has sometimes characterised criticism of Taylor's actions is demonstrated by this letter. In their introduction to *The Shepherd's Calendar* (p. ix), Robinson and Summerfield denounce as 'palpably false' Taylor's strictures on 'July', quoted on p. 116 above. But for some reason, they do not quote the lines *immediately* following in his letter, in which he praises sixteen lines which are undoubtedly amongst the very best in the whole section. Certainly, Taylor's criticism of 'July' as a whole was exaggerated and unjust; but to quote his strictures and to omit his praise scarcely makes for an accurate account of his general reaction.

59 *Poems Descriptive*, pp. xvii–xviii.

60 Egerton MS. 2245, fol. 225; 27 September 1820.

61 *The Collected Writings of Thomas De Quincey*, ed. David Masson, 14 vols., 1889–90; III, pp. 144–5.

62 Egerton MS. 2246, fol. 43; probably 18 March 1822.

63 Egerton MS. 2245, fol. 90; 18 April 1820.

64 Egerton MS. 2247, fol. 152; 4 March 1826.

65 *SC*, 1964, pp. viii–ix.

66 XXVII, June 1827, p. 519.

67 V, June 1827, p. 277.

68 Egerton MS. 2246, fol. 322; [3 August 1827].

69 *Clare Letters*, p. 200.

70 Egerton MS. 2248, fol. 378; 19 July 1831.

71 In the end, Taylor allowed the whole question of Clare's debts, real or imagined, to lapse. The £100 entered in Radstock's Subscription List remained a gift from the firm.

72 *KP*, p. 194.

73 *Clare Letters*, p. 253.

74 *ibid.*, p. 283.

75 Quoted by June Wilson in her *Green Shadows: The Life of Clare*, 1951, p. 221.
76 Bakewell MSS; 12 December 1836.
77 June Wilson, *Green Shadows*, pp. 226–7.
78 *Clare Letters*, p. 285.
79 Egerton MS. 2249, fol. 377; 13 June 1837.
80 *Clare Letters*, p. 53.
81 Egerton MS. 2246, fol. 308; 8 March 1824.
82 For example, in the same letter in which Taylor angrily criticised Clare for his illegible manuscripts (see p. 106 above), he could still write to him: 'My Regard for you remains undiminished & whenever I can have the opportunity of proving it I shall always be ready.' And in 1830, when disappointment over the statement of accounts had not completely subsided, Clare could yet write of Taylor: 'I am happy so far to find that altho in the first instance I mistook Collins Ready Reckoner for a Treatise on Friendship John Taylor is not among the number of those professions for I should have been very down at heel to find at last that he had not been a Friend & I am happy to find that I am not dissapointed' (*Clare Letters*, p. 245).
83 Egerton MS. 2249, fol. 295; 3 August 1835.
84 *The Village Minstrel*, I, p. xxvii.

Chapter 5   The *London Magazine*: 1821–5

1 Bakewell MSS; 8 October 1817.
2 Single word obliterated by tear.
3 *ibid.*, to his father, 9 December 1818.
4 King, p. 125.
5 *ibid.*, p. 124.
6 *ibid.*, p. 126.
7 Bakewell MSS.
8 On 18 July 1821, Taylor & Hessey also bought Gold and Northhouse's *London Magazine*, a declining rival of Baldwin's periodical, for which they paid £50 (*KP*, p. 123).
9 Bakewell MSS; 28 April 1821.
10 *ibid.*, to his father, 7 August 1821.
11 P. P. Howe, *William Hazlitt*, p. 266.
12 VIII, October 1820, p. 81.
13 *ibid.*, p. 81.
14 King, p. 125.
15 Bakewell MSS; to James, 28 April 1821.
16 *ibid.*, 28 April 1821.
17 Bakewell MSS.
18 *ibid.*, to his father, 31 May 1821.

19 Jonathan Curling, *Janus Weathercock: the Life of Thomas Griffiths Waine-wright*, 1938, p. 127.

20 Egerton MS. 2245, fol. 351; 7 August 1821.

21 King, p. 171.

22 *Collected Writings*, ed. David Masson; III, p. 127. According to the *New European Magazine* (III, October 1823, p. 298) De Quincey received twenty guineas a sheet for his *Confessions*.

23 J. C. Reid, *Thomas Hood*, 1963, p. 37.

24 Bakewell MSS; to his father.

25 Reid, p. 37. These were Hood's own words.

26 Jerrold, p. 100.

27 T. Rowland Hughes, 'John Scott: Editor, Author and Critic', *London Mercury*, XXI, 1930, p. 525.

28 Jerrold, pp. 100–1.

29 *Lamb Letters*, II, p. 306.

30 Bakewell MSS; 22 August 1821.

31 Berg Collection MSS; vol. 6 of Taylor's Commonplace Books. The note from which these extracts are taken is dated 16 December 1821.

32 *KP*, p. 241.

33 Bakewell MSS; to his father, 29 December 1821.

34 H. A. Eaton, *Thomas De Quincey*, 1936, p. 284. This conversation was related to Woodhouse, who recorded it in the notebook he kept of De Quincey's conversations during the latter months of 1821. The reason for De Quincey's suspicion of Wilson was that the critic had been in London in November 1821, and had seen Taylor and several writers to the magazine. There was a widespread feeling that this was a sounding out in preparation for an attack upon the *London* and its contributors.

35 *ibid.*, p. 286.

36 *ibid.*, p. 291.

37 Bakewell MSS; to James, 12 July 1824.

38 Pierpont Morgan Library MSS. Brief extracts from this article were quoted by Richard H. Byrns in 'Some Unpublished Works of De Quincey', *PMLA*, LXXI, no. 5, December 1956, pp. 990–1003. The final quotation on p. 142 above, in which De Quincey expresses the house's determination to avoid 'any one presiding mind studiously impinging its' own stamp upon the whole body of the articles', is in fact part of a cancelled passage. I have quoted it as a firm expression of the firm's policy because it is clear that the only reason De Quincey struck it out was that he realised he was wandering from his immediate point – the *specific* improvements which Taylor and Hessey proposed to effect in the magazine.

39 *London Magazine*, I, p. 5.

40 Jerrold, p. 104.

41 *ibid.*, p. 129.

42 *Sketches in the Life of John Clare*, ed. Edmund Blunden, 1931, p. 112.

43 B. W. Procter, *Charles Lamb: a Memoir*, 1866, p. 158.

44 B. W. Procter, *An autobiographical Fragment*, 1877, p. 207.

45 King, p. 144.

46 B. W. Procter, *Charles Lamb*, p. 157.

47 Jerrold, p. 121.

48 *Sketches in the Life of John Clare*, ed. Blunden, pp. 109–11.

49 Jerrold, p. 112.

50 *ibid.*, p. 113.

51 *Sketches in the Life of John Clare*, ed. Blunden, p. 113.

52 Jerrold, p. 116.

53 *Sketches in the Life of John Clare*, ed. Blunden, p. 111.

54 B. W. Procter, *Charles Lamb*, p. 159.

55 B. W. Procter, *An Autobiographical Fragment*, p. 212.

56 T. G. Wainewright, 'The Delicate Intricacies', *London Magazine*, VI, July 1822, p. 72.

57 *KP*, p. 144.

58 *Lamb Letters*, II, p. 307.

59 Bakewell MSS; to James, 8 December 1821.

60 B. W. Procter, *Charles Lamb*, p. 156.

61 Jerrold, p. 132.

62 *London Magazine*, VII, February 1823, p. 194.

63 *ibid.*, II, December 1820, p. 686.

64 *ibid.*, IV, July 1821, p. 75.

65 For these examples of influence, I am indebted to Josephine Bauer's excellent study of the magazine, pp. 154–8.

66 National Library of Scotland MS. 1808, fol. 204; 8 February 1822.

67 Bakewell MSS; to James, 14 September 1822.

68 *ibid.*, 18 December 1822.

69 *ibid.*, to his father, 16 August 1821.

70 *ibid.*, to his father, 31 December 1821.

71 *Lamb Letters*, II, p. 323.

72 J. C. Reid (*Thomas Hood*, p. 42) suggests that Hood may well have continued as sub-editor after this date; but no more pieces by him were ever printed in the magazine.

73 *Lamb Letters*, II, p. 385.

74 *ibid.*, II, pp. 394–5.

75 *ibid.*, II, p. 385.

76 Harvard University MSS; n.d.

77 *KP*, p. 137. Within months, Hazlitt too had begun to contribute increasingly to rival publications such as Henry Colburn's *New Monthly Magazine*.

78 Harvard University MSS; n.d.

79 King, pp. 174–5.

80 Harvard University MSS; n.d.

81 Bakewell MSS; to James, 28 April 1821.

82 National Library of Scotland MS. 7209, fol. 115; to George Combe, 4 June 1822.

83 *KP*, p. 136.

84 Jerrold, p. 161.

85 Bakewell MSS; to James, 8 December 1821.

86 Egerton MS. 2246, fol. 296; 1 March 1824.

87 *Lamb Letters*, II, p. 456.

88 See Bauer, p. 87.

89 Bakewell MSS; 4 December 1824.

90 *Lamb Letters*, II, p. 460.

91 Bakewell MSS; to James, 22 February 1825.

92 Egerton MS. 2247, fol. 43; 9 July 1825.

93 *Lamb Letters*, III, p. 19.

94 *ibid.*, III, p. 23.

95 LXXVI, May 1823, pp. 370–1.

96 X, December 1821, p. 499.

97 Jack, p. 320.

98 National Library of Scotland MS. 1706, fol. 189; n.d.

99 Egerton MS. 2246, fol. 241; 2 October 1823.

100 III, October 1823, p. 298.

101 *KP*, p. 245. As Blunden suggests, in this advertisement 'we have almost certainly Taylor's own interpretation of the character of his periodical'.

102 Bakewell MSS; 4 December 1824.

103 *ibid.*, 7 June 1825.

104 This repetition of material was strongly criticised by, amongst others, the *New European Magazine* in October 1823. There was an 'unpalatable sameness' in Cunningham's tales, Elia was 'but the *ghost* of what he once was', and the similarity in contributors' offerings in general had become 'tiresome' (III, p. 298).

105 Berg Collection MSS; to Taylor, 26 [?] October, n.y. The square brackets indicate a single word which is indecipherable.

106 Jerrold, pp. 102, 101.

Chapter 6 The years 1821–5:
Lamb, De Quincey, Carlyle, Landor, and Coleridge

1 Bakewell MSS; to James, 28 April 1821.

2 *ibid.*, to James, 28 January 1825.

3 *ibid.*, 14 February 1823.

4 *ibid.*, 18 December 1822.

5 *ibid.*, 18 December 1822.

6 *Lamb Letters*, II, p. 410.

7 'Description &c of the University of London', 1828.

8 As ever, it is almost impossible to judge the impact of such a remark upon sales. Certainly, Southey's criticism and Lamb's response to it in the *London* created some stir in literary circles, but Crabb Robinson's belief that Southey by his remark had 'utterly ruined the sale of Elia, and perhaps the popularity of Lamb for ever as a writer' seems an exaggeration. The *Quarterly* number for January 1823, in which Southey made his comment, did not in fact appear until the summer of that year, and *Elia* had thus at least six months' sale without the stigma of 'infidelity'. The fact too that the house had not exhausted the first edition of 1,000 copies even as late as 1828 (when the remark would presumably have been forgotten by most readers), suggests that Southey's criticism played only a minor part at best in reducing sales.

9 R. W. King's notes.

10 Egerton MS. 2246, fol. 218; 9 July 1823.

11 National Library of Scotland MS. 1764, fol. 259; to Carlyle, 29 September 1823.

12 *ibid.*, 29 September 1823.

13 National Library of Scotland MS. 1764, fol. 259; 29 September 1823.

14 *KP*, p. 131.

15 National Library of Scotland MS. 1765, fol. 12; copy of a letter from Carlyle to Taylor & Hessey, 6 August 1824, and Hessey's reply, 31 August 1824.

16 Berg Collection MSS; to Taylor, 29 July 1824.

17 National Library of Scotland MS. 1765, fol. 23; 10 February 1825.

18 Berg Collection MSS; 30 December 1827.

19 National Library of Scotland MS. 1765, fol. 82; 14 January 1828.

20 McFarland, p. 62.

21 Malcolm Elwin, *Savage Landor*, 1941, p. 204.

22 Berg Collection MSS; 4 March 1823.

23 *ibid.*, to Hare, 16 April 1823.

24 *ibid.*, to Hare, 19 April 1823.

25 Malcolm Elwin, *Savage Landor*, p. 204.

26 Berg Collection MSS; to Hare, 26 April 1823.

27 *ibid.*, 26 April 1823.

28 Page torn: Goal? God?

29 See McFarland, pp. 62–3.

30 Berg Collection MSS; 26 April 1823. In fact, after still more protracted argument, this dialogue was included in the 1824 edition published by the firm. But a comparison of this edition with that of 1826 reveals that Taylor did in the end censor several passages. Whether this censorship was on Wordsworth's or Southey's advice, I have been unable to discover.

31 *ibid.*, to Hare, n.d.

32 *ibid.*, to Hare, 12 July 1824.

33 *ibid.*, 12 July 1824.

34 Bakewell MSS; to James, n.d., but almost certainly written in late 1824 or early 1825.
35 Berg Collection MSS; to Hare, 29 November 1824.
36 *ibid.*, a copy in Hessey's hand of a letter from Landor to Hare, [April 1825].
37 *ibid.*, 19 April 1825.
38 McFarland, pp. 67–8.
39 Berg Collection MSS; to Hare, 22 April 1825.
40 *ibid.*, a memorandum of expenses, drawn up by Hessey, and included in Taylor's letter to Hare of 29 April [1825].
41 *ibid.*, 22 April 1825.
42 *ibid.*, 29 April [1825].
43 *ibid.*, 29 April [1825].
44 Bakewell MSS; to James, 18 March 1827.
45 *KP*, p. 143.
46 Berg Collection MSS; a letter to Hessey, [1824].
47 *KP*, p. 154.
48 See *KP*, p. 151.
49 Egerton MS. 2247, fol. 34; 31 May 1825.
50 *ibid.*, fol. 41; 30 June 1825.
51 Add. MS. 34569, fol. 227; 9 August 1825.
52 Bakewell MSS.
53 *ibid.*, 13 July 1825.
54 *ibid.*, 5 June 1821.
55 *ibid.*, 7 June 1821.
56 *ibid.*, 30 June 1821.
57 *ibid.*, to one of his sisters, 18 December 1821.
58 Egerton MS. 2246, fol. 79; 28 June 1822.
59 Bakewell MSS; Taylor to James, 2 September 1821.
60 *ibid.*, to James, 2 September 1822.
61 Egerton MS. 2246, fols. 270, 278.
62 Egerton MS. 2247, fol. 65; 6 September 1825.
63 Egerton MS. 2245, fol. 235; 6 November 1830.
64 Bakewell MSS.
65 Egerton MS. 2245, fol. 235; 6 November 1830.
66 Bakewell MSS.
67 Egerton MS. 2247, fol. 65; 6 September 1825.
68 *ibid.*, fol. 74; 22 September 1825.

Chapter 7 'No publisher of poetry now': the years 1826–64

1 Seton Dearden, *The Gypsy Gentleman, a Study of George Borrow*, 1939, p. 120.
2 *ibid.*, pp. 122–3.
3 Bakewell MSS; 13 December 1825.

4 *Passages of a Working Life*, II, p. 39.
5 Bakewell MSS.
6 Jack, p. 421.
7 Egerton MS. 2247, fols. 322, 352; [3 August 1827] and 20 November 1827.
8 *Clare Letters*, p. 200.
9 IX, April 1824, pp. 424–7.
10 *Englishman's Magazine*, September 1831.
11 *Lamb Letters*, III, p. 225.
12 ibid., III, p. 144.
13 Jack, p. 38.
14 *Lamb Letters*, III, p. 179.
15 C. Colleer Abbott, *The Life and Letters of George Darley*, 1928, p. 74.
16 A. S. Collins, *The Profession of Letters*, p. 157.
17 ibid., p. 182.
18 Harold G. Merriam, *Edward Moxon*, 1939, pp. 27–8.
19 Bulwer Lytton, *England and the English*, quoted by Jack, p. 423.
20 IV, July 1825, pp. 151, 166.
21 Amy Cruse, *The Englishman and his Books in the early Nineteenth Century*, 1930, p. 148.
22 *Bibliophobia*, 1832, p. 15.
23 Bakewell MSS; to James, 18 July 1831.
24 ibid., to James, 29 June 1831.
25 Royal A. Gettmann, *A Victorian Publisher: A Study of the Bentley Papers*, 1960, p. 10.
26 No. 212, 19 November 1831, p. 755.
27 Bakewell MSS; 29 May 1826.
28 University College London MSS; Record Office, Minutes of the University Council, vol. 1.
29 Egerton MS. 2247, fol. 322 [3 August 1827]; and MS. 2248, fol. 99, 31 December 1828.
30 Bakewell MSS; to James, 15 October 1825.
31 ibid., to James, 17 November 1827.
32 ibid., Taylor to James, 18 March 1827.
33 ibid., to James, 31 January 1828.
34 ibid., 21 December 1829.
35 *KP*, p. 189.
36 Bakewell MSS; to James, 28 January 1823.
37 ibid., to James, 10 October 1829.
38 Egerton MS. 2247, fol. 275; 30 March 1827.
39 Egerton MS. 2248, fol. 208; 6 January 1830.
40 ibid., fol. 261; 15 September 1830.
41 P. P. Howe, *The Life of William Hazlitt*, p. 386.
42 Hessey too seems to have felt the same at times. See, for example, his letter to Taylor in 1858, *KC*, II, pp. 473–4.

43 *Lamb Letters*, III, p. 357.

44 *ibid.*, III, p. 358.

45 E. V. Lucas, *The Life of Charles Lamb*, 1 vol. ed. 1907, p. 647.

46 Egerton MS. 2249, fol. 259; 9 January 1835.

47 *KP*, p. 199.

48 Egerton MS. 2249, fol. 259; 9 January 1835.

49 *KC*, II, pp. 468–9.

50 C. Colleer Abbott, *The Life and Letters of George Darley*, p. 270.

51 *KC*, II, p. 473.

52 *ibid.*, II, pp. 315–16.

53 Bakewell MSS; one of Taylor's notebooks. A note dated 17 June 1854.

54 *KP*, p. 215.

55 *ibid.*, p. 224.

56 In a letter to James of 1 September 1857, Taylor writes: 'I am thinking of going to Northampton tomorrow . . . with Hessey' (Bakewell MSS). I assume that this journey was a visit to Clare since, to my knowledge, none of Taylor's friends or relatives lived in this area. But whether a meeting between poet and publisher did in fact take place must remain in doubt.

57 Edmund Blunden (*KP*, p. 251) lists these books.

58 Keats House MSS; 27 June 1861.

59 *KP*, p. 223.

60 Bakewell MSS; to James, 28 November 1861.

61 Richardson, p. 228.

62 Egerton MS. 2249, fol. 153; 27 July 1833.

63 *KP*, p. 230.

64 Richardson, p. 229.

65 R. H. Horne, *Exposition of the False Medium* . . ., pp. 248–9.

66 *ibid.*, p. 251.

Chapter 8 Literature, the publisher, and the reading public

1 *The News of Literature*, 10 December 1825.

2 *London Magazine*, VII, January 1823, p. 90.

3 *Lamb Letters*, III, p. 179.

4 *Biographia Literaria*, ch. xi.

5 *Clare Letters*, p. 200.

6 *Keats Letters*, I, pp. 266–7.

7 *ibid.*, I, p. 415.

8 *The Poetical Works of Wordsworth*, ed. Thomas Hutchinson, 1908, p. 935.

9 *ibid.*

10 *England and the English*, I, p. 171.

11 *The English Review*, XV, October 1913, pp. 334–5.

12 *Miscellanies of Literature*, 1840, p. 86.

13 National Library of Scotland MS. 1765, fol. 82; 14 January 1828.

14 Berg Collection MSS; vol. 6 of Taylor's Commonplace Books, pp. 12–14.
15 *KP*, p. 156.
16 Stout, p. 224.
17 Egerton MS. 2245, fol. 302; 26 March 1821.
18 See, for example, Taylor's letter to Haydon of 5 November 1824. Haydon had apparently proposed a work of criticism about painting, which he offered to the firm. But Taylor replied: 'I should think your Genius would vindicate itself best in teaching the Art of Painting by your own splendid Examples, leaving to others who cannot paint so well the Province of writing about it. I assimilate the two to Poetry & Criticism – the latter comes after Poetry in historical order – is founded upon what the Poet has done – & confessedly implies an Inferiority of Mind' (*KP*, p. 156).
19 J. W. and A. Tibble, *John Clare: His Life and Poetry*, p. 31.
20 *KP*, p. 214.
21 Egerton MS. 2247, fol. 261; 15 September 1830.
22 *KP*, p. 241.
23 *ibid.*, pp. 240–1.
24 Bakewell MSS; 20 October 1808.
25 Egerton MS. 2246, fol. 308; 8 March 1824.

Select bibliography of books and manuscript sources

Of necessity, the following bibliography contains only the most important or useful works studied during the writing of this book. For ease of reference I have divided it into four sections. Section A contains general studies of publishing, the reading public, and the book trade, and includes also the chief literary histories and books of historical background consulted. Section B comprises studies of particular publishing houses, and includes those books and articles specifically concerned with the firm of Taylor & Hessey. Section C follows the order of chapters in the text and contains the chief works consulted in the writing of each chapter, in addition to the more general books listed in previous sections. Section D contains the most valuable of the unpublished manuscript sources I have drawn upon, both for direct quotation and for general reference.

Since I hope to present a full bibliography of Taylor & Hessey publications in the near future, no mention is made here of the original editions of the works they brought out. Invariably, the most modern standard edition of each author is quoted instead.

CLSB	*Charles Lamb Society Bulletin*
ELH	*English Literary History*
K-Sh J	*Keats–Shelley Journal*
K-Sh MB	*Bulletin of the Keats–Shelley Memorial Association*
JEGP	*Journal of English and Germanic Philology*
LM	*London Mercury*
MLN	*Modern Language Notes*
MLQ	*Modern Language Quarterly*
MLR	*Modern Language Review*
MP	*Modern Philology*
PMLA	*Publications of the Modern Language Association of America*
REL	*Review of English Literature*
RES	*Review of English Studies*
SP	*Studies in Philology*
TLS	*Times Literary Supplement*

Section A

Altick, R. D., *The English Common Reader: A Social History of the Mass Reading Public*, 1957.

Bryant, Arthur, *The Age of Elegance, 1812–1822*, 1950.

Collins, A. S., *The Profession of Letters: A Study of the Relation of Author to Patron, Publisher and Public, 1780–1832*, 1928.

Cruse, Amy, *The Englishman and his Books in the early nineteenth century*, 1930.

—— *The Victorians and their Books*, 1935.

Dibdin, T. F., *The Bibliomania; or Book-Madness*, 1809.

—— *Bibliophobia: Remarks on the Present Languid and Depressed State of Literature and the Book Trade*, 1832.

D'Israeli, Isaac, *Calamities of Authors*, 2 vols, 1812.

—— *Curiosities of Literature*, 3 vols, 1817 ed.

—— *Essay on the Literary Character*, 1818 ed.

Gross, John, *The Rise and Fall of the Man of Letters*, 1969.

Halévy, Elie, *Histoire du peuple anglais au XIXme siècle*. The relevant volumes are *England in 1815*, 1924; *The Liberal Awakening, 1815–1830*, 1926; *The Triumph of Reform*, 1927. Rev. eds 1949–50.

Hauser, Arnold, *The Social History of Art*, 4 vols, 1962 ed.

Hoggart, Richard, *The Uses of Literacy*, 1957.

Horne, R. H., *Exposition of the False Medium and Barriers Excluding Men of Genius from the Public*, 1833.

Howe, Ellic, *The London Compositor . . . 1785–1900*, The Bibliographical Society, 1947.

Jack, Ian, *English Literature, 1815–1832*, 1963.

James, Louis, *Fiction for the Working Man, 1830–1850*, 1963.

Knight, Charles, *Passages of a Working Life*, 3 vols, 1864–5.

—— *Shadows of the Old Booksellers*, 1865.

—— *The Struggles of a Book against Excessive Taxation*, [1850] ed.

Leavis, Q. D., *Fiction and the Reading Public*, 1965 ed.

Lytton, Bulwer, *England and the English*, 1833.

Munby, Frank, *Publishing and Bookselling: A History from the Earliest Times to the Present Day*, 1956 ed.

Plant, Marjorie, *The English Book Trade*, 1965 ed.

Rees, T. and J. Britton, *Reminiscences of Literary London*, 1853.

Sadleir, Michael, *XIX Century Fiction: A Bibliographical Record*, 2 vols, 1951.

Saunders, J. W., *The Profession of English Letters*, 1964.

Schucking, Levin L., *The Sociology of Literary Taste*, 1944.

Steinberg, S. H., *Five Hundred Years of Printing*, 1959 ed.

Unwin, Stanley, *The Price of Books*, 1925 ed.

—— *The Truth about Publishing*, 1946.

Webb, R. K., *The British Working Class Reader, 1790–1848: Literacy and Social Tension*, 1955.

Williams, Raymond, *Culture and Society, 1780–1950*, 1958.

Allen, Walter, *et al.*, 'The Changing Face of Publishing', *New Statesman*, 13 April 1957.
Blackburn, Thomas, 'The Poetry Adviser', *REL*, viii, January 1967.
Eliot, T. S., 'The Publishing of Poetry', *Bookseller*, 6 December 1952.
Monteith, Charles, 'The Cost of Publishing Poetry', *Guardian*, 5 June 1964.
Stallworthy, Jon, 'Poet and Publisher', *REL*, viii, January 1967.
White, Eric W., 'Public Support for Poetry', *REL*, viii, January 1967.

Section B

Besterman, T., *The Publishing Firm of Cadell & Davies: Select Correspondence and Accounts, 1793–1836*, 1938.
Blakey, Dorothy, *The Minerva Press, 1790–1820*, 1939.
Blunden, Edmund, *Keats's Publisher: A Memoir of John Taylor (1781–1864)*, 1936.
Constable, T., *Archibald Constable and his Literary Correspondents*, 3 vols, 1873.
Cox, H. and J. E. Chandler, *The House of Longman, 1724–1924*, 1925.
Faber, Geoffrey, *A Publisher Speaking*, 1934.
Gettmann, R. A., *A Victorian Publisher: A Study of the Bentley Papers*, 1960.
Keir, D., *The House of Collins*, 1952.
Keynes, Geoffrey, *William Pickering, Publisher*, 1924.
Merriam, Harold G., *Edward Moxon, Publisher of Poets*, 1939.
Oliphant, Margaret, *Annals of a Publishing House: William Blackwood and his Sons*, 2 vols, 1897.
Page, Walter, *A Publisher's Confessions*, 1924.
Smiles, Samuel, *A Publisher and his Friends: Memoirs and Correspondence of the late John Murray*, 2 vols, 1891.

Anon., 'John Murray: the Anax of Publishers', *TLS*, 26 June 1943.
Blunden, Edmund, 'John Taylor, 1781–1864', *K-Sh MB*, xv, 1964.
Morgan, Peter F., 'Taylor and Hessey: Aspects of their Conduct of the *London Magazine*', *K-Sh J*, vii, 1958.
Richardson, Joanna, 'John Taylor and James Hessey, a Centenary Address', *CLSB*, No. 171, May 1963.
Taylor, Olive M., 'John Taylor, Author and Publisher', *LM*, xii, June and July 1925.

Section C

Chapter 1   Apprenticeship

Lackington, James, *Memoirs of the Forty-Five First Years of the Life of James Lackington, Bookseller*, 1791 and 1827 eds.

Taylor, John, *The Identity of Junius with a Distinguished Living Character Established*, 1816 and 1818.

Hewlett, Maurice, 'J. Lackington, Bookseller', *LM*, iv, 1921.
Richardson, Joanna, 'Richard Woodhouse and his Family', *K-Sh MB*, v, 1953.

Chapter 2   Keats

Garrod, H. W. (ed.), *The Poetical Works*, rev. ed. 1958.
Milnes, R. M. (ed.), *Life, Letters, and Literary Remains*, 2 vols, 1848.
Rollins, H. E. (ed.), *The Letters of John Keats, 1814–1821*, 2 vols, 1958.
—— *The Keats Circle: Letters and Papers, 1816–78*, 2 vols, 1948.
—— *More Letters and Papers of the Keats Circle*, 1955.

Bate, Walter J., *John Keats*, 1963.
Finney, C. L., *The Evolution of Keats's Poetry*, 2 vols, 1936.
Gittings, Robert, *John Keats: The Living Year . . .*, 1954.
—— *John Keats*, 1968.
Hewlett, Dorothy, *A Life of Keats*, 1949.
Lowell, Amy, *John Keats*, 2 vols, 1925.
Richardson, Joanna, *The Everlasting Spell*, 1963.
Ward, Aileen, *Keats: The Making of a Poet*, 1963.

Blackstone, Bernard, 'The Authorship of *The Poet*', *TLS*, 13 November 1959.
Brooke, E. L., 'The Poet, an Error in the Keats Canon', *MLN*, lxvii, November 1952.
Marsh, G. L. and N. I. White, 'Keats and the Periodicals of his Time', MP, xxxii, 1934.
Steele, Mabel A. E., 'The Authorship of *The Poet* and other Sonnets', *K-Sh J*, v, 1956.
Thorpe, C. D., 'Keats and Hazlitt: A Record of Personal Relationship and Critical Estimate', *PMLA*, lxii, 1947.

Chapter 3   Cary, Hazlitt, Leigh Hunt, Reynolds, and the Reviews

Cary

Cary, Henry (jun.), *Memoirs of the Rev. Henry Francis Cary . . . with his Literary Journal and Letters*, 2 vols, 1847.
King, R. W., *The Translator of Dante*, 1925.

King, R. W., 'Charles Lamb, Cary, and the "London Magazine"', *The Nineteenth Century and after*, dlix and dlx, 1923.
Parker, W. M., 'Henry Francis Cary, 1772–1844', *TLS*, 19 August 1944.
Roscoe, S., 'Cary: "Dante"', *Book Collector*, ii, 1952.
Toynbee, P., 'The Centenary of Cary's Dante', *MLR*, vii, 1912.

Hazlitt

Howe, P. P. (ed.), *The Complete Works*, 20 vols, 1930–4.

Baker, Herschel, *William Hazlitt*, 1962.
Howe, P. P., *The Life of William Hazlitt*, rev. ed. 1947.
Maclean, Catherine M., *Born Under Saturn: A Biography of Hazlitt*, 1943.

Carver, P. L., 'Hazlitt's Contributions to the *Edinburgh Review*', RES, iv, 1928.
Howe, P. P., 'Hazlitt and *Blackwood's Magazine*', *Fortnightly Review*, cxii, 1919.
Strout, A. L., 'Hunt, Hazlitt and *Maga*', *ELH*, iv, 1937.

Leigh Hunt

Milford, H. S. (ed.), *The Poetical Works*, 1923.

Blunden, Edmund, *Leigh Hunt*, 1930.
Landré, Louis, *Leigh Hunt*, 2 vols, 1935–6.

Stout, G. D., 'Leigh Hunt's Money Troubles', *Washington University Studies*, xii, Humanistic Series, No. 2, 1925.
—— 'The Cockney School', *TLS*, 7 February 1929.
Wheeler, P. M., 'The Great Quarterlies and Leigh Hunt', *South Atlantic Quarterly*, 1930.

Reynolds

Marsh, G. L. (ed.), *John Hamilton Reynolds: Poetry and Prose*, 1928.

Blunden, Edmund, 'Friends of Keats' in *Votive Tablets*, 1931.
Morgan, Peter F., 'John Hamilton Reynolds and Thomas Hood', *K-Sh J*, xi, 1962.
Pope, W. B., 'J. H. Reynolds', *Wessex*, iii, 1935.

The Reviews

Blunden, Edmund, *Leigh Hunt's 'Examiner' Examined*, 1928.
Brightfield, M. F., *John Wilson Croker*, 1940.
Clark, Roy B., *William Gifford, Tory satirist, critic and editor*, 1930.
Clive, J., *Scotch Reviewers*, 1957.
Coppleston, Edward, *Advice to a Young Reviewer, with a Specimen of the Art*, 1807.
Crawford, Thomas, '*The Edinburgh Review' and Romantic Poetry, 1802–29*, 1955.
Graham, Walter, *English Literary Periodicals*, 1930.
—— *Tory Criticism in the Quarterly Review, 1809–1853*, 1921.
Mineka, F. E., *The Dissidence of Dissent: 'The Monthly Repository', 1806–1838*, 1944.
Thrall, Miriam M. H., *Rebellious Fraser's*, 1934.
Wain, John (ed.), *Contemporary Reviews of Romantic Poetry*, 1953.

Carnall, G., 'The *Monthly Magazine*', *RES*, v, 1954.
Cox, R. G., 'The Great Reviews', *Scrutiny*, vi, 1937.
Derby, J. Raymond, 'The Paradox of Francis Jeffrey: reason versus sensibility', *MLQ*, vii, 1946.
Elwin, M., 'The Founder of the Quarterly Review', *Quarterly Review*, cclxxxi, 1943.
Graham, W., 'Some Infamous Tory Reviews', *SP*, xxii, 1925.
McCutcheon, R. P., 'The Beginning of British Reviewing in English Periodicals', *PMLA*, xxxviii, 1922.
Ward, W. S., 'Some Aspects of the Conservative Attitude toward Poetry in English Criticism: 1798–1820', *PMLA*, lx, 1945.
Welker, J. J., 'The Position of the Quarterlies on some Classical Dogmas', *SP*, xxxvii, 1940.

(For studies of the *Westminster Review* and the *Athenaeum*, see under chapter 7)

Chapter 4   Clare

Blunden, Edmund (ed.), *Sketches in the Life of John Clare, written by himself*, 1931.
Grigson, Geoffrey (ed.), *Poems of John Clare's Madness*, 1949.
Robinson, Eric and Geoffrey Summerfield (eds), *The Shepherd's Calendar*, 1964.
—— *The Later Poems of John Clare*, 1964.
—— *Clare*, New Oxford English Series, 1966.
Tibble, J. W. (ed.), *The Poems of John Clare*, 2 vols, 1935.
Tibble, J. W. and A. Tibble (eds), *The Letters of John Clare*, 1951.
—— *The Prose of John Clare*, 1951.
—— *Selected Poems of John Clare*, 1965.

Martin, Frederick, *Life of John Clare*, 1964 reprint of the original 1865 ed., with introduction by Eric Robinson and Geoffrey Summerfield.
Tibble, J. W. and A., *John Clare: A Life*, 1932.
—— *John Clare: His Life and Poetry*, 1956.
Wilson, June, *Green Shadows: The Life of Clare*, 1951.

Blunden, Edmund, 'Clare on the Londoners', *LM*, 1923.
Robinson, E. and G. Summerfield, 'Taylor's editing of *The Shepherd's Calendar*', *RES*, xiv, 1963.

Chapter 5   The London Magazine *– general studies, Cunningham, De Quincey, Hood, Lamb, Procter, and Wainewright*

General

Bauer, Josephine, 'The London Magazine, 1820–29', *Anglistica*, I, 1953.
Blunden, Edmund, 'Clare on the Londoners', *LM*, vii, February 1923.

Butterworth, S., 'The Old London Magazine and some of its contributors', *Bookman*, October 1922.

Hughes, T. Rowland, 'John Scott: Editor, Author and Critic', *LM*, xxi, 1930.

Prance, C. A., 'The London Magazine', *CLSB*, No. 101, May 1951.

Zeitlin, Jacob, 'The Editor of the London Magazine', *JEGP*, xx, 1921.

Brooks, Elmer L., 'Studies in the London Magazine', unpublished doctoral dissertation, Harvard, 1954.

Hughes, T. Rowland, 'The London Magazine', unpublished doctoral dissertation, Jesus College, Oxford, 1931.

Cunningham

Gilfillan, G., *Galleries of Literary Portraits*, 1856.

Hogg, D., *A Life of Allan Cunningham, with Selections from his Works and Correspondence*, 1875.

Hall, S. C., 'Allan Cunningham', *Art Journal*, xviii, 1866.

De Quincey

Masson, David (ed.), *Collected Writings*, 14 vols, 1889–90.

Eaton, H. A., *Thomas De Quincey: a biography*, 1936.

Sackville West, E., *A Flame in Sunlight: the life and work of De Quincey*, 1936.

Byrns, Richard H., 'Some Unpublished Works of De Quincey', *PMLA*, lxxi, No. 5, December 1956.

Hood

Jerrold, Walter (ed.), *Poetical Works*, 1920.

—— *Hood: His Life and Times*, 1907.

—— (ed.), *Thomas Hood and Charles Lamb: The Story of a Friendship*, 1930.

Reid, J. C., *Thomas Hood*, 1963.

Morgan, Peter F., 'John Hamilton Reynolds and Thomas Hood', *K-Sh J*, xi, 1962.

Lamb

Lucas, E. V. (ed.), *The Works of Charles Lamb*, 7 vols, 1903–5; 6 vols, 1912.

—— (ed.), *The Letters of Charles and Mary Lamb*, 3 vols, 1935.

Blunden, Edmund, *Charles Lamb and his Contemporaries*, 1933.

—— (ed.), *Charles Lamb: His Life Recorded by his Contemporaries*, 1934.

Jerrold, Walter (ed.), *Thomas Hood and Charles Lamb: The Story of a Friendship*, 1930.

Lucas, E. V., *The Life of Charles Lamb*, 2 vols, 1905; 1 vol., 1907; rev. ed., 1921.

Procter, B. W., *Charles Lamb: A Memoir*, 1866.

—— *An Autobiographical Fragment*, 1877.

King, R. W., 'Charles Lamb, Cary and the "London Magazine"', *The Nineteenth Century and after*, dlix and dlx, 1923.

Prance, C. A., 'A Forgotten Skit by Charles Lamb', *TLS*, 9 February 1951.

Procter

Procter, B. W., *Charles Lamb: A Memoir*, 1866.

—— *An Autobiographical Fragment*, 1877 (ed. Coventry Patmore).

Armour, R. W., *Barry Cornwall: A Biography*, 1935.

Wainewright

Hazlitt, W. Carew (ed.), *Essays and Criticisms*, 1880.

Curling, Jonathan, *Janus Weathercock: The Life of Thomas Griffiths Wainewright*, 1938.

Lindsey, J., *Suburban Gentleman*, 1942.

Chapter 6   Carlyle, Coleridge, and Landor

Carlyle

Traill, H. D. (ed.), *Collected Works*, 30 vols, 1896–1901.

Neff, Emery, *Carlyle*, 1932.

Wilson, David A., *Carlyle*, 6 vols, 1923–34.

Coleridge

Griggs, E. L. (ed.), *Collected Letters of Coleridge*, 6 vols, 1956– .

Chambers, E. K., *Coleridge: a biographical study*, 1950 ed.

Landor

Crump, C. G. (ed.), *Imaginary Conversations*, 6 vols, 1891.

Welby, T. Earle and S. Wheeler (eds), *The Complete Works*, 16 vols, 1927–36.

Elwin, Malcolm, *Savage Landor*, 1941.

—— *Landor: A Replevin*, 1958.

Super, R. H., *Walter Savage Landor: A Biography*, 1957 ed.

—— *The Publication of Landor's Works*, Bibliographical Society, 1954.

McFarland, G. F., 'The Early Literary Career of Julius Hare', *Bulletin of the John Rylands Library*, xlvi, 1963, and xlvii, 1964.

Wheeler, S., 'Landor and his Publishers', *TLS*, 19 January 1922.

Chapter 7   Borrow, Darley, and the Reviews

Borrow

Dearden, Seaton, *The Gypsy Gentleman, A Study of George Borrow*, 1939.

Darley

Abbott, C. C., *The Life and Letters of George Darley*, 1928.
—— 'Further Letters of George Darley', *Durham University Journal*, xxxiii, 1940.

The Reviews

Marchand, L. A., *The Athenaeum: A Mirror of Victorian Culture*, 1941.
Nesbitt, George L., *Benthamite Reviewing: The Westminster Review 1824-1836*, 1934.

Section D

Add. MSS. MSS 27781 and 34569 in this collection in the British Museum contain a few letters by Taylor.

Bakewell MSS. This collection is by far the most valuable and extensive source of unpublished material relating to Taylor. It contains many notebooks and hundreds of letters written by him to his mother and father and, most especially, to his brother James at Holywell House, Bakewell. The letters date from 1801 to 1864, and are now in the possession of Mr R. W. P. Cockerton of Bakewell.

Berg Collection MSS. The Henry W. and Albert A. Berg Collection in the New York Public Library, contains much important material, including nine of Taylor's Commonplace Books, letters from him to Julius Hare concerning Landor's *Imaginary Conversations*, letters to him from Carlyle and De Quincey, and to Hessey from Coleridge.

Brooke-Taylor MSS. This collection is a further source of important material relating to the firm, and from the letters now in the possession of Michael Brooke-Taylor, I have quoted several extracts.

Egerton MSS. The Egerton MSS 2245-9 in the British Museum contain an extensive and valuable collection of letters from Taylor, Hessey, Mrs Emmerson, Lord Radstock, and many others to John Clare. Many have been published by previous biographers, though some important ones are quoted here for the first time.

Harvard University MSS. The Houghton Library at Harvard contains an interesting series of thirty-one letters from B. W. Procter to Taylor & Hessey, chiefly concerning *The London Magazine*. All the letters are undated, but almost certainly belong to the period summer 1822—early 1824.

National Library of Scotland MSS. The collection in Edinburgh contains a small but interesting group of letters concerned with the firm. Materials in MSS 1706, 1764, 1765, 1808 and 7209 consist of letters from Horatio Smith to John Scott, from Taylor & Hessey to Carlyle and from him to them, from Cunningham to Hessey, and from Taylor to George Combe.

Northampton MSS. The material relating to Clare in the Northampton Public Library is, together with the manuscripts in Peterborough Museum, the finest primary source which now exists about the poet, comprising no fewer than 1350 poems in manuscript as well as hundreds of his letters. From this collection, which contains a good deal of unpublished material relating to Taylor, I have quoted from MSS 34, 43, and 44.

Peterborough MSS. The collection in Peterborough Museum is an invaluable source for students of Clare's poetry, containing as it does so many original manuscripts. MSS A 20 and F 1, which I have made particular use of, comprise a volume of Clare's poems for the *Shepherd's Calendar*, and certain letters from Van Dyk to Clare about the editing of this book.

Pierpont Morgan Library MSS. The Pierpont Morgan Library, New York, contains interesting letters from De Quincey and Carlyle to the firm, as well as a series of letters from Coleridge to H. F. Cary. But, as far as Taylor & Hessey are concerned, by far the most valuable item is the first draft of the article by De Quincey on the *London*, which is discussed on pp. 141–3 and p. 224 above.

University College London MSS. The Record Office of University College contains information about Taylor's appointment as publisher and bookseller to the University.

University of Texas MSS. The Miriam Stark Library of the University of Texas at Austin contains Taylor's own copy of *The Literary Diary*, in which many of his poems composed between 1811 and 1818 are transcribed.

Wilton MSS. Mrs Flecker of Wilton, Marlborough, a great-granddaughter of Hessey, has a small but interesting collection of material relating to her ancestor, containing family letters by Hessey, and a manuscript biography of his son.

Index

For the sake of reasonable brevity, the entries in this index do not include merely passing references to the most frequent recipients of Taylor & Hessey's letters, such as Clare and James Taylor, jun. Purely incidental references to the firm's major writers have also been omitted.

Hessey, James Augustus—*contd.*
96–8, 104, 111–12, 122; and the
London, 129, 130, 137, 146, 148–51,
153–4, 160–1, 194, 210; and De
Quincey, 139–41; and Carlyle, 167;
and Coleridge, 176–7; dissolves
partnership, 178–9; and T.'s illness,
180–2; bankrupt, 188; later life,
189–91, 193–7
Hessey, James Augustus (son), 8
Hessey, Kate (wife), 17, 196
Hilton, William, 2, 84, 123, 125, 191,
194–5
Hodgson, Rev. Francis, 207
Hogg, James, 73
Hood, Thomas, *sen.*, 9–11, 84
Hood, Thomas, *jun.*: and the London
dinners, 84, 143–6, 153, 160; and the
magazine, 135–7, 147, 159–60, 180,
193; leaves the London, 150–2; later
life, 190, 194
Horne, R. H., 197–8
How & Whittaker, house of, 124, 195
Howard & Evans, firm of, 66–7
Hugo, Victor, 143
Hume, David, 11
Hunt, John, 174
Hunt, Leigh: and Keats, 23, 29, 31–5,
55; and Queen Caroline, 51; and
T. & H., 59–62, 208; and the reviews,
75, 95, 112; on periodicals, 156
Hurst Robinson, house of, 184
Hussey, William, 12

Irving, Edward, 166–7

Jeffrey, Francis, 70, 76–7, 79
Johnson, Samuel, 141, 200
Jones, Isabella, 39, 43, 193, 211
Joyce, Mary, 103
'Junius', 17–19, 87

Keats, Fanny, 53
Keats, George, 24, 38
Keats, Georgiana, 38
Keats, John: meets T. & H., 22–3; 1817
Poems, 23–4; on imagination, 26–8,
35–6, 86, 120; finances, 27–8, 52–3;
and Endymion, 28–35, 37, 68, 71–2,
112; on the reviews, 37–8, 73–4;

attacks reading public, 38–41, 44, 74,
202–5; and St Agnes, 40–3, 169;
Lamia published, 45–7, 50–2, 68,
206–7; illness, 46–8, 129; defended
by T., 48–50; last months, 53–4; and
T.'s Memoir, 55, 61; and his epitaph,
56–7; presiding genius of T. & H.,
58; visits Fleet Street, 70, 84; on
Clare, 119–21; his literary remains,
191, 194
Keats, Tom, 29–30
Keepsake, 185
Kemble, Fanny, 186
Kent, Elizabeth, 60–1, 207
Kirkman, Mr, 7
Knight, Charles, 6, 78, 183

Lackington, James, 6–8, 11, 66, 201
Lamb, Charles: and London dinners, 84,
129, 143–6, 153; writes for London,
132–3, 135–7, 141, 148, 159, 163, 193;
on the decline of London, 149–55;
Elia published, 161, 163–4, 168, 206;
on the reading public, 185, 202;
argues with T., 190–1, 210; death,
191, 211
Landor, Walter Savage: and Hazlitt,
79–80, 175; quarrels with T., 79,
174–6; published by T. & H., 159,
161, 170–3, 178
Landor, Walter (of Rugeley), 174
Lang, Andrew, 76
Lardner, Dionysius, 188, 193
Leighton, Archbishop, 176
Leopold, Prince, 20
Liverpool, Lord, 66
Lockhart, John Gibson, 32–3, 70, 132
London Magazine (Baldwin's), 74, 131–3
London Magazine (Gold's), 47
London Magazine (T. & H.'s), 167–9,
173, 176, 194; bought from Baldwin, 129–30, 132–3; circulation of,
133–4, 149, 158, 162; decline of,
149–55; dinners, 143–8, 153; editorial
policy of, 141–3, 156–8; lack of
focus in, 156, 158–9; liberalism of,
156–7; loss on, 158, 178; payment
to writers, 135, 139; sold, 154–5, 182;
spirit of, 143–8, 163